THE
Big Book
of Bible
Bloopers

J. STEPHEN LANG

HARVEST HOUSE PUBLISHERS

EUGENE, OREGON

Published in association with the literary agency of Mark Sweeney & Associates

Cover design and illustration © Dugan Design Group, Bloomington, Minnesota

THE BIG BOOK OF BIBLE BLOOPERS
Copyright © 2007 by J. Stephen Lang
Published by Harvest House Publishers
Eugene, Oregon 97402
www.harvesthousepublishers.com

Library of Congress Cataloging-in-Publication Data
Lang, J. Stephen.
    The big book of Bible bloopers / by J. Stephen Lang.
        p. cm.
    ISBN-13: 978-0-7369-2136-7
    ISBN-10: 0-7369-2136-2
    1. Bible—Miscellanea. I. Title.
    BS534.L24 2007
    220—dc22

                                                    2007012932

Printed in the United States of America

07 08 09 10 11 12 13 14 15 / BP-SK / 12 11 10 9 8 7 6 5 4 3 2 1

To Marshall Gilliam

recalling college classes

leavened with laughter

Contents

Introduction

Here's some good news: More people read the Bible than any other book in the world. Now the bad news: Those people misunderstand, misquote, misuse, and misconstrue it more than any other book in the world. That's what the book you are now holding is all about—people's misconceptions about the Bible. People have been arguing for centuries about whether the Bible contains errors. But one thing is absolutely certain: People who read the Bible (or claim to) make *lots* of errors.

This broad category of "Bible bloopers" includes items that will make you laugh, make you think, and (we hope) make you dig more deeply into the Bible itself. After all, you can't actually detect Bible bloopers unless you know what the Bible *really* says, can you? One section of the book deals with some of the most common misconceptions about the Bible—things that "everyone knows" even though they aren't based on the Bible at all. Another section looks at some of the often hilarious errors that students have made on Bible tests. You can chuckle at the foolishness of the famous and infamous in a section dealing with celebrities' ridiculous ideas about the Bible. Another section deals with the various sects and movements that have misconstrued the Book.

(This is a section that will convince you that truth is stranger than fiction. Can you guess what the Adamites were famous for?) The book of Revelation, probably the most misunderstood book of the Bible, has its own section. The numerous boo-boos made by translators (sometimes deliberate, sometimes not) have their own chapter. So do the many printer errors (like "Thou shalt commit adultery") made over the centuries.

Despite my attempt at organization, this book is for browsing. It was made to fill up your time commuting on the train, the hour spent in the dentist's waiting room, the few minutes before dinner is on the table, the hours on a long road trip (not while you're behind the wheel, of course). The book is designed to be read randomly, anywhere, and with no preparation of any kind. One purpose of the book is simply to entertain, but a more serious purpose is at work too: By getting a close look at human errors about the Bible, you're also getting a closer look at the truth of the Bible—what it really says, not what its critics and other misguided people have said about it.

I hope you enjoy reading this as much as I enjoyed writing it.

ONE

Bible Students Say the Weirdest Things

The following questions and (goofball) answers are taken from actual tests administered in college-level courses in the Bible. Some are from a state community college, the others are from a Christian college. For obvious reasons, the colleges and the professors who administered the tests will remain anonymous. That goes double for the students who supplied these answers.

Some of these are misspellings, some are just plain dumb (and funny), and some fall into the category of "I didn't know the answer, so I figured I'd give the professor a good laugh."

Q: Where was Solomon's temple?
A: On the side of his head.
Correct: Jerusalem.

Q: Eglon, a very obese king in the book of Judges, ruled over what nation?
A: The Cellulites.
The Hiptites.
Correct: Moab.

Q: Name as many of the Ten Commandments as you can.

A: You shall kill.

Honor your father and mutter.

Do not bow down before any greasy images.

Remember the Sabbath day, and keep it holey.

Sing around the campfire, join the Campfire Girls.

Be prepared.

Do a good deed daily.

Go placidly amid the noise and confusion.

Love your neighbor as your shelf.

Be the wind beneath someone's wings.

Thou shalt not commit adulthood.

Zoom, zoom, zoom, and forgot the other seven.

You shall have no other dogs before me.

The Lord is my shepherd, and so I won't.

You shall not cover your neighbor's house.

Do not take God's name in your vein.

See Rock City.

Have a nice day.

Honor your fodder and murder.

You shall knot steel.

Come alive, you're in the Pepsi generation.

Just do it.

Have friends in low places.

You shall not kill your mother.

Go for it.

Q. The prophet Ezekiel had a famous vision of a valley of dry _____.

A. Saunas.

Skin.

Diapers.

Correct: Bones.

Q: What prophet was beheaded by the order of Herod?
A: Johnny the Southern Baptist.

Q: What prophet walked around naked for three years?
A: Nudel.
    Correct: Isaiah.

Q: Name the first man and woman.
A: Adam and Pocahontas.

Q: Where were Jesus' followers first called Christians?
A: At First Christian Church.
    Correct: Antioch.

Q: Who was Israel's first judge?
A: Judge Judy.
    Judge Dredd.
    Correct: Othniel.

Q: What man in the Bible was called "beloved physician"?
A: That cute guy on *ER.*
    Dr. Kildare.
    Correct: Luke.

Q: Who lived to the ripe old age of 969?
A: Yoda.
    Probably some Galapagos tortoise.
    Dr. Doolittle's parrot.
    Joan Collins.
    Mike Wallace.
    Mick Jagger.
    Cher.
    Correct: Methuselah.

Q: In the book of Exodus, the first plague on the Egyptians was turning the river waters into what?

A: Perrier.
Starbuck's.
Sewage.
Gatorade.
Correct: Blood.

Q: Complete this verse from Psalms: "Keep me as the _____ of thine eye."

A. Idol.
Pupil.
Lash.
Correct: Apple.

Q: Who was the first king of Israel?

A: Soul.
Elvis.
George Washington.
Correct: Saul.

Q: According to Jesus, you cannot serve both God and ___.

A: Pork.
Satan.
Buddha.
Ted Turner.
Correct: Mammon (money).

Q: The rainbow was God's sign of a covenant with what man?

A: The guy who invented Skittles.
Jesse Jackson.
Correct: Noah.

Q: In Genesis, Joseph was given a beautiful coat of many
   _____.
A: Paints, but they had to put on primer first.
   Correct: Colors.

Q: In Genesis, what happened to the serpent after God cursed
   it?
A: It had a hissy fit.
   Correct: It was made to crawl on its belly.

Q: Which two books of the Bible do not mention God's name?
A: Esther and the Gong of Solomon.
   Correct: Esther and the Song of Solomon.

Q: What is the meaning of the number 666 in the book of
   Revelation?
A: It's really 999 turned upside down.
   *Correct: It's the number of the Beast, but no one knows for
   sure what it means.*

Q: In the book of Daniel, King Nebuchadnezzar had a dream
   of a statue made of what four metals?
A: Gold, aluminum, fiberglass, and heavy.
   Correct: Gold, silver, brass, iron.

Q: Who was the father of King David?
A: His mom's husband.
   Correct: Jesse.

Q: What important Bible character was also known as
   Jedidiah?
A: The old guy on *The Beverly Hillbillies.*
   Correct: Solomon.

Q: What is the first murder in the Bible?
A: Abel was killed with a cane.
   Correct: Cain killed Abel.

Q: In the book of Jonah, where does God tell the prophet to go?
A: Sea World.
   The beach.
   Fishing.
   On a cruise.
   Red Lobster.
   Correct: Nineveh.

Q: The great heroic strong man Samson was famous for not cutting his what?
A: Toenails.
   Teeth.
   Taxes.
   Correct: Hair.

Q: The child with the long name Maher-shalal-hash-baz was the son of whom?
A: A parent with a sick sense of humor.
   Correct: The prophet Isaiah. This is the longest name in the Bible.

Q: Lot's wife was turned into a pillar of what?
A: The community.
   Fire.
   Goose feathers.
   Prozac.
   Correct: Salt.

Q: What is the Golden Rule?
A: Share and share alike.
    Win some, lose some.
    Never give a sucker an even break.
    Curiosity killed the cat.
    Life is just a bowl of cherries.
    Brush and floss daily.
    Invest in no-load mutual funds.
    Never invite a porcupine to a nudist camp.
    Every man for himself.
    Let a smile be your umbrella.
    Correct: Do to others what you would have them do to you
    (Matthew 7:12 NIV).

Q: Complete this statement made by Paul in the book of Acts:
    "I appeal to _____."
A: Women who go for missionaries.
    Correct: Caesar.

Q: Who built pagan temples to please all his foreign wives?
A: Donald Trump.
    Larry King.
    King Henry VIII.
    Correct: Solomon.

Q: Who was the wife of Uriah the Hittite?
A: Uriette.
    Mrs. Uriah.
    Correct: Bathsheba.

Q: Jemima, Keziah, and Keren-happuch were whose names?
A: The Trinity.

The three little pigs.
The fairies in Sleeping Beauty.
The three wise women.
Three of Solomon's 700 wives.
The Supremes.
Correct: Job's daughters.

Q: Name the four Gospels.
A: Matthew, Mark, Duke, and George.
John, Paul, George, and Ringo.
Gospels I, II, III, and IV.
Correct: Matthew, Mark, Luke, and John.

Q: The prophet Daniel was thrown into a den of what?
A: Cub Scouts.
Thieves.
Women selling Tupperware.
Correct: Lions.

Q: What was the notable physical difference between twins Jacob and Esau?
A: Esau was a girl.
One of them was left-handed.
Esau had better abs.
Jacob had a mole in a really embarrassing location.
Correct: Jacob was smooth-skinned, and Esau was hairy. Also, Esau's hair was red, and Jacob's wasn't.

Q: According to Jesus, what sin cannot be forgiven?
A: Returning a video after the due date.
Wearing white after Labor Day.
Stealing a Gideon's Bible from a hotel.
Laughing in church.

Eating crackers and trying to whistle "Yankee Doodle."
Pulling a Do Not Remove tag off a mattress.
Adultery with the minister's wife.
Admitting to people you are a *Star Trek* geek.
Correct: Blasphemy against the Holy Spirit.

Q: King Solomon was paid a visit by what famous queen?
A: Elizabeth II.
Latifah.
Victoria.
Ru-Paul.
Camilla.
Correct: The queen of Sheba.

Q: The prophet Joel had a vision of a plague of what?
A: Acne.
Used car salesmen.
Jehovah's Witnesses going door to door.
Lawyers.
Hip-hop artists.
Correct: Locusts.

Q: What was Gideon famous for?
A: Putting Bibles in hotel rooms.
Correct: He was one of the judges and military leaders in ancient Israel.

Q: Who went to live in the land of Nod?
A: Winken and Blinken.
My granddad.
Rip van Winkle.
Sleeping Beauty.
Correct: Cain.

Q: For quarreling with her brother Moses, Miriam was afflicted with what?

A: A long time-out and no Kool-Aid.
Her credit cards were taken away.
The heartbreak of psoriasis.
Correct: Leprosy.

Q: What did Isaiah say when he had his vision of God in the temple?

A: Whoa, it's me!
Correct: Woe is me!

Q: King Ahab was married to whom?

A: Moby Dick.
The queen.
Mrs. Ahab.
Correct: Jezebel.

Q: Who cursed the day he was born?

A: I don't know, but someone should have washed that kid's mouth out with soap.
A rapper.
Correct: Job.

Q: Moses' wife belonged to what tribe?

A: The Mennonites.
Correct: Midianites.

Q: Who invented farming?

A: John Deere.
Correct: Adam.

Q: What relation were Moses and Aaron?
A: Business partners.
   Fishing buddies.
   Correct: Brothers.

Q: Who invented wine making?
A: Mogen David.
   The apostle Paul Masson.
   Correct: Noah.

Q: Who was the first hunter?
A: Charlton Heston.
   Ted Nugent.
   Correct: Nimrod.

Q: Where was Peter when he preached the Pentecost sermon?
A: First Assembly of God.
   Correct: Jerusalem.

Q: The book of Revelation was written by whom?
A: I don't know, but 666 was his pen name.
   The beast.
   Correct: John.

Q: What mighty empire conquered Jerusalem in 586 BC?
A: Mexico.
   North Korea.
   Baby Lawn.
   Correct: Babylon.

Q: What language was the New Testament written in?
A: Corny Greek.
   Correct: Koine Greek.

Q: In the Old Testament, what woman "painted her face"?
A: Mary Kay.
Tammy Bakker.
Merle Norman.
Correct: Queen Jezebel.

Q: After his baptism, Jesus was tempted by whom?
A: A lawyer.
An Amway salesman.
Girl Scouts selling cookies.
Correct: The devil.

Q: Name three of the ancient empires that the Jews were subject to.
A: Babylon, Nylon, and Orlon.
Correct: Babylon, Medo-Persia, and Greece (Rome also).

Q: What were the Urim and Thummim?
A: Cousins of Tweedledee and Tweedledum.
Ancient rock groups.
Correct: Two stones used in determining the will of God.

Q: Which of King David's many wives "despised him in her heart"?
A: The one who had to change all the diapers.
Correct: Michal.

Q: Who denied Jesus three times?
A: His bank's loan officer.
Correct: The apostle Peter.

Q: What is the shortest Gospel?
A: The one in Reader's Digest.
Correct: Mark.

Q: The wicked cities of Sodom and Gomorrah were destroyed by fire and what?
A: The Flintstones.
   Broom stones.
   Correct: Brimstone.

Q: Who is the first king mentioned in the Bible?
A: King James.
   Elvis.
   Correct: Nimrod.

Q: Judas betrayed Jesus for 30 pieces of what?
A: Fudge.
   Real estate.
   Sheet music.
   Correct: Silver.

Q: The Bible tells us to love God with all our heart, soul, mind, and _____.
A: Liquid assets.
   Inner child.
   Remote control.
   Correct: Strength.

Q: Tithing means giving what to God?
A: A tithe.
   Correct: A tenth. Tithe *means tenth, so this goofy answer is correct, but the teacher marked it wrong anyway!*

Q: When the Israelites were wandering in the wilderness, what did they follow by day?
A: The Wal-Mart smiley face.
   A blue light.

The pied piper.
The bouncing ball.
The soaps.
Correct: A pillar of cloud.

Q: According to Revelation, what place is never dark?
A: Motel 6 because they leave the light on.
7-Eleven.
A fraternity house.
Alaska in the summer.
Las Vegas.
Correct: Heaven.

Q: Name the three sons of Adam and Eve.
A: Abel, Cain, and Bravo.
Huey, Dewey, and Louie.
Dewey, Cheatham, and Howe.
John, Paul, and George.
Abel, Cain, and Adam Junior.
Correct: Abel, Cain, and Seth.

Q: Complete this saying from Genesis 4: "Sin is _____ at the door."
A: Knocking really hard.
Selling Avon.
Trick-or-treating.
Salivating.
Passing out tracts.
Getting in touch with its inner child.
Correct: Crouching.

Q: Who was 500 years old when he fathered his sons?
A: The dad on *My Three Sons.*

Billy Bob Thornton.
Mick Jagger.
Obi-Wan Kenobi.
Correct: Noah.

Q: In the Gospels, what two people walked on water?
A: Jesus and that little fast blond kid in *The Incredibles*.
Correct: Jesus and Peter.

Q: What did Moses' staff turn into?
A: A bunch of lazy loafers playing Internet poker.
Unemployed people.
Correct: A snake.

Q: In Exodus, what plague was sent upon Egypt's cattle?
A: Mad cow disease.
They all jumped over the moon.
Correct: They were killed.

Q: When Jesus healed a paralyzed man, what did the man
pick up and carry back to his home?
A: His insurance claim forms.
Correct: His mat that he had lain on.

Q: How did Joseph learn about Mary's miraculous concep-
tion?
A: In a chat room.
Instant messaging.
A little bird told him.
Correct: In a dream.

Q: What is the first medicine mentioned in the Bible?
A: The tablets God gave to Moses.
Correct: A merry heart.

Q: Why was Moses buried in the land of Moab?
A: He was dead.
    Correct: He disobeyed God and was not able to enter the promised land.

Q: To be baptized by John the Baptist, what did a person have to do?
A: Get wet.
    Correct: Repent of his or her sins.

Q: According to Jesus, what is the greatest commandment?
A: Don't worry, be happy.
    Keep your sunny side up.
    Marry in haste, repent at leisure.
    Praise the Lord and pass the ammunition.
    Let the good times roll.
    Never buy ice cubes from an Eskimo.
    Buy now, pay later.
    Do not pass Go, do not collect $200.
    Beware the Ides of March.
    Correct: Love God with all your heart, soul, mind, and strength.

Q: What expensive ointment was Jesus anointed with?
A: Probably some Clinique product.
    Tinactin.
    Gold Bond.
    Retin-A.
    The kind with no flies in it.
    Correct: Nard or spikenard.

Q: What men in Israel were anointed with holy oil?
A: Professional wrestlers.

Body builders.
Correct: Priests and kings.

Q: Who wore a camel's hair coat?
A: A used car salesman.
   A guy trying to meet women in a bar.
   Correct: John the Baptist. Some translations say he wore a tunic.

Q: Was the prodigal son the older or younger son?
A: Yes.
   Correct: The younger.

Q: According to Malachi, who will return to earth to turn the hearts of the children to their parents?
A: Dr. Phil.
   Barney the dinosaur.
   Michael Jackson.
   Correct: The prophet Elijah.

Q: Which son was Isaac partial to?
A: The favorite.
   Correct: Esau.

Q: According to the Old Testament Law, what is the penalty for someone who strikes his mother or father?
A: No theme parks, ever.
   Vacation at colonial Williamsburg.
   Long visits with grandparents.
   He can't get a tattoo.
   No MTV.
   No PlayStation.
   Correct: Death.

Q: Who said we must all change and become like little children?
A: Barney the dinosaur.
    Peter Pan.
    Robin Williams.
    Correct: Jesus.

Q: King Solomon had 700 wives and 300 _____.
A: Cummerbunds.
    Cucumbers.
    Bathrooms.
    Correct: Concubines.

Q: Jesus brought to life a woman's son in the town of _____.
A: Nair.
    Nine.
    Correct: Nain.

Q: Who said that Christian widows were better off not to remarry?
A: Their tax accountants.
    Correct: Paul.

Q: Who gave birth to a son when she was 90 years old?
A: Cher.
    Joan Collins.
    Correct: Abraham's wife Sarah.

Q: In between the Old and New Testaments, who were the Hellenists?
A: People who believed in hell.

Admirers of Helen of Troy.
Correct: Hellenes *is another name for the Greeks. Hellenists were non-Greek people who admired and copied Greek culture.*

Q: Who had a huge bed made of iron?
A: Superman, the man of steel.
Arnold Schwarzenegger.
Rush Limbaugh.
Correct: Og, king of Bashan.

Q: In Revelation, what falls on earth's waters and makes them bitter?
A: Acid rain.
Spoiled mayonnaise.
Correct: A star named Wormwood.

Q: Name the five books of the Law.
A: Civil, Criminal, Traffic, Divorce, and Small Claims.
Matthew, Mark, Luke, John, and Judge Judy.
Jennysits, Exits, Libidinous, Mumblers, and Trigonometry.
Correct: Genesis, Exodus, Leviticus, Numbers, and Deuteronomy.

Q: Who is seated at the right hand of God?
A: His right-hand man.
An attorney.
Correct: Jesus.

Q: What king had a feast where a mysterious hand wrote on the wall?
A: Burger King.
Correct: Belshazzar.

Q: What is fasting?
A: The opposite of slowing.
    Correct: Abstaining from eating.

Q: In Exodus, what was the last plague sent on the Egyptians?
A: The stock market crash.
    Their hard drives crash.
    All cell phones went dead.
    Correct: The death of all the firstborn.

Q: Jesus said, "You shall love your _____ as yourself."
A: Clone.
    Evil twin.
    Stand-in.
    Rottweiler.
    Secret Santa.
    Valentine.
    Bridge partner.
    Stockbroker.
    Chiropractor.
    Imaginary friend.
    Plastic surgeon.
    Internet technician.
    Correct: Neighbor.

Q: Who lived in the land of Uz?
A: The Wizard.
    Judy Garland.
    Correct: Job.

Q: Who was swallowed by a "great fish"?
A: Mrs. Paul's.
    Pinocchio.

Nemo.
The Gorton's fisherman.
Correct: Jonah.

Q: According to Revelation, the gates of heaven are made of
     what?
A: PVC.
     Clouds.
     Correct: Pearl.

Q: The high priest of Israel wore a gold plaque containing 12
     what?
A: Disciples.
     Correct: Stones representing Israel's 12 tribes.

Q: What were the names of Noah's three sons?
A: Simon, Theodore, and Alvin.
     Peter, Paul, and Mario.
     Bert, Ernie, and Elmo.
     Curly, Larry, and Moe.
     Shem, Ham, and Bacon.
     Correct: Shem, Ham, and Japheth.

Q. The city of Jericho's walls fell down when the Israelites blew
     their _____.
A: Noses.
     Cover.
     Correct: Trumpets.

Q: What three persons make up the Trinity?
A: Father, Son, and Grandson.
     Father, Sun, and Moon.

Auburn, Alabama, and Georgia Tech.
Blue, Red, and Yellow.
Correct: Father, Son, and Holy Spirit.

Q: What did Jesus feed to the crowd of 5000?
A: Happy Meals.
   Kit-Kat bars.
   Correct: Fish and bread.

Q: What was Samson's final dramatic act?
A: He invented Samsonite luggage.
   He spiked his hair with gel.
   He showed up at Wrestlemania.
   He opened a salon.
   Correct: He destroyed the Philistine temple.

Q: Paul had a divine vision while on the road to _____.
A: Rehab.
   Disney World.
   His graduation.
   A family reunion.
   A fraternity party.
   Correct: Damascus.

Some Dopey (and Sometimes Dangerous) Ideas

In the Middle Ages, church authorities tried to keep laymen from reading the Bible. Why? Because they feared the laymen couldn't interpret it properly and might fall into all kinds of weird beliefs and behaviors. Well, today we give people credit for being able to read the Bible for themselves. However, the items below will make you wonder if everybody can read the Bible and stay sane—or whether everybody can read the Bible sanely.

In many of the entries in this chapter, you'll encounter the word *heresy,* which signifies a belief or set of beliefs that Christian leaders regarded as wrong. Today we don't have a high opinion of people who hunt out heretics because those people strike us as intolerant—one of the dirtiest labels in our language. Even Christians today pride themselves on tolerance and wonder how Christians of an earlier time could have been so very harsh on heresies. Wouldn't "live and let live" have been the right attitude—even the right *Christian* attitude? But those Christians of an earlier age might ask us, don't you care about the truth? Don't you see that everyone's beliefs can't all be right, especially when some beliefs clearly contradict others? Isn't your tolerance just a way of excusing your mental laziness, meaning you're just too indifferent or too unclear in your thinking to make important distinctions?

Keep those questions in mind as you read this chapter. Also keep in mind that this book in no way approves of persecution of heretics. One of the saddest things in the history of Christianity—or any other religion—is the cruelty that believers show to each other. Christians have no excuse for using violence against other people, especially in the name of the faith. Another sad feature of church history is that the heretics, though wrong in their beliefs, often lived saintly lives that made more orthodox Christians look bad by comparison. We can hold the right beliefs and not be particularly good people—just as we can be misguided in our beliefs and yet behave well.

Adamites

Before they sinned, Adam and Eve were naked and unashamed. Afterward, they felt compelled to cover themselves (Genesis 3). Throughout history, various groups on the fringes of Christianity have tried to get back to Eden by making nakedness a part of their lives. A group of so-called Adamites existed as early as the year 300, and many have appeared since.

Some of the groups have practiced sexual promiscuity, some have not. Even when they didn't, the accusation is understandable. Regardless how spiritual such groups are in theory, adult human males are...well...adult human males, and the presence of nude bodies has an effect that is hardly spiritual.

In the early years of Christianity, the Egyptian wilderness drew all sorts of men pursuing the monastic life. Some of these men were genuinely devout believers, but others were genuine crackpots—misreading the Bible, trying to draw attention to themselves, or both. One very saintly old hermit who had lived to be nearly 90, meditating and praying in his hut all day and eating very little, suddenly decided at his advanced age that he had drawn so close to God that he had reentered Eden, undoing the disobedience of Adam and Eve. He left his hut and wandered around naked for more than a year, preaching to others that they too could reenter Eden if they were spiritual enough. Because the old man already had a reputation for being saintly, many people followed him in the practice of walking around naked—but most did not, and in time his reputation began to slide. He disappeared rather mysteriously, and his followers said he had been taken directly into heaven, but his opponents said he had been divinely punished by being eaten by crocodiles.

Not all Adamites thought they had achieved spiritual perfection. Some decided to go naked as a way of punishing themselves, disciplining their bodies. In southern Spain in the late 1500s, a group of men were impressed by the order of Carmelite monks. Some of the more strict monks were *discalced,* which means they were shoeless. They went barefoot as a way of modeling the life of saintly poverty. The men who were impressed by the discalced monks went even further and began going fully naked, and several of them took up residence in an abandoned castle. Things seemed to go fine—until winter came, and their life as nudists came to a chilly halt.

Near Naples, Italy, a young woman calling herself Eve wandered naked in the vicinity of Mount Vesuvius. She wrapped a dead snake around her neck and said it was the serpent of Eden. She claimed she had conquered the devil, embodied in the snake, by treading on its head, fulfilling the prophecy of Genesis that the children of Eve would strike the serpent's head (3:15). Townspeople later discovered that the young woman had become pregnant by her local priest, her scandalized family had turned her out of the house, and she had gone slightly mad.

Around the year 1480 in York in northern England, a village priest named William Bolden read the Bible (in Latin, since

translations into English were illegal then) and became fascinated
by the story of Adam and Eve in Genesis. Bolden was slightly
mentally unstable, and he began walking around the village at
night naked. He believed nakedness was the God-given state
of man, but he was wise enough to realize that walking around
naked in the daytime would get him into trouble. However, word
travels fast in small towns, and soon the whole area knew about
Bolden's naked nocturnal walks. Several people, both men and
women, eventually joined him on these nighttime rambles, and
before long they were calling themselves Adamites. Their rambles
always ended at—you guessed it—an apple orchard, where Bolden
preached to them about the need to live as God intended, urging
them to go naked in the daytime.

Finally several of them got up the nerve to do so, but on the
first day of full exposure, some aides of Bolden's bishop arrived
and took Bolden and the other naked folks into custody. They
were kept in a cold, damp dungeon until they begged their
captors for clothing or at least some blankets to wrap themselves
in. The bishop allowed them some blankets and gave them a
sound scolding, telling them that in this sinful world, God did
not intend for people to run around nude.

Several months later, three women who had joined Bolden's
Adamite band were discovered to be pregnant—and all three
claimed that Bolden was the father. Bolden's sermons about the
innocence of the garden of Eden had evidently been part of a
flimsy excuse for his own sexual promiscuity. The bishop punished Bolden by imprisoning him—naked—in a cage on the
village green for several days. The humiliation seemed to cure
him permanently of wanting to "go Adam" again.

In the mid 1800s in the United States, some Seminole Indians
in southern Florida converted to Christianity—sort of. These particular converts took a fancy to the story of Adam and Eve being
naked and unashamed in the garden of Eden. They noticed that

their own region was much like the garden of Eden (except for the alligators and venomous snakes) and that the climate allowed for going naked, so they began calling themselves "children of Adam" and cast their clothing aside. The missionaries who had evangelized them had to explain that Adam and Eve had fallen into sin, so nakedness was no longer God's will for humans.

Aside from these real instances of Adamites, several fictional groups existed not in reality but in the minds of people trying to smear their opponents. Throughout human history, people have depicted their enemies as promiscuous and immoral. (Oddly, this happens even in societies that seem to tolerate promiscuity and immorality.) In England in the 1500s, rumor spread that a group of Puritans called the Family of Love met for worship naked—and that the worship always degenerated into a sexual orgy. The Family of Love probably never existed except in the minds of people who hated the Puritans. (For what it's worth, the Puritans weren't slack about spreading rumors about their critics either.)

People who were accused falsely of being Adamites might have taken some comfort in knowing that the early Christians were also accused of degenerate sexual practice and that the innocent practice of calling each other brother and sister was misconstrued to indicate that incest was taking place among the Christians.

The Proslavery Argument

When the Bible was written, slavery was an accepted part of life—so much so that the Bible never actually says that slavery is wrong. On the other hand, the key event of the Old Testament is the miraculous freeing of the Hebrew slaves in Egypt. We would expect the Old Testament Law to prohibit slavery, but it doesn't. However, it does mandate freeing any slave after seven years, so the only lifelong slaves in Israel chose to be so. As far as we know, slavery among the Israelites was much less burdensome than the brutal slavery the Israelites endured under the Egyptians.

Jesus Himself said nothing at all about slavery—or at least nothing that is recorded in the Gospels. The apostle Paul did address the subject:

> All who are under the yoke of slavery should consider their masters worthy of full respect, so that God's name and our teaching may not be slandered. Those who have believing masters are not to show less respect for them because they are brothers. Instead, they are to serve them even better, because those who benefit from their service are believers, and dear to them (1 Timothy 6:1-2 NIV).

The shortest of Paul's epistles, the brief letter to Philemon, encourages Philemon to take back his runaway slave, Onesimus, and to treat him as a Christian brother. So Paul doesn't prohibit slavery, though he commands Christian slave owners to be humane, especially if the slave himself is a Christian. The apostle Peter exhorts, "Slaves, submit yourselves to your masters with all respect, not only to those who are good and considerate, but also to those who are harsh" (1 Peter 2:18 NIV).

In America in the 1800s, slavery was a hot issue. Abolitionists (many of whom were Christian ministers) wanted slavery abolished totally, and many of them based their beliefs on the Bible, saying that Christian civilization had changed since Bible days and that Christians should no longer tolerate the practice. The abolitionists also pointed out that though the Bible never says not to own slaves, several passages do command paying people for their labor. (Slave owners countered this by saying that though slaves were not paid in money, they received room, food, and clothing from their masters.) Abolitionists also pointed out that the command "Thou shalt not steal" applied to stealing human beings and that Exodus 21:16 commands the death penalty for anyone who kidnaps a man and sells him.

But in the South, opponents of abolition felt no shame in basing their proslavery arguments on the Bible. Virginia author Thomas Stringfellow published *A Brief Examination of Scripture Testimony on the Institution of Slavery.* In the book he points out (correctly) that the Bible does not actually prohibit slavery and that Paul even directed Onesimus to return to Philemon. Another writer, a minister named Josiah Priest, covered some of the same ground in *Bible Defense of Slavery.* Like many authors, Priest not only discussed the Bible's acceptance of slavery but also frightened readers by describing the horror that would occur if the slaves were ever freed—or worse, if they revolted and went on a murderous spree, as the slave Nat Turner had done.

The proslavery side used the command "Thou shalt not steal" against their abolitionist opponents. Slave owners regarded slaves as their personal property (and the U.S. Supreme Court at that time agreed), so in their view, the abolitionists were trying to steal their property. Both sides interpreted the commandment "Thou shalt not steal" to say what they wanted it to say.

Probably the most perverted use of the Bible among the proslavery writers was the story of Noah and his three sons. In Genesis 9:18-27, Noah gets drunk on wine and lies naked in his tent. His son Ham finds it amusing, so he tells his brothers, Shem and Japheth. These two are respectful enough to drape a cloth over their father without actually seeing him naked. When Noah awakes, he blesses Shem and Japheth but curses Ham—or, more precisely, Canaan, the son of Ham, and all his descendants: "'Cursed be Canaan! The lowest of slaves will he be to his brothers.' He also said, 'Blessed be the LORD, the God of Shem! May Canaan be the slave of Shem. May God extend the territory of Japheth; may Japheth live in the tents of Shem, and may Canaan be his slave'" (NIV). The genealogy that follows in Genesis 10 identifies Ham as the ancestor of Egypt, Cush, and other people believed to live in Africa. Slave owners reached the conclusion that Africans were the descendants of Ham and Canaan and that God had ordained them to live in slavery. This is evident in M.T. Wheat's book *The Progress and Intelligence of Americans: Collateral Proof of Slavery, From the First to the Eleventh Chapter of Genesis, as Founded on Organic Law, and From the Fact of Christ Being a Caucasian.*

For the record, this ridiculous belief that Africans were under the curse of Ham wasn't the worst racial idea circulating in the 1800s. Some people—many of them claiming to be scientists— held to a theory called *polygenesis,* which claimed that the different races of man were descended not from Noah and his three sons but from different *species* of humankind—Africans being (so the theory went) the descendants of an inferior ancestor. In a sense, polygenesis taught that keeping black-skinned people as slaves was acceptable because they weren't fully human—or at least were a definitely lower form of human. History has witnessed not only silly beliefs about the Bible but also some very silly science.

One of the great tragedies of American history—and the history of Christianity also—is that our nation divided not only politically but religiously. In fact, most of the larger Christian denominations split into Southern and Northern branches years before the Southern states broke away and formed the Confederacy. What might have happened if Southern clergymen had agreed with their Northern counterparts that slavery was simply wrong, even if it wasn't specifically prohibited in the Bible? Harriett Beecher Stowe, author of the phenomenally popular antislavery novel *Uncle Tom's Cabin,* originally subtitled the book *The Man Who Was a Thing.* She understood that any Christian who claimed to guide his life by the Bible should treat his fellow humans as people made in God's image, not as things to be used and bought and sold.

After Abraham Lincoln became president, Southern states began to secede, 11 of them forming the Confederate States of America. Many Southerners compared Lincoln to the biblical king Rehoboam, the tactless son of Solomon who alienated some of the tribes of Israel, leading them to break away and form a new nation. In the Bible, Rehoboam is seen as a bad king, and the Confederates felt they were right in breaking away from such a ruler. But Confederates also compared Lincoln to another biblical ruler, the oppressive Pharaoh in Exodus. Naturally they compared themselves to Israel, God's chosen people, and their president, Jefferson Davis, to Moses, leading his people away from the tyranny of Pharaoh. They compared the Civil War to the Egyptian army's quest to kill or capture the released Israelites. Ironically, the Southerners saw themselves as slaves freed from bondage even though they formed a new nation committed to the institution of slavery.

Nat Turner, Preacher and Murderer

In the tense years before the American Civil War, many American slave owners feared a bloody uprising of the slaves. The fears seemed to come to gory life in the person of Nat Turner, a preacher and ex-slave who led a slave revolt in Virginia in 1831. He and his followers murdered more than 50 whites, and Turner was caught and hanged.

Turner knew the Bible well, but like many revolutionary leaders, he chose to ignore the Bible's teachings on forgiveness and compassion. However, he did not neglect such Bible verses as this one from Exodus: "And he that stealeth a man, and selleth him, or if he be found in his hand, he shall surely be put to death" (Exodus 21:16). In Turner's opinion, the passage justified the murder of slaveholders. (In the county where Turner went on his rampage, the county seat was named Jerusalem.)

St. John the Killer

John Brown (1800–1859) was an important figure in American history, and one of the strangest. The poor man had a large brood of children (20 to be exact) and had done a poor job of providing for them. He found something that gave his life meaning and purpose: abolishing slavery. Unfortunately, Brown had no intention of waiting to abolish it through the political process. He intended to use violence against slave owners (or even against people who condoned slavery) and to arm slaves and lead them in a revolt. Brown firmly believed God wanted the slaves freed—by violence if necessary. He felt no qualms about mentioning God's will and bullets in the same sentence.

Brown and some of his followers trekked to the new territory of Kansas, which was up for grabs in terms of legalizing slavery. Both proslavery and antislavery people were settling there, and in 1856 Brown and his gang brutally murdered several proslavery people. Although many people protested the horror, the East Coast intellectual elite applauded the acts. In October 1859, Brown and his gang seized the federal armory in Harper's Ferry, Virginia, hoping to arm slaves with the weapons and ignite the revolt he had prayed for. The U.S. Marines captured Brown, who was found guilty of treason and hanged. Brown's plan had been so ridiculous and badly planned that he apparently wanted to become a martyr for the antislavery cause. His sympathizers in the Northeast considered him a saint. Writer Henry David Thoreau called him the Angel of Light. (Perhaps Thoreau had forgotten that Paul had written that Satan masquerades as an angel of light. At any rate, this "angel" had a lot of blood on his hands.)

Like Nat Turner, the slave who had led a violent revolt in Virginia, Brown had a selective way of reading the Bible. He liked to focus on the Old Testament, particularly the book of Joshua, where the Israelites used violence against their enemies. Although his sympathizers regarded him as a Christian martyr, Brown had no interest in the New Testament with its pray-for-your-enemies, turn-the-other-cheek morality.

Anne Morrow Lindbergh

Anne Morrow Lindbergh, widow of American aviator Charles Lindbergh, became a celebrity in her own right with such books as *Gift from the Sea* (1955). Mrs. Lindbergh represented something new in America: a kind of mystical blending of Christianity, pagan thought, and the vague new religion of self-help and looking inward. In her books she used phrases from the Bible such as *kingdom of heaven,* but invested them with egocentric meanings that appealed to readers of the 1950s and '60s.

Cosmic Consciousness

The New Age movement is actually quite old, though the New Age name is fairly recent. As far back as 1901, a self-styled seer named Richard Maurice Bucke published *Cosmic Consciousness,* in which he drew on the insights of Jesus and Paul—and also Buddha, various Christian heretics, and many anonymous Americans who testified to living on "a new plane of existence" and to having been "illuminated." Two of the illuminated, Walter and Lao Russell, put Bucke's ideas into practice at their University of Science and Philosophy, which they founded in Virginia in 1957. The university's curriculum was only loosely connected to the message of the Bible.

Licking the Sun King's Boots

At the court of French king Louis XIV (the "Sun King"), court preacher Jacques Bossuet found many Bible quotations "proving" that the people should submit to and reverence the vain and powerful king. Bossuet began as preacher in the royal chapel, and in

1670 he was appointed tutor to the king's heir. Bossuet's book on the divine right of kings was *Politique tiree des propres paroles de l'Ecriture Sainte (Politics Derived from the Very Words of Holy Scripture)*, written for the instruction of the heir. Part 2 of the book defends Bossuet's belief that hereditary monarchy is the best form of government (overlooking Samuel's words about the perils of monarchy in 1 Samuel 8). He compared Louis to David and Solomon, and he claimed that the sources of authority were the king, the church, and God. Obviously, Bossuet designed his writings to praise the king rather than to interpret Scripture accurately.

Baptism by Bible

The Bogomiles were a group of Christian heretics living in the Balkans in the eleventh century. Though Christian in some ways, they disregarded the Old Testament, saying it was the work of Satan, not God. Also, the patriarchs of Israel had been inspired by Satan, not God. Satan was originally God's right-hand helper but had rebelled. Satan, they said, made the material world, so all matter is evil. Because matter is evil, Bogomiles didn't practice the traditional rituals of water baptism and the Lord's Supper but rather turned both into entirely spiritual acts. They baptized a convert by placing a copy of John's Gospel on his head while reciting the Lord's Prayer.

Compulsive Inquisition

The Inquisition is one of the ugliest examples of violent oppression in the history of Christianity. It existed in Catholic Europe and was intended to root out suspected heretics. The tactics of arresting people, seizing their property, torturing them, and even executing them were horrible. Did you ever wonder how an institution that was supposedly Christian could justify such behavior? Blame it on a bad misconstruing of the Bible. The Inquisition used Jesus' parable of the great supper in Luke 14, emphasizing verse 17: "Compel them to come in." The Inquisitors took this to mean that Christians whose beliefs were going astray had to be compelled into right belief—even if the compelling included torture and death.

Random Guidance

The word *bibliomancy* refers to the practice of opening a sacred book at random to receive guidance from whatever passage appears first. Theologians have never approved of this, but a few high-profile Christians have practiced it, including John Bunyan, the author of *Pilgrim's Progress,* and John Wesley, the founder of the Methodist movement. Augustine attributed his conversion to hearing a child repeating the singsong phrase, "Take it and read it, take it and read it." A copy of Paul's letter to the Romans happened to be within reach, and after reading the first passage his eyes rested on, Augustine became a new man. Incidentally, many of the ancient Greeks and Romans applied the same principle to the epic poems of Homer and Virgil.

No Surgery, Thanks

In times past, some Christians opposed the surgical removal of limbs, saying that when bodies are raised at the resurrection they shouldn't have limbs missing. Obviously these folks gave no thought to the many martyrs (such as Paul) who were beheaded or the many others who were burned at the stake. A physician named James Simpson put forward the argument that God Himself was the first surgeon because He put Adam to sleep and removed his rib to form Eve.

Stylish Quoting

A preacher who was opposed to women wearing their hair in a knot or ball on top of their heads searched for a Bible verse to back him up until he found this saying of Jesus: "Let him which is on the housetop not come down" (Matthew 24:17). The preacher whittled the verse down to "top (k)not come down" and made it the basis of a sermon.

The Adventists' Diet

Seventh-day Adventists' biblical position regarding their diet—that is, their adherence to the kosher foods laws of the Old Testament—is incorrect. In fact, the New Testament is rather clear on this matter: The old food laws no longer apply because Jesus Himself pronounced all foods clean (Mark 7:19). In Jesus' teaching, what comes out of a man (his words and deeds) are what make him unclean, not the food he takes into his body. The book of Acts records Peter's famous vision of a sheet containing unclean (nonkosher) animals and a voice from heaven telling him that all these beasts, which he had been taught were unclean, had been declared clean by God (Acts 10). The apostle Paul, a faithful Jew in his younger days, saw that the old Jewish laws were obstacles to bringing non-Jews into the church. In Galatians and other writings, he emphasized that Christians were freed from the old Jewish laws—not the moral laws, such as those against murder, stealing, and adultery, but the laws about sacrifices, clean and unclean foods, and other ritualistic concerns.

The Adventists weren't the first or the last believers to try to "re-Judaize" Christianity. Most of the sects that try to reinstitute the kosher laws do so in the belief that God must have had His reasons for the kosher laws—that is, the Old Testament diet must be the healthiest way for people to eat. So, no pork, no shellfish, no catfish—interesting idea, but definitely not an accurate interpretation of the Bible.

The Sabbath Is When?

Not to pick on Seventh-day Adventists, but the practice of

worshipping on Saturday is a confusion of the Old Testament (Jewish) Sabbath and the New Testament (Christian) "Lord's Day." Numerous sects over the centuries tried to reinstitute the Old Testament practice of worshipping on the seventh day (Saturday) instead of Sunday even though we know that the early Christians rather quickly began worshipping on Sunday in memory of Jesus being raised from the dead on the first day of the week.

Merciful Marcion

Marcion was probably one of the first scholars to use the "pick and choose" approach to the Bible—that is, he based his beliefs not on the whole Bible, but only on those parts he happened to agree with. Marcion saw two Gods in the Bible—the righteous God of the Old Testament and the kind God of the New Testament. The Old Testament God created the world and was jealous, angry, and eager to punish people. The New Testament God pitied mankind and sent Jesus to rescue humanity. The devotees of the Old Testament God were the ones who crucified Jesus. Jesus' death was a kind of bargain between the righteous God and the kind God—the crucifixion "paid off" the righteous God. In Marcion's teaching, the angry God was powerful, but not as powerful as the loving God. Jesus, Marcion believed, was not fully human but only appeared to be.

Marcion wasn't the last to misread the descriptions of God in the Old Testament and the New. The fact is, both Testaments witness to the same God—the God who is merciful and loving but also angry at human sin. Jesus spoke often not only about His loving Father but also about the serious consequences of sin. In other words, God in both Testaments is a God of tough love, whereas Marcion and those who follow him see the tough God and the loving God as two different beings. Marcion wrote a book called *Antitheses,* contrasting the Law of the Old Testament's angry God with the Gospel of the loving God of the New Testament.

So Marcion discarded the Old Testament completely, but he also had to discard parts of the New Testament he didn't like. In the Gospels, Jesus said that He came not to destroy the Law but to fulfill it. Since Marcion completely disregarded the Old Testament Law (which was given by the angry God), he changed Jesus' words to "not to fulfill the Law but to destroy it." Marcion accepted only Luke's Gospel, and he even tweaked that to fit his own beliefs. He accepted Paul's letters as inspired Scripture but revised them too.

Marcion not only tossed out the Old Testament and edited the New, but also taught that all created matter was evil (because matter was created by the angry God of the Old Testament). He taught that man's body was an evil thing and that Jesus did not have a physical body. Therefore, the key event of the New Testament (Jesus' bodily resurrection from the tomb) was not literal. The belief that matter is evil and spirit is good is called *dualism,* and it isn't based on the Bible, despite the fact that the New Testament authors did warn against the dangers of the world and the flesh. In the Bible, God's created world is good, but human sin has corrupted it to some extent.

Marcion lived sometime in the second century, but the sect he founded lasted several centuries after that. As it turned out, he had a beneficial effect on Christianity because his edited version of the Bible caused Christian leaders to identify which books were divinely inspired. Amazingly, his belief that the Old Testament God was not the same as the God of the New is still around.

Paul, the Faith Corrupter

One idea that's been floating around for centuries is that Jesus Christ taught a simple faith that the apostle corrupted terribly. This is a curious idea, especially considering that a huge chunk of the New Testament was written by Paul and that all his writings were in circulation before the four Gospels were written.

In our days of political correctness, Paul is still the bad boy of Christianity because he spoke out boldly against homosexuality and because he told wives to be submissive to their husbands. Hard-line feminists and pro-gay activists generally see Paul as an intolerant, unloving chauvinist whose faith was nothing like the faith of the loving, tolerant Jesus. In the 1988 film *The Last Temptation of Christ,* Paul is depicted as being so fanatical and coldhearted that he even murders Lazarus, the friend Jesus raised from the dead. Toward the end of that movie, Paul meets Jesus and tells him that the faith Paul preaches doesn't even need Jesus—Paul has created his own intolerant, legalistic religion that bears scant resemblance to what Jesus taught. This misconception is ironic because Paul was the great preacher of a faith that was *not* legalistic. As one scholar said, "Paul is the great libertarian of religious history."

Paul and Jesus both spoke of God as a loving Father who offers salvation to all repentant sinners. And both Paul and Jesus hated sin and urged people to live as sinlessly as they could—all the while remembering that God was patient with human failings. The idea that Paul's God was judgmental and exclusive while Jesus' God was tolerant and inclusive is plain silly. Christian author C.S. Lewis pointed out that attacking Paul is really an indirect way of attacking Christianity—that is, attacking Jesus directly isn't smart because most people have a high opinion of Him, but attacking Paul is okay because the public at large doesn't have as much sentimental attachment to him. But Jesus and Paul taught essentially the same beliefs and the same morality, so when people sling mud at Paul, they inevitably splatter it on Jesus also.

Ever wonder why so few films about the life of Paul have been made? The reason is that he's either depicted as non-Christian in his actions (as in *The Last Temptation of Christ*), or he isn't depicted at all, thanks to the foolish belief that he somehow changed and corrupted the loving, inclusive gospel of Jesus.

Some anti-Paul folks point out that Jesus did not say a word about homosexuality and that Paul spoke out boldly against it in 1 Corinthians 6 and Romans 1. Jesus, as a devout Jew, must have felt about homosexual behavior the same way Paul did: It was an abomination. Homosexual novelist Gore Vidal took fiendish delight in his novel *Live from Golgotha* in depicting Paul as a repressed homosexual whose antihomosexual remarks were rooted in his own guilt and self-hatred—an interesting idea but totally without merit.

Liberation Theology

One of the most controversial theological trends of the twentieth century was the so-called liberation theology, which at its worst was essentially communism with a very thin veneer of Christianity laid on top. The basic idea of this extreme liberation theology was that God was the great Liberator who wanted all oppressed people to rise in revolt against their capitalist oppressors. Liberation theologians liked to point to the story of Moses and the Exodus as the great pattern of freedom from bondage, but they overlooked the fact that in Exodus, deliverance comes from God, not from human revolutionaries. Some of the more radical theologians turned a blind eye to the New Testament teaching about mercy, forgiveness, not seeking vengeance, and living peaceably, putting themselves in the very unbiblical position of saying that killing an oppressor or a whole social class of oppressors may be God's will in certain situations. By the end of the twentieth century, this extreme liberation theology had pretty much run its course because communism (which most liberation theologians admired) had failed in so many instances. In the more liberal seminaries, a few aging liberation theologians keep the flame alive.

The Ebionites

From the very beginning of the church, various groups split off from Christianity, preserving some Christian beliefs but adding some distinctive features of their own. The group known as the Ebionites used the Gospel According to the Hebrews, which apparently was an altered version of Matthew's Gospel without the parts about the virgin birth. They believed Jesus was the son of Mary and Joseph and that He became Son of God at His baptism. They regarded Jesus as more of a teacher and moral role model than a Savior, and they rejected the authority of Paul's epistles. They also circulated the strange story that Paul was not born a Jew but had had himself circumcised in order to marry a priest's daughter; when that didn't work out as planned, he became seriously anti-Semitic. In other words, he became a Christian not because of any attraction to the faith but out of a desire to spite the Jews. In short, the Ebionites were Jewish Christians who appeared more Jewish than Christian. In their view, the new religion was just a new and improved edition of the old, and they still ordered their lives around the Old Testament laws—something that all the writers of the New Testament said was no longer necessary.

The Gnostics

A system of thought called Gnosticism competed with Christianity for centuries, and at times it threatened to triumph over it. The Gnostics were never organized in their thinking or organization, so their teachings varied widely. We can say generally that they believed matter is evil and spirit is good, that the material world was created by an evil god, and that the human spirit's goal is to be released from the material world and enter the pure realm of spirit. In Gnostic teaching, God Himself wasn't that important. After all, He created the material world, which was bad, and He was not "with" human beings but was way off in some distant realm, unconcerned with life on earth. In other words, He wasn't much like the watchful, human-loving God of the Bible.

In Gnostic teaching, people need to be saved not from their sins but from ignorance. Salvation comes through recognizing one's inner divinity.

Some of the Gnostics considered themselves Christians, and they tried (not too successfully) to mix their own beliefs with the teachings of the New Testament. Marcion (see page 45) was a kind of Christian Gnostic, and other Christian Gnostics followed him in editing the New Testament to make it reflect Gnostic beliefs. Many Gnostic Gospels floated around, and some of them are being studied widely today, including the famous Gospel of Thomas. The writers of these false Gospels lived long after the time of Jesus and His disciples, but they generally published their Gospels under the names of the disciples to gain credibility. In the Gnostic Gospels, Jesus isn't the Savior sent to free people from their sins; He's the Cosmic Teacher sent to enlighten certain people who are worthy to enter the spiritual realm. Many of the Gnostics taught that Jesus was not really human but only appeared to be.

Some of the Gnostics honored Simon the magician, a character in the book of Acts. Simon submits to baptism and is supposedly a Christian, but he is so astounded by the apostles' power to work miracles that he offers to purchase it from them. He is scolded for this, and he asks the apostles to pray for him. That is all the Bible says about him, but legends about him proliferated, some of them making him a sort of Gnostic guru who continued to make trouble for Christians.

The Gnostics didn't take the Bible itself at face value or as historical truth. For them the Bible was a kind of divine code book to be interpreted only by those initiated into Gnostic wisdom. They had no interest at all in Jesus as a real human being who walked the earth. For them, Jesus Christ was an inner reality, quite separate from the real world. When they read the Gospels, they tended to spin the text, imposing their own interpretation on it. For example, many of them believed that when Jesus on the cross cried out, "My God, my God, why have you forsaken me?" this was the sign that the spark of divinity within Jesus had departed.

The Gnostics' contempt for the material world could lead in two directions: One direction was in rejection of the material world, swearing off marriage and sex, living with few material goods, and keeping one's diet as simple as possible. But the other direction was the indulging of one's sensual appetites. If the material world really isn't important, what a person does with his own body (or someone else's) is of no significance. In Romans 6:15, the apostle Paul had written, "Shall we sin, because we are not under the law, but under grace? God forbid." Instead of saying, "God forbid," some of the Gnostics said, "Sure, let's sin and enjoy it!" Needless to say, a religion that teaches "Do whatever you like" always finds fans.

Gnosticism is still around. There will always be people who like to think of themselves as spiritual, but who don't like to think of God watching over them and judging their moral state. The polls that show an increasing number of people who identify themselves as spiritual but not religious are a witness to the survival of Gnosticism. A religion that emphasizes being "in the know" instead of living a moral life will always be popular.

Gnosticism might have remained buried in libraries had it not been for the 1979 book *The Gnostic Gospels* by Elaine Pagels. It sold well, and people were intrigued by the author's belief that Christianity had deliberately narrowed its tolerance, branding many worthy books and ideas as heresy. In Pagels' telling, Gnosticism was a great might-have-been of history, something wonderful that was snuffed out by an oppressive Christianity.

Pagels and many other fans of Gnosticism are feminists who oppose Paul's teaching on women in the New Testament. Paul did tell wives to be subject to their husbands (Ephesians 5:21-22), though people often forget that in the same passage he told husband and wife to submit to each other. And frankly, Gnosticism isn't really feminist at all. Most of the Gnostic Gospels don't show women in a favorable light. In fact, the most famous of them, the Gospel of Thomas, has Jesus saying that women have to become male before entering the kingdom of heaven. This surely degrades women more than anything Paul said.

Cainites

Cain, the first murderer, is hardly an admirable character, yet one Gnostic group called itself the Cainites. Active around the year 150, the group said that God was evil and that rebels against Him (such as Cain, Esau, and the men of Sodom) were the real heroes. The Cainites flipped the Bible's morality upside down: If God said not to do it, they said to do it. The group even made a hero of Judas Iscariot and circulated a Gospel of Judas, which made headlines in 2006 when *National Geographic* published it in English.

In this very strange document, Jesus makes Judas His favorite disciple, trusting him with the true teachings that the other 11 disciples are not worthy to hear. In fact, Jesus literally laughs at the other 11 disciples when they try to act religious. Jesus says that the God who made the material world with all its suffering is the God of the Old Testament and is not worthy to be worshipped. Rebels like Cain and the men of Sodom are heroes because they opposed this cruel God. Some fortunate people, Jesus says, are worthy to receive the "mysteries of the kingdom." They recognize the "seed" of divinity within them, and on their death they are released from this crude material world and enter the realm of light, called Barbelo. These enlightened people are called the "great generation with no ruler over it."

In the Gospel of Judas, as in many other Gnostic writings, Jesus is not actually human but only appears to be. In fact, He sometimes assumes the form of a child, sometimes an old man—and can appear in different guises and in different places simultaneously. This Gospel ends not with Jesus' resurrection, but with Judas betraying Jesus to the authorities. Judas has done his Master the supreme favor, for in death Jesus is released from this world.

Whoever wrote the Gospel of Judas believed that Jesus' other 11 disciples were misguided—they were "ministers of error"—and so were the Christians who honored them. If the teachings in the Gospel of Judas are true, the writings in the New Testament are false because they show the God of this world as loving and kind. Jesus is His Son, sent to save mankind from sin, and this is accomplished by His death and resurrection. This dichotomy explains why this musty old Gnostic Gospel was resurrected in the twenty-first century: It offers an alternative view of Christianity that many people find appealing.

The Sethians

One of the many Gnostic Christian groups that flourished in ancient times called themselves Sethians, after Seth, the third son of Adam and Eve. Abel was dead, and Cain had gone into exile, so the Sethians believed Seth represented a new beginning for the human race. Yet strangely, they also identified Seth with Jesus Christ—"Setho, who is called Christ." The Sethians' way of reading the Old Testament was quite interesting. They were aware that the original Hebrew Bible uses several different names for God: Yahweh, Elohim, Adonai, and others. But they believed these were not different names for God, but different gods. The true God, the one Jesus called Father, was several generations earlier than the gods named in the Old Testament.

The Paulicians

This sect, which started sometime around 650 in the Middle

East, named itself after the apostle Paul or after some other Paul they honored. The Paulicians threw out the Old Testament altogether but studied Paul's epistles and the Gospel of Luke. They were adoptionists, believing that Jesus became the Son of God at His baptism. In their communion service they used water instead of wine. Most of them were celibate, and quite a few were vegetarians. They believed that marriage and sex were wrong, so any pregnancies among the women Paulicians were "corrected" by forced abortions. They also believed all matter was evil, so they encouraged suicide among their members because death was an escape from the evil material world. In fact, they practiced assisted suicide, helping a person who lost his nerve to finish the final act.

The Christians regarded the Paulicians as heretics. The Paulicians proved to have a much longer life than most heresies, however, for some Paulicians were living in Armenia and Russia as late as the 1800s. In the Middle Ages they suffered severe persecution under some of the Byzantine emperors, although one emperor was himself a Paulician, who during his reign gave them a rest from persecution. Some of the Paulicians living in the Middle East welcomed the Muslim conquerors, believing the Muslims would treat them better than the Christians did.

Arius and His Followers

One of the great mysteries of Christian belief is the Trinity—the belief that God is three Persons: one in three and three in one. Jesus told His disciples to baptize people "in the name of the Father, and of the Son, and of the Holy Spirit" (Matthew 28:19). The disciple Thomas referred to Jesus as "my Lord and my God" (John 20:28), and John's Gospel spoke of Jesus as "the Word," and "the Word was with God, and the Word was God" (1:1). Some of the early Christians liked to speculate how Jesus could be both the Son of God and God Himself, and how the Trinity existed. Did the Son and the Spirit both exist eternally with God the Father, or was God older? And were the Son and the Spirit somehow subordinate to the Father?

This kind of discussion makes many people's eyes glaze over, and most Christians are content to simply accept the Trinity as a divine mystery that needn't be explored too deeply. But some of the early Christians wanted to define the belief in the Trinity very precisely. One who wished to do so was Arius, who lived in the early 300s. He was a Christian priest in Alexandria, Egypt, who taught that Jesus was indeed divine and the Son of God but that He was subordinate to the Father and that He did not exist from all eternity as the Father did. Some would say that this is hairsplitting by people who have too much time on their hands. But in fact the so-called Arian controversy proved to be one of the most divisive issues in the history of Christianity.

Arius was a handsome man and eloquent speaker, and he attracted many followers because of his demeanor and because many people thought he was reading the Bible correctly. The controversy became so heated that Constantine, the Roman emperor who had become a Christian and ended persecution, called a council to decide once and for all whether Arianism was acceptable or heretical. The council met in 325 in the city of Nicea, and after some long and heated debates, it ruled against Arius. The precision was amazing: Arius taught that Jesus was of "similar substance" (Greek word *homoiousios*) with the Father, while the council ruled that Jesus was of the "same substance" *(homoousios)* as the Father. In other words, one tiny letter made the difference between right belief and heresy. The church approved a statement of faith called the Nicene Creed (still recited in many churches), which affirms that Jesus was "of one substance with the Father."

Constantine considered the matter settled, and he thought he was reigning over an empire where all Christians thought alike—but he was wrong. Arianism continued to attract people, and one of Constantine's own sons, later to be emperor, was an Arian. The Arians took their form of Christianity to the mission field, and many European converts to the new religion were Arians. Politics became mixed up with religion, and people living outside the Roman empire, such as the Goths in northern Europe, found Arianism attractive because it had been condemned by the empire. Inside the empire, persecution usually took the form of prominent Arians being exiled to some unpleasant locale. This is a curious thing: Pagan persecution of Christians had ended under Constantine, but now Christians persecuted those they considered heretics. Aside from government persecution, horrible and violent riots erupted between Arians and Christians. People literally killed each other over a theological point represented by the letter *i*.

Several centuries later we can safely say that Arius was wrong and his opponents were right—that is, Arius had not interpreted the New Testament in quite the right way. However, the average Christian is probably not enough of a theologian to distinguish Arianism from Christianity. (Many people are probably Arians without realizing it!) Phrases like "one substance" are difficult to understand, especially since God, a spiritual being, can't really have a substance in the way that the material world has. The theologians were groping for the right words to describe the divine, and any attempt to do that is always doubtful.

One prominent group that teaches a form of Arianism is the Jehovah's Witnesses, who, like Arius, deny that the Son existed with the Father from all eternity.

The Nestorians

The Council of Nicea, mentioned in the last entry, stated that Jesus Christ, the Son of God, was of "one substance with the

Father." That didn't settle the question of just how Jesus—fully divine but also fully human—was somehow both man and God. The New Testament clearly demonstrated that he was both—but how could that be?

One person who tried to answer that deep question was Nestorius, who had been made the bishop of Constantinople, the capital of the Roman empire at that time. Nestorius' teaching is difficult to summarize in a few sentences, but essentially he taught that Jesus existed as a kind of split personality with divine and human natures existing in Him side by side.

Nestorius also taught that it was wrong to call Jesus' mother, the virgin Mary, by the name *Theotokos*—"God bearer." Nestorius said she could only be called *Christotokos*—"Christ bearer." His teaching about what to call Mary got him into even worse trouble than his teaching about the two natures existing in Jesus. Tactless and arrogant, he was condemned at a church council in 431 and sent into exile in Egypt, where he died in 451.

Nestorius' teaching lasted a lot longer than he did. It spread eastward, where it had the attraction of being a religion that had been condemned in the Roman empire. In Persia, Nestorius' homeland, thousands of people converted to his form of Christianity, and Persia was largely Nestorian in religion when the Muslims conquered the country centuries later. Nestorianism spread as far away as India and China. The Nestorian church was large enough in China that the city of Peking had a Nestorian archbishop. The religion still exists in the Middle East, where the group calling itself Assyrian Christians treats Nestorius as a saint, not a heretic.

The Monophysites

In Christian history, one heresy usually leads to another. The Christian church officially condemned the teaching of Nestorius, described in the paragraphs above. Nestorius presented Jesus as a kind of split personality, the divine and human in Him existing side by side. At the other extreme was the heresy known as Monophysitism, from the Greek words meaning "one nature." The Monophysites taught that Jesus' humanity was absorbed into His divinity, so He really was of just one nature, the divine. Most Christians saw this as denying Jesus His full humanity, and the New Testament certainly presents Jesus as both fully human and fully divine. Even so, Monophysitism spread far and wide, and one prominent Monophysite was Theodora, wife of the Roman emperor Justinian. Although Justinian was hard on people he regarded as heretics (he literally killed the last of the Montanists), he wasn't going to be rid of the Monophysites so easily, especially with his wife supporting them. Theodora even sent Monophysite missionaries into Ethiopia ahead of the orthodox missionaries her husband had sent. In fact, Justinian was leaning toward Monophysitism himself when he died in 565.

The movement spread widely in some areas, especially Egypt, where it was bound up with resentment against the Roman empire. In some areas, violent riots broke out between Monophysites and orthodox Christians. When invading Muslims conquered Egypt, many of the Monophysites welcomed them, seeing them as a good alternative to the Romans. Many Christians in Egypt, Ethiopia, and other Middle Eastern nations still proudly identify themselves as Monophysites. Their theological distinctiveness prevents them from entering into close relations with other Christian denominations.

A kind of spin-off of Monophysitism was called Monothelitism—from the Greek words for "one will." The Monothelites taught that Jesus had both a divine will and a human will, but that the human will was absorbed into the divine will. The church authorities condemned Monothelitism and chose the position called Dyothelitism—meaning "two wills."

The Spirit Fighters

Is the Holy Spirit divine? Is the Spirit, in some sense, God? Christians have traditionally answered yes to these questions, basing their belief on Jesus' command to baptize people in the name of the Father, Son, and Spirit. The traditional belief, rooted in the Bible, is that Father, Son, and Spirit are the Holy Trinity—God existing as three persons.

One group that did not accept the Spirit as God was known as the Pneumatomachi—the name means "fighters against the Spirit." Some of them accepted the decree of the Council of Nicea (which met in the year 325) that Jesus was of the same substance as the Father, but not that the Spirit was of the same substance. Some of the Pneumatomachi went further and denied that either the Son or the Spirit was of the same substance as the Father.

The group's beliefs weren't around for very long because they fell prey to the Emperor Theodosius' strict antiheresy laws.

The Waldensians' Lunatic Fringe

One of the most admirable groups in Christian history was the Waldensians, named after their founder, Peter Waldo, a rich French merchant who disposed of his fortune in the late 1100s and gathered around him men and women who took seriously Jesus' words about going out in pairs, spreading the faith, and owning few material possessions. Calling themselves the Poor in Spirit, they were at first smiled on by the pope, but when they began preaching against corruption in the pope's court, his attitude changed dramatically, and these saintly people were persecuted. Some were burned at the stake; others were thrown into prison. Some survived in remote villages in the mountains, and in time some of them immigrated to the English colonies in America.

We can easily admire the Waldensians, for they were trying to behave as true Christians in a society that was only Christian on the surface. Yet nearly every good movement has a few lunatics on its edges. In southern France, one Waldensian decided that the Old Testament practice of polygamy was still an option for God's people, so he took a second wife, then another, and finally seven. Perhaps he wasn't aware that the New Testament and the Christian tradition make no place for polygamy. At any rate, he was thrown into prison, and all of his marriages were declared invalid except for the first.

The Pure Ones

One of the most prominent heresies of the Middle Ages went by several names. Its devotees were known as the Cathari (meaning "Pure Ones") but also as Albigenses and Paterenes. Although they considered themselves Christians, they believed in two eternal principles, one evil and one good, and the evil held the power over the church hierarchy. They believed (as did the Gnostics centuries earlier) that the material world was evil and that the body's physical needs had to be denied as much as possible. Marriage was frowned on, and producing children was regarded as horrible. Because matter was evil, Jesus was not truly a physical being, and the crucifixion, resurrection, and ascension were all illusions. Jesus wasn't truly human but rather a pure spirit who appeared on earth to teach mankind. The Cathari, like many sects, picked what they liked from the Bible and discarded the rest, throwing out most of the Old Testament and much of the New. They had their own organization of bishops and ministers. In some parts of Europe, especially southern France, they comprised a huge percentage of the population.

Like the Waldensians, the Cathari embarrassed the official church by their own self-denying morality, and the church took pains to stamp them out. In 1179 the Catholic church's Third Lateran Council proclaimed a crusade against the Cathari—the first crusade directed against heretics. Many of the Cathari were killed, and others were persuaded to return to the Catholic church. Others fled east to the Balkan Mountains. The Inquisition rooted out what was left of the movement.

British Israelites

The kings of England descended from King David of Israel? Sounds silly, but that idea has been floating around for several centuries. In its usual form, the legend says that when the Babylonians conquered Jerusalem in 586 BC and carried its leading citizens into exile, the daughter of King Zedekiah fled to Ireland and became the ancestor of a ruling dynasty there. The same dynasty later ruled in Scotland, and when the Scottish king James VI became James I, king of England, the Davidic bloodline passed to the English.

This was total nonsense, of course, but since it couldn't be disproven (or proven), it did add a little mystique to the British kings, making them the descendants of the most famous king in the Bible. Even the many illegitimate sons of the kings were descendants of David. Also, since David was a descendant of the patriarch Abraham, God's promise to make a great nation of Abraham's descendants could be applied to the British. The British were the chosen people of modern times, as the Jews had been in the ancient world. Many Americans of English origin found the idea appealing also, and some even believed America had replaced Britain as the favored nation of God.

The idea of England being a new Israel was many centuries old. King Alfred the Great, who died in the year 901, explicitly based his laws on the Old Testament laws, especially the three chapters following the Ten Commandments. Alfred saw the English as the new Israelites, subject to God's laws as the old Israelites were.

Adoptionism

Was Jesus always the Son of God, or did He become the Son at His baptism? Many early Christians taught that Jesus of Nazareth was fully human and became God's Son at His baptism. They based this belief on the voice of God declaring "This is my beloved Son" at the baptism (Matthew 3:17). Christian theologians have generally taught that this view—called adoptionism, because it seems to hold that the man Jesus was adopted by God at the baptism—is a heresy.

Adoptionists also believed that when Jesus cried out on the cross, "My God, my God, why have you forsaken me?" the divine spirit inside Christ departed, leaving the human body of Jesus to die on the cross.

Basilides' Biblical Bungling

In ancient times, one of the most difficult ideas for people to swallow was that Jesus Christ was actually God in human form. People could accept the idea that God—or *a* god—would walk the earth in disguise for a while. The Greeks had myths about such occurrences, with Zeus, Apollo, Athena, or some other divinity assuming human shape now and then. But the idea that a god actually became human was difficult to grasp. They couldn't imagine a god accepting human limitations, enduring pain, even (in the Gospels) dying. Many people chose to spin the Gospel stories about Jesus. One example was the heresy known as Docetism, which basically taught that Jesus only appeared to be a human but really wasn't. In the Docetists' view, Jesus' flogging and crucifixion were really just an act because a divine being couldn't really shed blood and experience excruciating pain.

One heretic, a man named Basilides, went a step further, saying that it wasn't Jesus on the cross, nor Jesus' phantom. The one who was crucified was Simon of Cyrene. In the Gospels, Simon was an innocent bystander whom the Romans forced to carry Jesus' cross to the place of crucifixion. In Basilides' version, Jesus at that point engaged in instant identity theft. He used his divine power to make Himself look like Simon and Simon look like Him, so in fact it was Simon of Cyrene (poor man!) who suffered and died on the cross. An interesting idea, but certainly not one that makes Jesus looks good. His alleged switch would have sent an innocent bystander to a painful death.

The Prosperity Gospel

One of the most beautiful sayings in all the Bible is John 10:10, where Jesus says, "I have come that they may have life, and have it to the full" (NIV). Perhaps the King James Version here is a little more poetic: "I am come that they might have life, and that they might have it more abundantly." The idea of abundant life has given many people hope and courage over the centuries. Lovely as it sounds, though, what does it actually mean? Is Jesus teaching a prosperity gospel, promising His followers health, happiness, and success in this life? Or the hope of a happy eternity? Or both?

The so-called prosperity gospel has been a divisive issue among Christians. In times past, it was the teaching of fringe preachers like Reverend Ike, who mocked Christians who were content to wait for "pie in the sky, by and by." But the prosperity gospel has become more mainstream. Is it really rooted in the Bible?

If you read just the Old Testament, you would definitely see prosperity as the blessing of those who live good lives. Psalm 1 states that the person who follows the Lord's command prospers in all he does. That idea is echoed throughout the Old Testament. But other passages lament that, in this world, the righteous often suffer while the wicked prosper—which no one can doubt, assuming they look at the world through clear eyes. The book of Ecclesiastes advances another idea: Prosperity is like many other achievements in life, a meaningless "chasing after the wind." In other words, even success doesn't necessarily bring satisfaction. The Old Testament is a mixed bag of attitudes toward prosperity, but it most often teaches that a godly life will lead to some form of prosperity—usually.

The New Testament is radically different. In this sinful world, good people suffer. The Son of God was persecuted and executed, and His followers can expect the same treatment. So when Jesus told His disciples they would have "life to the full," clearly He meant something other than material prosperity. Paul gave a rather detailed account of the abundant life he had as an apostle:

> Five times I received from the Jews the forty lashes minus one. Three times I was beaten with rods, once I was stoned, three times I was shipwrecked, I spent a night and a day in the open sea, I have been constantly on the move. I have been in danger from rivers, in danger from bandits, in danger from my own countrymen, in danger from Gentiles; in danger in the city, in danger in the country, in danger at sea; and in danger from false brothers. I have labored and toiled and have often gone without sleep; I have known hunger and thirst and have often gone without food; I have been cold and naked. Besides everything else, I face daily the pressure of my concern for all the churches (2 Corinthians 11:24-28 NIV).

Doesn't sound like a cozy, comfortable existence in a gated community, does it? And yet Paul often used the word *joy* in his letters. "We also rejoice in our sufferings, because we know that suffering produces perseverance" (Romans 5:3 NIV). "Be joyful in hope, patient in affliction, faithful in prayer" (Romans 12:12 NIV). "The fruit of the Spirit is love, joy, peace, patience, kindness, goodness, faithfulness" (Galatians 5:22 NIV). "Rejoice in the Lord always. I will say it again: Rejoice!" (Philippians 4:4 NIV). In spite of all he endured, Paul was not a whiner, nor did he seem to care much for material comfort. "I know what it is to be in need, and I know what it is to have plenty. I have learned the secret of being content in any and every situation, whether well fed or hungry, whether living in plenty or in want" (Philippians 4:12 NIV). "Godliness with contentment is great gain" (1 Timothy 6:6 NIV).

In short, the prosperity gospel does not exist in the New Testament. Christians are encouraged to go about their daily lives, content with what they have, focused on a better life in the next world—a hope that gives them life in this one. The only real success is living a godly life.

The Rappites

Christian communes represent an interesting idea based on Acts 2:41-47, which describes how the Jerusalem Christians shared all their property in common. This has been tried many times in history, and it inevitably fails. One attempt at it that lasted quite a while was the Harmony Society, a German group also known as the Rappites after their leader George Rapp. The group founded a Christian commune in New Harmony, Indiana, in 1816, and then relocated to Pennsylvania, where their commune survived until 1916. Like many other Christian communes, the Rappites were industrious, well-organized, and devout. Their commitment to celibacy probably had something to do with their decline.

The First Muslim?

The Jews consider Abraham their physical and spiritual ancestor—and so do the Muslims. The Jews trace their descent from Abraham's son Isaac; Muslims trace theirs from Abraham's other son, Ishmael (called *Ismail* in the Muslim holy book, the Koran). According to the Koran, God revealed the true religion to Abraham, and with his son Ismail, he built the holy site known as the Ka'aba. Jews and Christians, the Muslims believe, have distorted the pure religion God gave to Abraham.

"Two Seed" Predestination

Many Christians have held to the doctrine of predestination, and they can quote Bible passages to support their position. One extreme form of the teaching has no basis in the Bible, however. This was the "Two Seed" theology taught by American frontier preacher Daniel Parker in the 1800s. According to Parker, mankind fell into two groups, depending on whether they were descended from Eve's good seed or bad seed. Parker said that the good seed was planted by God, the bad seed by Satan. This, Parker said, explained why some people accepted the gospel and others did not.

Landmarkism

Some Baptists have taken baptism by immersion very seriously—so much so that they believe that any other form of baptism is wrong. "Landmarkers" were Baptists who taught that since the New Testament period, true believers passed on the belief and practice in baptism by immersion. Only where this was done was Christianity truly present. Thus the Middle Ages, when almost all baptism was by sprinkling, was a time of spiritual darkness. Likewise for any Protestant churches that baptize by sprinkling. Any church that practices immersion is a true church; any that does not is a false church.

The Smith Revision

Joseph Smith (1805–1844) was founder of the Church of Jesus

Christ of Latter-day Saints—known generally as Mormons. Smith claimed to be a faithful Christian and follower of the Bible (which in his day meant the King James Version). But Smith claimed he received a "direct revelation" of the Bible in 1830, and this led to his revision of the Bible. This was, Smith said, necessary because "ignorant translators, careless transcribers, or designing and corrupt priests have committed many errors." Curiously, Smith's "corrected" Bible contains numerous references to Jesus Christ in the Old Testament. For example, Noah makes a call to repentance and includes a challenge to "be baptized in the name of Jesus Christ" centuries before Christ had been born on earth. In all, Smith made changes in more than 3000 verses of the King James Bible. His revision is often called the Inspired Version. The Mormons officially teach that Smith was a translator, even though he worked from the English Bible, not the original Hebrew and Greek. Still, most Mormons today use the KJV, and that's the version used on the LDS website.

Our Bibles contain the Old and New Testaments. Most Christians believe that though Christ is not mentioned by name in the Old Testament, His life and work were predicted there, so in a sense both Old and New Testaments are Christian books. The Mormons believe there is a third Testament, their own Book of Mormon, which actually has the subtitle Another Testament of Jesus Christ. Mormons believe that the New Testament does not contain the fullness of the gospel, so the Book of Mormon is necessary for right belief.

Another of the sacred books valued by Mormons is The Pearl of Great Price, which takes its name from Jesus' parable of the man finding a valuable pearl (Matthew 13:45-46). The Mormons' Pearl contains several sections in which Mormon founder Joseph Smith elaborates on stories found in the Bible.

Most Christians claim the Bible alone as the basis of belief and morality. The Mormons count the Bible as only one of their standard works, the others being the Book of Mormon, Doctrine and Covenants, and The Pearl of Great Price.

According to the Old Testament, the mighty Nebuchadnezzar, king of Babylon, conquered Jerusalem and carried off many of its people to Babylon (see 2 Kings 24–25). The Book of Mormon carries the story far beyond the Bible: God instructed a prophet named Lehi to take his family and a few others and leave Jerusalem for a new home in…America! The Book of Mormon claims to contain the record of Lehi's people from the time of Nebuchadnezzar until the fifth century after Christ.

The Order of Jacob

This phrase is what the Mormons used to refer to their practice of polygamy. As the patriarch Jacob (and so many other wealthy men in the Old Testament) had multiple wives and concubines, so men today might have the same. The first Mormons were aware that both Christians and non-Christians reacted with horror at this, and for a time it was kept secret. Various other Christian or semi-Christian sects and cults throughout history have attempted to reinstitute Old Testament polygamy. The Mormons banned it in 1890.

The Reorganized Bible

Joseph Smith's widow, who was with the Reorganized Church of Latter-day Saints, had a manuscript of Smith's Inspired Version of the Bible, which she claimed he prepared under the inspiration of God. A revision of the King James Version, it was published in Iowa in 1867 and was the favored version of the Reorganized Church. The Book of Mormon states that "they have taken away from the Gospel of the Lamb, many parts which are plain and most precious…that they might pervert the right ways of the Lord." Smith's revelations of the Bible were designed to correct the KJV. One notable change was that when God repents in the Old Testament, He does not do so in the Mormon version. Nor does He harden anyone's heart: "I will harden [Pharaoh's] heart" becomes "Pharaoh will harden his heart" (Exodus 4:21). "An evil spirit from the Lord troubled him" becomes "An evil spirit not from the Lord troubled him" (1 Samuel 16:14). The Lord's Prayer is changed to "and suffer us not to be led into temptation." Interestingly, "thou shalt not suffer a witch to live" becomes "thou shalt not suffer a murderer to live." The Last Supper rite is changed dramatically from "this is my blood" to "this is for you in remembrance of my body—this in remembrance of my blood."

But the biggest changes are in Genesis, with Smith's version introducing Christ, the Lamb of God, the resurrection, the necessity of being born again, and so forth. Smith's version omits the Song of Solomon. Odd that a man with several wives would omit the one book of the Bible that so openly celebrates physical attraction.

Jesus as a Late Bloomer

Unitarians, as you might guess from their name, do not believe Jesus was the Son of God or part of the Holy Trinity. A Unitarian version of the Bible, edited by a committee headed by Thomas Belsham of London, made it clear that Jesus was not equal with God. A note attached to John 1 states that "in the beginning" refers not to the creation of the world but to the beginning of Jesus' ministry. The stories of Jesus' virgin birth are printed in italics as additions to the original text. In places referring to Jesus as the Son of God, they substituted "a son of God."

The Reincarnation Treadmill

Is reincarnation taught in the Bible? Hardly. Hebrews 9:27 is a pretty neat summary of what the Bible says faces man after death: "Man is destined to die once, and after that to face judgment." That seems clear enough. Life on earth, judgment, and then either heaven or hell.

But as noted elsewhere in this book, people tend to find what they're looking for in the Bible, especially if they are willing to ignore the parts they happen not to agree with. Sometimes even a familiar and easily understandable verse gets twisted. For example, consider this well-known saying of Jesus: "You must be born again" (John 3:7). It's very clear in this passage that "born again" refers to a spiritual rebirth. In fact, John 3 makes it clear that Jesus is *not* referring to a physical rebirth. Some translations include a footnote stating that "born again" can also be translated "born from above." In any case, John 3 in no way teaches (or even hints) that the human soul must be born again into another physical body.

Another passage from John's Gospel is used to support belief in reincarnation. John 9 tells of the miraculous healing of a man born blind. Jesus' disciples ask Him this question: "Rabbi, who sinned, this man or his parents, that he was born blind?" (John 9:2 NIV). Admittedly this is a difficult verse to explain. The man was *born* blind, so how could his affliction be a punishment for his own sins—unless he had committed sins in a previous life? Jesus' disciples weren't believers in reincarnation. Instead, they were speaking as Jews of their time spoke, assuming that every sin has its punishment and that a man could be born with some physical handicap as a kind of preemptive punishment. The Bible doesn't actually teach this, but apparently it was widely believed by many people of that era, including Jesus' disciples. Jesus' reply to His disciples' question isn't the answer they expected: "Neither this man nor his parents sinned…but this happened so that the work of God might be displayed in his life" (9:3 NIV). Instead of seeing a physical affliction as a chance to start assigning blame, Jesus saw it as an opportunity to display the divine power to heal.

Reincarnation does not square with the Bible, but people have often tried to reconcile the two. A reincarnation Bible was published in 1881 in Philadelphia, weaving together the four Gospels and the first part of Acts with a lot of weird matter. The title page pretty much tells it all: *Christian Spiritual Bible, Containing the Gospel of the Type of the Emanation and God, the Only Ubiquitous Son, Being the Gospel of Our Lord in His Four Incarnations, Together with the Gospel of Our Lady, His Altruistic Affinity. Given Through the Angel Robert by His Intelligences.* Most people probably fell asleep by the time they finished reading the title!

The Sexless Shakers

You may have heard of the Shakers, the religious sect remembered for its simple and well-made furniture. The rest of their story is much more interesting than furniture. The group was founded by Englishwoman Ann Lee—"Mother Ann" to the group. She came to America in 1774 with her vision of getting back to Eden. She taught that God was both male and female, and that while Jesus, the first Messiah, was male, the second Messiah was female—namely, Ann Lee herself. Mother Ann liked to quote Jesus' words found in Matthew 22:30: "At the resurrection people will neither marry nor be given in marriage; they will be like the angels in heaven" (NIV). Her followers weren't awaiting the resurrection to put this into practice. They lived in dormitories, men and women under the same roof. Hallways were wide so that men and women would literally not bump into each other. A man and woman could only converse if a third party was present, and the sexes sat separately during worship. The famous ecstatic Shaker dances did not involve any touching. How the movement attracted 6000 people in its heyday is anybody's guess, but eventually numbers dwindled because they weren't recruiting new members and (obviously) weren't raising any children. Mother Ann taught that sexual intercourse was the cardinal sin.

Mother Ann's reading of Matthew 22:30 is a typical case of a Christian zooming in on one Bible verse and becoming obsessed with it. The New Testament includes no hint that God intended Christians to become sexless in this lifetime—nor to court temptation by having the sexes live together under one roof while adhering to a Don't Touch! policy. Mother Ann had let her own unhappy experiences as a wife and mother affect her reading of the Bible.

Incidentally, the Shakers' official name was United Society of Believers in Christ's Second Appearing. They were commonly called Shakers because their uninhibited worship style involved dancing and shaking.

The Swedenborg Condensed Bible

Ever heard of the Church of the New Jerusalem, better known as the Swedenborgians? The movement was begun by Swedish scientist Emanuel Swedenborg (1688–1772), who underwent a sort of conversion experience around 1744 and after that wrote numerous books outlining his spiritual beliefs. These included the eight-volume *Celestial Secrets*. Swedenborg regarded himself as a true Christian (as do most founders of sects), but his beliefs vary greatly from normal Christianity. He had no intention of starting his own church, but some of his admirers formed the Church of the New Jerusalem after his death. Following their master, the Swedenborgians omit these books from their Bible: Ruth, Chronicles, Ezra, Nehemiah, Esther, Job, Proverbs, Ecclesiastes, Song of Solomon, Acts, and all epistles. According to Swedenborg, the omitted books did not have "the internal sense" that the other books had. In 1865 a Swedenborg Bible was published in Boston with the title The Word of the Lord although it would have been more accurate to call it The Seriously Modified Word. Like many founders of sects, Swedenborg taught that the words of the Bible had a spiritual meaning that was much more important than the literal meaning—and he, of course, felt qualified to explain just what the spiritual meaning was.

The Christian Science Pastor

We think of a pastor as a human being, but one American religious sect has the Bible as its pastor: Christian Science. In 1895, Mary Baker Eddy, founder of Christian Science, officially ordained as pastors of her church the Bible and her own book *Science and Health, with Key to the Scriptures.* Most Christian sermons quote the Bible at some point, but in Christian Science sermons, fully half the time or more is devoted to readings from the Bible. However, the Christian Science service also devotes time and authority to Eddy's book.

In 1925, Arthur Overbury published his *People's New Covenant Scriptural Writing,* combining his revised King James Version text with quotations from Christian Science founder Mary Baker Eddy's *Science and Health.* It was never officially recognized by the Christian Science church. A sample text from John 1: "In original being the Word, or GOD-idea existed; and the GOD-idea existed in at-one-ment with GOD, and GOD-idea was GOD-manifest. The same existed in original being, at-one with GOD. All things came into being with this GOD-conception."

Joseph and the Pyramids

Genesis 41–42 tells the amazing story of young Joseph's rise from being prisoner to right-hand man of Egypt's Pharaoh. Because he could interpret Pharaoh's puzzling dreams about seven fat cows being devoured by seven skinny cows, Joseph was given charge of Egypt's grain supply, storing it up during the seven fat years and having enough to eat during the years of famine.

Believe it or not, in times past, travelers to Egypt were under the mistaken impression that the great pyramids were actually giant storehouses used for the grain in Joseph's time. Sir John Mandeville, an English pilgrim in the fourteenth century, wrote a widely read travel book with this bit of misinformation. Mandeville had been told that the pyramids were actually massive tombs for kings and other nobles, but he didn't believe it. Even as late as the 1970s, Israel's Menachem Begin, on a visit to Egypt, told Egyptian president Sadat that "our forefathers built these."

Resurrection on Monday?

Occasionally a zealous preacher will inform his congregation that Jesus was resurrected not on Sunday but on Monday. Since the New Testament says that Jesus was raised on the third day, this makes sense—after all, Monday is the third day after Friday. To our way of thinking, yes, but not to the thinking of those who wrote the New Testament. Their way of counting the days *included* the day they started from. Since Jesus was crucified on a Friday (something everyone seems to agree on), they counted this way: Friday (day 1), Saturday (day 2), and Sunday (day 3).

Martin Luther's Only Problem

Most people know that Martin Luther was the man who launched the Protestant Reformation in 1517. What many don't know is that Luther gave his native Germany—and the entire world—a fine translation of the Bible from the original Hebrew and Greek texts. Following Luther's lead, other Protestants gave people Bible translations in their own languages, ending the centuries-old Catholic tradition of a Latin Bible that most people couldn't read. Luther was the inspiration for English scholar William Tyndale to make his superb English translation. In fact, many of the explanatory notes in Tyndale's Bible were translations from Luther's German notes.

Luther, hiding away in the gloomy Wartburg castle in Germany, translated the New Testament into German in a mere three months, and it was published in September 1522. It was such a fine translation that it became *the* Bible in German, much the same as the King James Version became *the* Bible in English.

Luther not only translated from the Greek and Hebrew but also separated the books he called apocryphal from the Old Testament, indicating that they were worth reading, but were not divinely inspired in the way the other books of the Bible were. Protestant translators in other countries followed his lead in this while the Catholics continued their old tradition of having the books of the Apocrypha scattered throughout the Old Testament.

Luther didn't consider all of the New Testament to be equally inspired. In fact, he referred to the letter of James as "an epistle of straw" because he thought it taught people that they should be saved by their good works instead of by God's grace. In fact, Luther's main argument against the Catholic church was that it taught a system of good works, not salvation by faith. Luther was struck by the fact that in two of Paul's letters he used the phrase "the just shall live by faith" (Romans 1:17; Galatians 3:11). In translating these verses, he added the word (in German, of course) *alone* after *faith*. He knew this wasn't in the Greek text, but he added it anyway because he was convinced Paul believed that faith alone was what saved people. In Latin, *faith alone* is *Sola fide,* and this Latin phrase became a rallying cry for Protestants. Adding *alone* was a blooper on Luther's part but an intentional one. In time, he did soften in his attitude to the letter of James because he realized that the brief letter contained an indisputable truth: Faith without works is dead.

Incidentally, Luther had a low opinion of the book of Revelation. He translated it grudgingly. He found it so puzzling (as do most people) that he thought its title was all wrong: "A revelation should be revealing."

That Blasted Allegorical Method

Allegory is a genre of writing in which people and things are never taken at face value. Everything stands for something else. For several centuries people interpreted the Bible allegorically, believing that the allegorical meaning was much more important than the literal meaning.

Where did the method come from? Mainly the Greeks. They had numerous myths about their gods and heroes, and many of these characters were cruel, flighty, and blatantly immoral. The more sensitive among the Greeks felt that these stories about their gods couldn't have been intended literally. There had to be deeper meanings if only the wise person could discover them.

Some people applied this same reasoning to the Old Testament. Many people were offended by the violence and barbarity of characters in Joshua, Judges, Samuel, and Kings. Surely God didn't intend to reveal Himself through these stories of crude characters like Samson and Gideon. By the time of Jesus, many Jews interpreted the Old Testament allegorically, and before long, Christians applied the same method to the New Testament. Writers outdid each other in trying to find the real meaning of the Bible. A simple and understandable story like the parable of the good Samaritan was buried under layers of allegorical speculation.

The speculation is understandable if you remember that in the Middle Ages, the Bible was hardly ever read except by celibate monks living in monasteries. Out of touch with the real world outside, they let their imaginations run wild, totally losing sight of the fact that most of the Bible is pretty straightforward and understandable.

In the 1500s the Protestant Reformation began, and the Protestants insisted on getting the Bible into the languages of the people. All the new Bible translations had notes that explained the literal meaning of the text. English scholar William Tyndale said, "The Scripture hath but one sense, which is the literal sense, and that literal sense is the root and ground of all. And if thou leave the literal sense, thou canst not but go out of the way." Tyndale referred to the allegorical method of interpretation as "chopology," chopping up the Bible so that the true meaning was lost. Miles Coverdale, who completed Tyndale's translation of the Old Testament, wrote, "Let the plain text be thy guide, and the spirit of God (which is the author thereof) shall lead thee in all truth." Another English scholar of that time, John Colet, wrote that "Except of the parables, all the rest has the sense that appears on the surface, nor is one thing said and another meant."

Fortunately, the allegorical method fell out of use. Or is the current mania for finding hidden codes in the Bible just another way to bypass the Bible's clear meaning and to find the real meaning underneath?

One book of the Bible was and sometimes still is interpreted allegorically, and that is the Song of Solomon. The book doesn't mention God or sound remotely spiritual. It is a sensuous dialogue between a man and a woman who are head over heels in love, and they praise each other to the skies. Many modern interpreters take it at face value and say that it is written in praise of human love and shows that despite Christians' reputation of being sexually inhibited, the Song lets us know that physical attraction is not a bad thing.

Well, maybe. But in the past, the Song was admitted into the Bible only because readers allegorized it. It was, they said, not really about the desire of a man and a woman but about God (the man in the poems) and his chosen people Israel (the woman). The early Christians agreed, except they interpreted the woman as the Christian church—or the individual human soul that God cherishes. Otherwise, the old commentators asked, why was this very carnal, unspiritual book included in the Bible at all? As a sample of the typical allegorizing of the book, consider this verse from the Geneva Bible, and the footnote that accompanied it: "Behold his bed, which is Solomon's; sixty valiant men are about it, of the valiant of Israel"(3:7). Footnote: "By the bed is meant the temple which Solomon made."

In 1781 an English woman named Ann Francis published a translation of the Song of Solomon from Hebrew. Her notes were entirely devoted to the literal sense—an oddity at that time because it was always considered allegorical. Her version was widely mocked.

Well-Traveled Apostles

According to British legend, 12 missionaries came to England very soon after the time of Christ. They were supposedly sent by Philip the apostle and led by Joseph of Arimathea. (Joseph, you might recall, was the man who buried Jesus in his own family tomb.) Supposedly they settled at Glastonbury in Somerset in southern England. This is pure legend, but we do know that Christians were in Britain as early as 200. Britain was part of the Roman empire then, and Christianity spread very quickly over the whole empire. Most of these early Christians were driven out by the Angles and Saxons, who invaded sometime after 400.

Supposedly Joseph of Arimathea is buried at Glastonbury Abbey.

Jesus Only

Most Christian baptisms are performed with the minister saying "I baptize you in the name of the Father, the Son, and the Holy Spirit." That formula is based on Jesus' Great Commission in

Matthew 28:19: "Go and make disciples of all nations, baptizing them in the name of the Father and of the Son and of the Holy Spirit." Early in the twentieth century, however, some Pentecostal Christians noticed something that believers had overlooked for centuries: In the book of Acts, the apostles never baptize anyone with that formula. On the contrary, all baptisms recorded in Acts are done in the name of Jesus. This led to a secession, with the "Jesus only" people forming their own denominations. Today they are called Jesus Only and also Oneness Pentecostals. They consider themselves true Christians but are to some degree snubbed by other Christians, including other Pentecostals. Some of their critics say that in addition to their baptismal formula being wrong, they also do not have a correct view of the Trinity.

Who is committing the blooper here? After all, the Oneness believers have a point—the apostles in Acts did not follow Jesus' Great Commission formula and baptize in the name of Father, Son, and Spirit.

Celebrities Say the Dumbest Things

Over the centuries, many famous people have had lots of praise for the Bible. But plenty of others have said some very mean—and often very dumb—things about the Book. In this chapter, you'll see that being a celebrity doesn't take much intelligence. You'll also see that people who criticize the Bible often don't know much about it.

Mary and Joseph Homeless?

In December 1997, Vice-President Al Gore made an interesting observation regarding the birth of Jesus: "Speaking from my own religious tradition, two thousand years ago a homeless woman gave birth to a homeless child in a manger because there was no room for her in the inn." Umm, Mr. Gore, Mary and Joseph had a home in Nazareth, and Jesus was born in a manger because Mary and Joseph had traveled to Bethlehem for a census. (At least Gore was correct about the inn being full.)

Mr. Turner versus Moses

In her autobiography, *My Life So Far,* actress Jane Fonda

reveals some interesting details about dating and marrying media mogul Ted Turner. On one of their first dates he bragged about replacing the Ten Commandments with his Ten Voluntary Initiatives, which included caring for the earth, having no more than two children per family, rejecting the use of force, and relying on the United Nations to settle all international disputes. He assured Fonda that in the modern world people just couldn't stomach being commanded to do anything.

Sam Spiegel

His may not be a household name, but Sam Spiegel (1904–1985) produced some of the most famous movies ever made, including *The African Queen, Lawrence of Arabia, The Bridge on the River Kwai,* and *On the Waterfront.* Someone proposed to Spiegel that he produce an epic film on the life of Jesus. Spiegel supposedly replied, "I don't know about that. It's so hard to find the actors to play Jesus and the ten disciples." *Ten,* Mr. Spiegel? There were *twelve.*

Big John D.

John Dillinger (1903–1934) was one of the most colorful characters of the Great Depression, a man who pulled off some amazing bank robberies and prison escapes. He became the most wanted man in America and was gunned down after emerging from a movie theater in Chicago. During one of his daring bank holdups, a woman in the bank threw her pocket Bible at him and said, "Mr. Dillinger, you really ought to read this." Dillinger didn't pick up the Bible but did reply, "Sorry, ma'am, but I've already broken all the Ten Commandments, including the one against drinking." We don't know for sure if the woman bothered to point out that drinking isn't mentioned in the Ten Commandments.

Clinton's Near Miss

At the 1992 Democratic convention, presidential candidate Bill Clinton misquoted (deliberately or not) a statement by the apostle Paul. First the Clinton version: "Eye hath not seen, nor ear heard, nor our minds imagined what we can build." Now, the King James Version: "Eye hath not seen, nor ear heard, neither have entered into the heart of man, the things which God hath prepared for them that love him" (1 Corinthians 2:9). Clinton secularized Paul's statement about the eternal bliss of Christians.

Salome Confused

Movie siren Rita Hayworth (1918–1987) was more famous for her celebrity marriages (to Orson Welles, for one) and her looks than for her acting ability. She played the title role in the 1953 film *Salome,* a rather bad movie that drastically revised the story of the stepdaughter of Herod, who danced to please Herod and then demanded the beheading of the great prophet John the Baptist. In this version, though, Salome is a good girl, not a bad one, and she actually tries to save John. At the end of the film, Salome becomes a follower of Jesus—an interesting idea but not one found in the Bible.

At any rate, Miss Hayworth was sought out to play the role of Potiphar's wife in a movie about the story of Joseph, son of Jacob, in the book of Genesis. The glamorous star wasn't exactly boned up on her Bible, for when she was asked about playing in a film about Joseph, she reportedly said, "Well, I just can't see myself playing the virgin Mary, but I'll give it some thought."

The Goddess on God's Word

Glamorous film queen Marlene Dietrich (1901–1992) was a skeptic about religion and the Bible. Her daughter claimed that

Dietrich said that "the Bible is the best script ever written, but you can't really believe it." Her daughter also noted that her mother, who hated and feared air travel, always carried a cross, a star of David, a St. Christopher medal, and a rabbit's foot whenever she flew. (Apparently even people who can't really believe the Bible feel an occasional need for some spiritual support.) In her old age, Dietrich said to her daughter that Christmas "has something to do with someone being born in a stable, doesn't it?" Her daughter admitted that Dietrich "wasn't too keen on theology."

Tallulah, Dahling

Daughter of a U.S. congressman, actress Tallulah Bankhead (1902–1965) was noted for her husky voice, throaty laugh, and extremely scandalous private life. Like many Hollywood celebrities, she visited Aimee Semple McPherson's church, Angelus Temple, not from religious conviction but because the famous Sister Aimee put on a good show. Supposedly she met Aimee after a worship service and had a brief chat in which Aimee asked her if she ever read the Bible. Tallulah replied, "Oh, yes, I've read all five Gospels several times." (This might have been a real blooper or just another of her jests.) Tallulah could also be blasphemous on occasion: According to one story, she entered a church on one Christmas day, saw a large picture of Jesus hanging on the cross, and said, "Why so glum? Smile—it's your birthday!"

Orson the Obese

Orson Welles (1915–1985) was regarded as Hollywood's wonder boy for many years. A talented actor, writer, and director, he was famed for *Citizen Kane* and other movie classics. Gaining weight in middle age, the once handsome Welles played a bloated, froglike King Saul in the 1960 Italian movie *David and Goliath*.

Though physically unattractive, he still possessed that magnificent, resonant voice, a voice put to use in another biblical epic, *King of Kings*. Welles served as narrator for this film about the life of Jesus, and his narration was majestic but had one minor problem: He insisted on pronouncing the *t* in the world *apostle*, which jarred the ears of everyone who knew that the *t* is silent.

Mr. American Auto

Auto manufacturer Henry Ford (1863–1947) had plenty of praise for the Bible: "The Bible is the most valuable book in the world... It is a true book of experience. My belief is that Jesus was an old person, old in experience, and it was this that gave him his superior knowledge of life." If you're wondering what Ford meant by "Jesus was an old person," he meant that Jesus had a very old soul, for Ford was a staunch believer in reincarnation. Perhaps if Ford had actually read the Bible on a regular basis, he might have noticed that it does *not* teach reincarnation.

Mencken the Mean

American writer H.L. Mencken (1880–1956) was noted for his cutting wit, which he directed at many categories of people, including Christians. He had a high opinion of his own intelligence and a low opinion of almost everyone else's, and he viewed most religious people as hypocrites and morons. Still, he had a certain affection for the English Bible and was not impressed with the various attempts to revise and improve it. "Many attempts have been made to purge the King James Version of its errors and obscurities, and many learned but misguided men have sought to produce translations that should be mathematically accurate, and in the plain speech of the everyday. But the Authorized Version has never yielded to any of them, for it is palpably and overwhelmingly better than they are." Mencken also stated that though the writers of the Bible had not kept the world from going to hell, they had at least given it "superb literature." He paid the writers another compliment: They were "honest men," a category of people he actually admired.

By the way, Mencken is sometimes credited with coining the term *Bible belt*. He did not mean it as a compliment.

Funny Lady and Bible Editor

Comedienne Phyllis Diller spent decades pleasing audiences with her outlandish hair and wardrobe and her comedy monologues dealing with marriage and housekeeping and mocking her own appearance. She gave her autobiography the provocative title *Like a Lampshade in a Whorehouse: My Life in Comedy*. She describes herself as being an atheist from an early age but also notes that she adopted her mother's favorite Bible verse, Romans 8:28: "All things work together for good to them that love God." But Diller admits she edited the verse by dropping the word "God" at the end: "All things work for good to them that love." Diller added, "I believe it. I am a loving person and that's why things work. It's karma."

The Fount of Goldwynisms

One of the most quotable people ever to work in Hollywood was the Polish-born producer Samuel Goldwyn (1882–1974). Goldwyn's mangling of the language resulted in such blooper gems as "Include me out," "In two words—impossible!" and "People stayed away in droves." The phrases were known as *Goldwynisms*. Though he was born into a Jewish family, Goldwyn's knowledge of the Old Testament was patchy to say the least. A writer proposed doing a film about Gideon, and he replied, "Who wants to see a movie about guys putting Bibles in hotel rooms?"

Pol Pot, Mass Murderer

One of the most loathsome characters of the twentieth century was Cambodian dictator Pol Pot (1925–1998). A dedicated communist, he hated all religions, especially Buddhism, the chief religion of his country. He destroyed many temples, but more importantly, he also destroyed an estimated four million people, many of them dying in the work camps his oppressive government ran. Supposedly the wicked man possessed a Bible in his native language, and some Cambodians who later settled in the United States said that he read the Old Testament book of Joshua and relished the parts about the Israelites trying to exterminate the peoples of Canaan. The dictator apparently did not get around to the New Testament with its very clear commands to shun violence and love one's enemies.

Mrs. Lennon

Yoko Ono, widow of Beatle John Lennon, has maintained her husband's strong attachment to liberal politics. And like him, she hasn't been friendly toward any religion, especially Christianity. However, on one occasion she said that she approved of "that 10 percent thing" practiced by some Christians—that is, she knew that some Christians gave 10 percent of their income to the church (presumably with some of it going to charitable causes), but she wasn't aware the practice is called *tithing*.

The Great Stone Face

One of the best-loved comics in silent films was the amazing Buster Keaton, "The Great Stone Face," who deadpanned his way through numerous comedy classics. Raised by vaudeville actors who were skeptical about religion in general and Christianity in particular, Keaton had no respect for the Bible, although he admitted once he'd never actually read it. While filming the movie *Limelight* with fellow comedian Charlie Chaplin, Keaton told Chaplin he had no time for "a religion that teaches someone was buried in a stable then brought to life again three days later." Buried in a stable, Mr. Keaton? Apparently no one told him Jesus was buried in a tomb.

Ah, Yes, Mr. Fields

Comic W.C. Fields was known for his red nose, hard drinking, and cynical wisecracks (such as "Start each day with a smile and get it over with"). Someone caught him reading the Bible once, and he claimed he was just looking for loopholes. On another occasion he claimed that "I scanned it once, looking for movie plots, but I found only a pack of wild lies." Fields' hard drinking was more a part of his stage act than reality, but he once claimed that "more people are driven insane by religious hysteria than by drinking alcohol."

Christ the Communist

In July, 2000, Cuban dictator Fidel claimed that "Christ chose the fishermen because he was a communist." Fidel's brother, Raul, claimed that Jesus was killed "for being a communist, for doing what Fidel defined as revolution."

Castro's remark got some media coverage, but the same remark had been made many times since the 1960s. But the Gospel and Marxism do not mix.

Jefferson and the Corruptions of Christianity

Thomas Jefferson was often criticized for his religious beliefs. Most people realized that Jefferson was not a Christian but a Deist. Jefferson did not like being criticized, and he claimed that his critics "know nothing of my opinions." To a friend he wrote,

"To the corruptions of Christianity I am opposed, but not to the genuine precepts of Jesus himself." Like many intellectuals of his day, Jefferson liked to think of Jesus as a good and moral man but not as the Savior or Son of God.

After his two terms as president were completed, Jefferson retired to Monticello, his Virginia home, where he kept busy with his cut-and-paste editing of the Gospels. In a book that he called *The Life and Morals of Jesus,* Jefferson recounted only the teachings of Jesus, none of the miracles or the resurrection. In fact, in his book, Jesus' story ends at John 19:30: "He bowed his head, and gave up the ghost." Jefferson told Charles Thomson, secretary to Congress and also a Bible scholar, that the "doctrines of Jesus are simple and tend to the happiness of all men" and that "a more beautiful or precious morsel of ethics I have never seen." Like many people who are skeptical about Christianity, he detested the apostle Paul, calling him "the first corrupter of the doctrines of Jesus." Jefferson believed the Gospels were a mixture of Jesus' true sayings and the authors' own opinions but that Jesus' actual words "were as easily distinguished as diamonds in a dunghill."

Although Jefferson was often criticized because he did not believe in the divinity of Christ or in the miracles in the Bible, he saw the value in people possessing and reading the Bible. In 1814, Jefferson, after his retirement from political life, sent a $50 contribution to one of the many Bible societies of the day.

Pudgy John and Tall Tom

America's second and third presidents could not have been more different—pudgy, combative John Adams and lanky, soft-spoken Thomas Jefferson. The two men had major political differences while they served in government, but in their retirement years they corresponded frequently, becoming "friends by letter," discussing political theories and the state of the nation. One thing they had in common: Neither was a practicing Christian (Adams was a Unitarian, Jefferson a Deist). Both admired Jesus as a moral teacher but not the Savior of man. Adams knew that Jefferson had edited the miracles out of the Gospels, and he wrote to Jefferson, "I admire your employment in selecting the philosophy and divinity of Jesus, and separating it from all mixtures." Like Jefferson, Adams believed that the Gospel authors had taken the simple teachings of Jesus and complicated His story by adding miracles and their belief that He was the Son of God.

Aldous Huxley

The English author who created *Brave New World* was a dabbler in drugs and Eastern religions and had little use for Christianity. He was familiar with the Bible but had the notion (a very modern one) that the only purpose religion might serve was a revolutionary one: "From Isaiah to Karl Marx, the prophets have spoken with one voice. In the golden age to which they look forward there will be liberty, peace, justice, and brotherly love." One wonders how the great prophet Isaiah would have responded to being lumped in with communist founder Karl Marx— particularly considering the incredible harm communism inflicted on the human race in the past 100 years.

Evangelist in Reverse

The English poet James Thomson (1834–1882) had an extremely religious mother who inadvertently turned him against Christianity and the Bible, which he learned at her knee. Thomson was a talented poet but an angry, depressed, and alcoholic man who considered himself an evangelist for atheism. Choosing an image from the Bible, he referred to himself as "Ishmael in the desert."

Before Marx, Hegel

The greatest influence on German philosopher Karl Marx was Georg Wilhelm Friedrich Hegel (1770–1831). Unlike Marx, Hegel was no atheist, but he was hardly a Christian either. For Hegel, the Bible and Christianity were a collection of myths, interesting only as illustrations of the truths of philosophy. Hegel said Christianity was "the religion of truth" but then immediately added that it was "not historically accurate." From Hegel, Marx took the idea that man was moving toward a heaven on earth and that it would be achieved without God or religion.

Engels and the Bible

Friedrich Engels (1820–1895) stands in the shadow of Karl Marx, his coauthor of the infamous *Communist Manifesto*. Engels did not despise religion quite as much as Marx did, and he noticed that communists and social reformers in general often took their inspiration from the Bible even when they rejected Christianity. Engels believed that Christianity in its original form was communistic, basing this belief on Acts 4:32, which states that the believers in Jerusalem "had all things in common." In fact, many communists (and even some very misguided Christians) have taught that Christianity and communism are basically compatible because the first Christians in Acts were really communists.

Congressional Approval

"Separation of church and state" is an issue that gets many people riled today. It was not such a sticky issue in the early days of the United States, and here is an example: In 1782 Robert Aitken published an American edition of the Bible, which contained, of all things, an endorsement from the Continental Congress. We can imagine the outcry today if Congress dared to give its official approval to any religious publication.

Chauncy and His Seasonable Thoughts

The Great Awakening was an amazing Christian revival movement of the 1700s, but not one that pleased all ministers. Some thought the Awakening aroused too much "enthusiasm" and that Christianity should be more rational and calm. One critic of the Awakening was Boston minister Charles Chauncy, who in 1743 published his *Seasonable Thoughts,* condemning the "enthusiasm" of some Christians. To ministers like Chauncy, a sermon was not an explanation of a passage from the Bible, but an academic lecture, presenting general moral truths in as calm (others would say boring) a manner as possible. Chauncy's book indicated a shift from the Puritan sermon ("The Bible tells us...") to the "sensible" sermon ("The light of reason tells us...").

The Positive Thinking Guy

Published in 1952, *The Power of Positive Thinking* was only one of many bestsellers by Norman Vincent Peale, pastor of the Marble Collegiate Church in New York. Peale was an orthodox Christian, but some critics—and he had many, though he had millions of admirers—said he was more of an "inspirationist" than a Christian prophet. In his many popular books he used (some might say abused) Bible passages by turning them into feel-good thoughts for the day. For example, in one book he made much of Paul's words "If God be for us, who can be against us?" (Romans 8:31). Peale individualized it: "If God be for me, who can be against me?" Critics pointed out that turning such verses into "feel-goodisms" leaves out the moral demands of the Bible. Critics also noted that Peale's books seemed to emphasize self-help and worldly success more than God-centered living.

"O Little Town" Without Sin

One of the superstars of American religion in the 1800s was Episcopal minister Phillips Brooks of Boston. Brooks is best remembered today for penning the words to "O Little Town of Bethlehem." In his own time he was a noted preacher, and his sermons reflect the optimistic view of human nature that was so popular then. Brooks preached that "the ultimate fact of human life is goodness, not sin." He advised people to "believe in yourself and reverence your own human nature." Whatever Bible Brooks read, it must have omitted verses such as "All have sinned, and come short of the glory of God" (Romans 3:23).

The Diamond Preacher

Baptist minister Russell Conwell of Philadelphia was a great believer in the lower classes becoming prosperous. Like many preachers of his day, he seemed to equate salvation with the desire to grow richer. Conwell delivered his famous "Acres of Diamonds" lecture 6000 times in his lifetime, and in it he admonished listeners, "You ought to get rich, and it is your duty to get rich...To make money honestly is to preach the gospel." In the same lecture he stated that "the grandest moment a human heart can know" is purchasing a home. Perhaps he lost sight of the many woes the Bible pronounces against the rich, including Jesus' statement that it's easier for a camel to go through the eye of a needle than for a rich man to enter heaven (Matthew 19:24).

Leapin' Lizards!

One of the best-loved comic strips of all time was *Little Orphan Annie,* drawn by Harold Gray (1894–1968). The strip, which debuted in 1924, featured the 12-year-old, curly-haired Annie (famous for "leapin' lizards" and other expressions) and her faithful dog, Sandy (famous only for saying "Arf!"). A fan once asked Gray how he summed up his own moral beliefs, and Gray replied in a letter that he "believed firmly in the Ten Commandments that Jesus received on Mount Sinai." Jesus on Mount Sinai? Hadn't Harold ever heard of Moses?

Mr. Psychotherapy

Sigmund Freud is regarded as the founder of psychotherapy, and he wrote several books on the subject. He also wrote one book on a subject in which he was definitely not an expert: religion. Freud was a Jewish atheist, and he seemed to despise the Jews' religious heritage. His 1939 book *Moses and Monotheism* revealed his theory that Moses was an Egyptian, not a Hebrew, and that Moses learned monotheism (belief in one God) from the Egyptian Pharaoh Akhenaten. The Hebrews accepted Moses as their leader, but they later found his divinely given laws too strict and killed him. They covered up their guilt by making him the great hero of the Old Testament.

Il Duce Antichrist?

Throughout history dictators have been accused of being the antichrist—sometimes to their faces. Italian fascist dictator Benito Mussolini, *Il Duce,* was told by some Belgian Christians that he was feared to be the antichrist. Mussolini was fascinated. "Is that really described in the Bible? Where is it found?"

Southey versus Byron

Robert Southey was Britain's Poet Laureate from 1813 until his death in 1843. Southey had some harsh things to say about some of the younger poets, whom he described as the "Satanic school" of poetry because of their immorality and opposition to traditional religion and morality. When King George III died in

1820, Southey wrote a long poem, "Vision of Judgment," in honor of the late monarch. In a preface to the poem he attacked the "Satanic school," using words drawn from the Bible (describing their attachment to the false gods Belial and Moloch, for example). Regarding this preface, Southey wrote that "I have sent a stone from my sling which has smitten their Goliath in the forehead." This "Goliath" was talented but immoral Lord Byron, who countered with his own "Vision of Judgment." In Byron's poem, Satan is suave and genteel, Peter is temperamental, and the archangel Michael is cowardly. Generations of readers have concluded that Byron was a better poet than Southey, but the two men's morals and values are another matter.

The Wicked Lord

Several poets of the early 1800s were loosely referred to as the "Satanic school" of poetry because of their contempt for religion and conventional morals. The best known of these was Lord Byron (1788–1824), whose life was pretty much the opposite of a Bible-guided morality. Even so, Byron was well-read in all fields, including the Bible. He wrote, "I am a great reader of these books and had read them through and through before I was eight years old; that is to say, the Old Testament, for the New struck me as a task, but the other as a pleasure." On one occasion a Methodist tried to convert Byron to a better life, but he found that Byron was quite adept at quoting the Bible. Late in his life, Byron wrote, "I do not reject the doctrines of Christianity; I only ask a few more proofs to profess them sincerely." Byron died young, before he had the chance to experience enough proofs.

Russia's Mad Monk

Grigori Rasputin (1869–1916) was one of the most colorful (and immoral) figures in Russian history. A monk in the Russian

Orthodox church, he became a trusted advisor to Alexandra, wife of Czar Nicholas II. Alexandra believed the monk helped control her son's hemophilia, and thanks to her, Rasputin had incredible clout in the court. The bearded, smelly peasant seduced several of the wealthy and perfumed court women. His drinking and womanizing brought shame on the czar's family. Though he presented himself as "God's servant" (and Alexandra believed he truly was), Rasputin's knowledge of Christianity and the Bible didn't run very deep. He told some of the women he seduced that they reminded him of "the virtuous St. Catherine of the Holy Bible"— even though there is no St. Catherine in the Bible. The immoral fraud was finally assassinated—poisoned, shot, and thrown in an icy river—by a relative of the czar.

The Funny Girl

Comedienne-singer Fanny Brice (1891–1951) was a well-loved entertainer whose life story was the basis of the film *Funny Girl.* Brice, famous as the bratty Baby Snooks on radio, was born Jewish but had little religious training as a child and not much use for religion as an adult. A reporter once asked her if she was planning to celebrate the upcoming Jewish holiday of Passover, and she supposedly replied, "Nah, I feel silly wearing a funny hat and blowing noisemakers." Perhaps she forgot that funny hats and noisemakers are associated with the holiday of Purim (rooted in the book of Esther) and not the much more somber holiday of Passover. (Come to think of it, why wouldn't this queen of comedy want to wear a funny hat?)

The Ragtime King

Composer Scott Joplin (1868–1917) was famous in his own time as king of the ragtime composers. His fame was revitalized in 1973 when his piano piece "The Entertainer" was used on the soundtrack of the popular movie *The Sting.* Joplin also wrote "Maple Leaf Rag," "Magnetic Rag," and other bouncy piano pieces. Joplin wrote an award-winning opera, but his style became passé as jazz became more popular. He became mentally unstable in his later years, perhaps because of syphilis, and he was eventually confined to an asylum. Joplin sometimes told other inmates of the asylum that he was "Solomon dancing before the ark of the Lord"—perhaps forgetting it was Solomon's father, David, who danced so exuberantly when the ark of the covenant was brought into Jerusalem (2 Samuel 6:14).

Walt Whitman

American poet Walt Whitman (1819–1892) is best known for his *Leaves of Grass,* a collection of free-verse poetry that readers either love or hate. Whitman was a homosexual, and his writings make clear that he despised Christianity. Even so, late in life he indicated that he had read and admired the Bible: "How many ages and generations have brooded and wept and agonized over this Book! What untellable joys and ecstasies, what support to martyrs at the stake!…Translated in all languages, how it has united this diverse world! There is not a verse, not a word, but is thick-studded with human emotion."

The Little Tramp, Slightly Confused

The legendary film comic Charlie Chaplin (1889–1977) was baptized in the Church of England as an infant and as a child was carried to church often by his mother, a former actress who had turned her back on the entertainment world. As an adult, Chaplin found fame and wealth more attractive than religion, and he scandalized many people with his numerous marriages (some of them to extremely young women) and divorce and paternity lawsuits. Chaplin was asked to play the part of Noah in the popular 1966 film *The Bible...in the Beginning* but turned it down. According to one story, when Chaplin heard about being offered the part of Noah, he asked, "Will they include the part about receiving the Ten Commandments on Mount Sinai?" Apparently his small dose of churchgoing as a child didn't help him distinguish Noah from Moses.

Hirohito, A Mere Mortal

Japan's emperor Hirohito (1901–1989) announced to his nation in 1946 that he was (gasp!) merely mortal. The Japanese had a long tradition of believing that their emperors were divine, the descendants of the sun goddess. The emperor, who was at least partly to blame for Japan's brutalities before and during World War II, continued on in a ceremonial rule after announcing his mortality.

He also traveled widely outside the country, something no previous emperor had ever done. His grasp of non-Japanese cultures was not always good, however. The story goes that while touring an art museum in Europe, he saw a painting of Jesus being baptized by John the Baptist, with a dove over Jesus' head. The emperor looked at the picture and said, "Ah, yes, I know these three—the Holy Trinity that Christians worship!" Actually, he wasn't totally wrong: The dove represents the Holy Spirit, and Jesus is the Son of God, so the only thing he was mistaken about was thinking that John the Baptist was part of the Trinity (the Father, the Son, and the Holy Spirit).

The Walden Pond Man

Famous for *Walden* and other writings, Henry David Thoreau

(1817–1862) was a friend and neighbor of author Ralph Waldo Emerson, and both men were part of that philosophical movement known as Transcendentalism. Thoreau did not consider himself a Christian and had harsh things to say about religion in general, but fairly late in life he did learn to appreciate the Bible. Having become fond of the New Testament, he wrote, "I know of no book that has so few readers. To Christians, no less than Greeks and Jews, it is foolishness and a stumbling block." In other words, Thoreau's reading of the Bible made him appreciate the Bible more but Christians even less.

Matthew Arnold

A noted poet and critic, Matthew Arnold (1822–1888) was the son of the devout Thomas Arnold, headmaster of the elite Rugby School and self-appointed shaper of "Christian gentlemen." Matthew did not have the religious certainty of his father. In his poem *Dover Beach,* he lamented the subsiding of the "sea of faith" that had once seemed so reliable. In addition to his poetry and literary essays, Arnold wrote such books as *God and the Bible, St. Paul and Protestantism,* and *Literature and Dogma.* Arnold was one of many people who thought Christianity and the Bible served useful social purposes even if they were not true. He was genuinely sad that in his day, not only the intellectuals but also the common people were doubting the Bible.

Bad Boy Shelley

One of England's great poets was Percy Bysshe Shelley (1792–1822), a lifelong radical who enjoyed mocking Christianity and conventional morality. Yet the loose-living Shelley was fascinated with the Bible, and he contemplated writing a long epic poem based on the book of Job. In her diary, his wife Mary (who wrote the novel *Frankenstein*) recorded that Shelley read the Bible almost every day. This was the same man who in his college days had written a book titled *The Necessity of Atheism.* Like many people of his time—including, across the Atlantic, Thomas Jefferson—Shelley wanted the high morality of the Bible without all the "mythology," yet he was clearly fascinated by those "myths."

Samuel Butler

"I hate God and my father" was the theme of novelist Samuel Butler's life. Butler (1835–1902), son of a Church of England minister, is most famous for his autobiographical novel *The Way of All Flesh,* in which the main character's father, a cold, narrow-minded minister, is clearly Butler's own father. Butler's hatred of Christianity and the Bible mostly stemmed from hatred of his father. He became convinced that the Gospel authors were con artists and that Jesus had not died on the cross but had been laid in the tomb still alive and later resuscitated. Butler's writings appealed to a whole generation that had turned against whatever their parents believed. For the record, Butler tried to demolish not only Christianity but also Darwinism, which he saw as being full of contradictions.

Voltaire Sadly Mistaken

The revered French author Voltaire (1694–1778) claimed to believe in God but was an avowed enemy of traditional Christianity and a severe skeptic of the Bible. In one of his optimistic (and anti-Christian) moods he wrote these words: "I will go through the forest of the Scriptures and girdle all the trees, so that in one hundred years Christianity will be but a vanishing memory." Like many skeptics, Voltaire was fascinated by the Bible—or more accurately, fascinated by what he believed were its errors. In his widely read *Philosophical Dictionary,* Voltaire included articles on the Bible and its important characters.

Moses the Juggler

Christopher Marlowe (1564–1593) was a contemporary of William Shakespeare and also a noted poet and playwright, famed for *Dr. Faustus* and other plays. Marlowe led a fairly wild and unconventional life, and some accused him of "atheistical opinions," meaning that his religious views were unorthodox. Like all educated men of his day, Marlowe read the Bible, but he referred to Moses as a "juggler" of words and said that if he were to create a new religion, it would be far superior to Christianity. Marlowe died young in a tavern brawl.

Ben Franklin, Paraphraser

The amazing Benjamin Franklin was an American original—Founding Father, scientist, philosopher, writer. He was wise enough to suggest that the beloved King James Version needed some modernizing. Unfortunately, wise Ben's paraphrasing of the opening chapter of the book of Job proved that his talents lay elsewhere. Judge this: "It being levee day in Heaven, all God's nobility came to court to present themselves before him; and Satan also appeared in the circle as one of the ministry. And God said unto Satan, You have been some time absent; where were you? And Satan answered, I have been at my country seat, and in different places visiting my friends. And God said, Well, what think you of Lord Job? You see he is my best friend, a perfectly honest man" (Job 1:6-8). Interesting, perhaps, but not an improvement over the King James.

James the Control Freak

Were you under the impression that Jesus Christ came into

the world to bring people salvation? According to King James I of England, "Christ came into the world to teach subjects obedience to the king." James had reason to be concerned about obedience: In his home country of Scotland, his Catholic mother, the famous Mary, Queen of Scots, had been booted out by her Protestant subjects. James grew up in fear of rebellions, especially if the rebels claimed they were doing God's will. And since he knew the Bible very well, he was aware that several passages in the New Testament urged Christians to be obedient to the civil government, which was instituted by God to keep order. Many of his subjects, however, put more stock in the verse from Acts where the apostles say, "We ought to obey God rather than men" (Acts 5:29).

By the way, although James has long been associated with a popular version of the Bible, his private life had its shady side. Although he married and fathered several children, he did not care about his wife enough to attend her funeral, and he generally shared his bed with some attractive young man. People joked that Queen Elizabeth I, James' predecessor, loved to surround herself with handsome men, and James kept the tradition going.

If James didn't abide by the Bible's moral teaching, he did know the Bible intellectually. At the age of eight he could translate passages from the Latin Bible into French, or French into English. He liked to have the court apple polishers refer to him as a Solomon, a king renowned for his amazing wisdom. One of James' fellow kings was not impressed and referred to James as the "wisest fool in Christendom."

Sir Isaac, Bible Scholar

If you think religion and science have always been at war with each other, think again, for one of the world's great scientists, Isaac Newton, took Christianity very seriously. Newton (1642–1727) was best known for his work in physics, and he believed that science was a "garden" God had given him to cultivate. All his scientific discoveries were, he said, communicated to him by the Holy Spirit. Newton probably spent as much time dabbling in the Bible and theology as he did in science, but he kept his religious views to himself because some of his beliefs were at odds with the Bible. He didn't accept the doctrine of the Trinity, and he had doubts about whether Jesus was truly divine. Like many people, he suspected that the New Testament had been corrupted from its original form and that Matthew, Mark, Luke, and John did not write the Gospels themselves. He was fascinated by the book of Revelation but believed no one had ever interpreted it correctly.

FOUR

Some Oh-So-Common Misunderstandings

Everyone knows that in the garden of Eden the forbidden fruit was an apple...but the Bible says nothing of the kind. In this chapter we will look at an assortment of generic bloopers, things that are common knowledge even though they really aren't based on the Bible at all.

The Coat of Many Colors

Generations of Bible readers have smiled at the familiar story of Jacob giving his favorite son, Joseph, a "coat of many colors." It has served as the basis of numerous paintings and the popular musical *Joseph and the Amazing Technicolor Dreamcoat.* But frankly, "coat of many colours" in the King James Version is probably not accurate. Most likely (though the scholars aren't absolutely certain) the item given to Joseph was a fine robe with long sleeves—something that would be worn by a man's designated heir. Thus Joseph's jealous brothers weren't envying the robe's beauty but rather its inference that Joseph, the next-to-the-youngest brother, was being elevated above his older brothers. (The ancient world took seniority very seriously!)

Still, it seems a shame to part with "coat of many colours," especially since many colorful garden plants are named Joseph's Coat, and since a Dolly Parton song immortalized the old Southern Appalachian practice of using scraps of quilt to make a "coat of many colors."

No Three Kings in the Bible

Nativity scenes usually depict the wise men (or magi) of Christmas as three kings, as does the popular song "We Three Kings of Orient Are." But this is legend, not the Bible. The story in Matthew's Gospel gives no hint that the wise men were kings, only that they were seeking the newborn king of the Jews, the baby Jesus. Later legend had it that they were kings themselves, paying their respect to an even greater king. The early Christians saw their visit as a fulfillment of the words of the prophet Isaiah: "The Gentiles [non-Jews] shall come to thy light, and kings to the brightness of thy rising" (60:3). In fact, the original Greek word Matthew used for *magi* refers to a class of priest-astrologers of either Persia or Babylon. Most likely these magi were from Persia and priests of the Persian god Ahura-Mazda. (In a world where most people worshipped numerous gods, the Jews and Persians did have in common the belief in only one God.) The magi were often advisors to kings but certainly not kings themselves. They were probably from the same country, so the old custom of showing them with different skin tones and clad in clothing very different from each other is probably not accurate.

Strictly speaking, the wise men don't belong in the nativity scene at all; they came later than the shepherds, after Joseph, Mary, and the baby had moved from a stable to a house (Matthew 2:11). However, this is an example of a Bible blooper that no one really wants to change because we like our Nativity scenes with their richly dressed kings mounted on camels. The shepherds side-by-side with the kings make a nice scene, both rich folk and common folk kneeling to the baby Jesus. The Catholic cathedral in Cologne, Germany, claims to possess the mortal remains of the three kings, and the spire on the cathedral bears a star to commemorate the star of Bethlehem.

By the way, the Bible never mentions how many wise men came to worship. The idea that there were three of them is based on the bringing of the three gifts, gold, frankincense, and myrrh. Early Christian artworks show as many as 12 wise men. The old custom of calling them Gaspar, Melchior, and Balthasar is not rooted in the Bible but in very old legends.

Adam's Apple

We call the protrusion in the human throat the *Adam's apple*, because of an old legend that when Adam ate the forbidden fruit in Eden, a piece of it stuck in his throat. An interesting notion, but just a legend—as is the identification of the fruit as an apple. The Bible doesn't give a clue what fruit Adam and Eve bit into. God had given them a great life in the garden with just one rule: Don't eat from the tree of knowledge of good and evil (Genesis 2:17). As we all know, the wily serpent tempted Eve to do so; she did, and she urged Adam to do the same. The partners in disobedience were booted out of Eden with no way to get back.

So what fruit did they eat? Artists have often depicted it as an apple but sometimes as an orange, a pomegranate, or a peach. Sometimes they let their imaginations run wild and painted a fruit that resembles nothing on earth. Perhaps the "tree of the knowledge of good and evil" was the only one of its kind. Or perhaps it was just an ordinary fruit tree, except that God had specifically said, "No, not *that* one."

If we knew where the garden of Eden was, that might at least narrow down the choices of what fruits would grow in that locale.

Many people would say Eden existed only in myth and legend. Others would say it was somewhere in the Middle East, the home-land of the Hebrews. If that was the case, it almost certainly wasn't an apple because apples don't grow well in that region. In fact, in those parts of English Bibles that actually do mention apples (such as the Song of Solomon), the translators were only guessing at what the Hebrew words meant. The names of plants and animals in Hebrew have always been difficult for translators, and identifying what species the text may have referred to is not easy.

Falling into Sex

As our culture grows less and less familiar with the Bible, odd ideas are circulated. One of these, which has actually been around for quite a while, is that the original sin of Adam and Eve was sex. As Genesis 3 makes clear, their sin was disobedience of God, defying His command not to eat the forbidden fruit in the garden of Eden. It is true, however, that there is no mention of Adam and Eve having sexual relations before this occurred (though we need not assume they didn't). We only know they were "naked and unashamed" before their disobedience, but not so afterward.

Incidentally, here is a bit of advice for people who believe the Bible is anti-sex: Read the sensual Song of Solomon in the Old Testament.

Mary Magdalene

Pop culture has had a field day with one very minor character in the New Testament—Mary Magdalene. She was a prominent character in the phenomenally popular play and film *Jesus Christ Superstar*, in the controversial film *The Last Temptation of Christ*, and more recently in the book and film *The Da Vinci Code* (see page 215 for more about *The Da Vinci Code*). Part of the reason writers have made so much of this character is that the Bible itself says very little about her, giving creative imaginations a chance to run wild.

Mary Magdalene is mentioned a grand total of 13 times in the New Testament. The Gospels say she was among Jesus' female followers and, more importantly, that she was the first person to see the risen Jesus. Granted, this was a special privilege, and she is worth remembering if only for that. But she is never mentioned in the book of Acts or any of the New Testament epistles, which gives a hint that she was not an important figure among the first Christians.

And what about her being a reformed prostitute? She wasn't. All the Gospels tell us, aside from her being a follower of Jesus, of being present at the crucifixion, and of seeing the risen Jesus, is this: Jesus expelled seven demons from her (Luke 8:2). This reference to Mary happens to follow the story (in Luke 7:36-50) of a dinner where a "woman who had lived a sinful life" is so touched by Jesus' presence that she anoints His feet with expensive perfume, shedding tears as she does so. Jesus is touched by this display of emotion and affection, and even though the host is appalled at this "sinful woman," Jesus says that the woman's sins are forgiven. Was the woman a prostitute? Possibly, or perhaps an adulteress. Then again, being "sinful" did not necessarily refer to sexual sin. At any rate, her name is never mentioned. It would seem odd for Luke to tell this story about Mary Magdalene without mentioning her name and then mention that Mary Magdalene had been cured of seven demons.

Mary was a common name in Bible times, and this leads to some confusion in reading the Gospels. In John 12, Mary, the sister of Lazarus, the man Jesus raised from the tomb, anoints Jesus' feet with expensive perfume. John doesn't mention her being an immoral woman or Jesus needing to forgive her. However, in this account, Judas Iscariot reprimands her for this "waste" of the perfume. In *Jesus Christ Superstar* Mary Magdalene is the woman Judas scolds. This is an error, for we know that Mary the sister of Lazarus and Mary Magdalene were two different people.

So it should be obvious that the Bible itself does not say— or even hint—that Mary Magdalene was ever a prostitute. One can only read that into the Bible by connecting Mary with the immoral woman in Luke 7—and these were almost certainly two different people.

One prominent person who was very confused about the Marys in the Bible was none other than Gregory the Great, who was pope from 590 to 604. In a sermon he preached in the year 591, he identified the sinful woman in Luke 7 with Mary Magdalene, adding that her seven demons were her vices. He even elaborated that the perfume she applied to Jesus' feet was the same perfume that, in her days of sinning, she had used as fragrance for her own wicked flesh. Having the pope's authority behind a story certainly gave it some credibility.

In the Middle Ages, one very popular devotional book was called *The Golden Legend*. True to its name, it recounted legends about many Christian saints, including some from the Bible. This book follows Gregory the Great in depicting Mary as a prostitute—or more precisely, a well-paid courtesan, living a lifestyle of the rich and famous. She reformed, however, on becoming a follower of Jesus. She has many adventures after Jesus' ascension, including being put out to sea in a boat, which eventually lands her on the coast of France. An interesting story but with hardly any connection to history.

Here's another error regarding Mary Magdalene: In *Jesus Christ Superstar* she is the only female in the band of Jesus' followers. This contradicts the Gospels, which mention her as just one in a group of several women: "Jesus traveled about from one town and village to another, proclaiming the good news of the kingdom of God. The Twelve were with him, and also some women who had been cured of evil spirits and diseases: Mary (called Magdalene) from whom seven demons had come out; Joanna the wife of Cuza, the manager of Herod's household; Susanna; and many others. These women were helping to support them out of their own means" (Luke 8:1-3 NIV). "Many others" certainly rules out the *Superstar* depiction of her as the one "groupie" traveling around with a band of 13 men.

One other notable error regarding Mary: In both *The Last Temptation of Christ* and *The Passion of the Christ,* she is depicted as the woman who is nearly stoned for adultery, the story found in John 8. This is almost certainly not the case. The woman in the story is unnamed, and John never even knew her name. But if it had been Mary, John would surely have said so.

Giving a Tenth, Like It or Not

A tithe is the same thing as a tenth. The Mosaic Law commanded the people of Israel to give a tenth of their income to God—meaning, in practice, to the Levites, the tribe of priests and other staff of the temple (Leviticus 27:30-32). Some of the tithe also went to aid the poor (Deuteronomy 14:29). So you might say the tithe was a sort of tax to support the ministers and aid the poor.

In the New Testament we learn that the most religious among the Jews were fussy about tithing, even giving a tenth of the herbs they grew for seasoning food (Matthew 23:23). Since most Jews lived within the Roman empire, they also had to pay taxes to Rome, so they had a double burden of the tithe and the Roman taxes.

Most of the first Christians were Jews, so they continued to pay the tithe. Christians from non-Jewish backgrounds felt no need to pay it, of course. We see in the New Testament that the Christians were very generous in helping each other in times of need. Paul wrote to some of his Christian brothers in Corinth, telling them to send money to aid the poor Christians of Jerusalem (1 Corinthians 16:1-3). He included no actual rule about giving a certain percentage. Rather, he encouraged them to give what they could to help people in need. But Christians were never required to continue the Old Testament practice of tithing.

In fact, there was no need for it. The Jewish culture required the tithe in order to maintain its priests and the temple. But Christians had no infrastructure or overhead—no buildings to maintain and few paid leaders. As centuries passed, of course, that changed—huge church buildings, huge staffs of ministers and their assistants. These had to be supported financially. Some church officials began to encourage—and later require—Christians to pay the tithe, citing the command in the Old Testament. For hundreds of years Christians in Europe were required to pay the tithe. Many of them grumbled about paying money to support clergy who were often lazy or immoral, or to build enormous churches, but some of the tithe did go to aid the poor. However, sensitive Christians like John Wycliffe read the New Testament and recognized the huge difference between the practice of their own time and the practice of the first Christians. Wycliffe wrote, "Men wonder highly why [clergy] are so severe in exacting tithes, since Christ and his apostles took no tithes, nor even spoke of them, either in the Gospel or the Epistles. Christ lived on alms, as the Gospel telleth, and the apostles lived sometimes by the labor of their hands, and sometimes took a poor livelihood and clothing, given of the people's free will."

The United States has no state church, so no one is required to tithe. Many Christians do it voluntarily, although people disagree over whether the tithe is the 10 percent before taxes or after taxes. Some churches are fairly aggressive in urging members to tithe. The New Testament does not mandate it, and the Old Testament laws no longer apply, so these churches cite the words of the prophet Malachi, who depicts God as saying, "Bring the whole tithe into the storehouse, that there may be food in my house. Test me in this...and see if I will not throw open the flood-gates of heaven and pour out so much blessing that you will not have room enough for it" (3:10). This "floodgates of heaven" verse is often quoted in the letters that churches and other Christian ministries send out to prospective donors.

Many churches sponsor what is called Stewardship Sunday, which could be more accurately called Fund-Raising Day. Usually on that Sunday the pastor will preach on good stewardship, prob-ably reading Jesus' great parable of the shrewd steward in Luke 16:1-8. Stewardship refers to looking after something in the place of the rightful owner, and broadly speaking, Christian steward-ship could refer to our wise handling of our finances, our homes, our time, ourselves. But in most churches, "urging good steward-ship" works out as "urging you to tithe or go beyond the tithe." People who don't attend church find this whole concept rather offensive, but certainly it is no more offensive than public tele-vision stations sponsoring pledge drives or charities constantly asking for donations.

Money and the Roots of Evil

Here's one of the most misquoted verses in the whole Bible: "Money is the root of all evil" (1 Timothy 6:10). True, that is a correct quotation—but it leaves out the words "love of," which precede "money." Money isn't the root of all evil, but the love of it is.

Granted, the Bible has a lot to say about money, most of it pretty negative. To be more accurate, money isn't evil at all, but people's obsession with it is. The Bible is full of compassionate words about the poor and how they should not be exploited or neglected. It is also full of stern warnings to people who are rich and self-satisfied.

Jesus famously said that we "cannot serve both God and mammon" (Matthew 6:24). "Mammon" here is often translated "money" in modern versions, but the word actually means something more like "material goods" or "possessions." Jesus wasn't saying that serving God required living without money but that if your heart is fixated on material things, you won't have time for the spiritual things, which are far more important.

One other correction: The King James Version says "the love of money is the root of all evil." That isn't quite right. Consider a more modern translation (such as the NIV): "The love of money is a root of all kinds of evil." Notice the difference? Not "the root" but "a root." And not "all evil" but "all kinds of evil." After all, plenty of evils in the world are not caused by money—adultery, for example, or malicious gossip about someone, or vandalism. Rather, the love of money leads to "all kinds of evil"—and we definitely know that it does.

Delilah's Scissors?

In so many paintings, the wily Delilah is shown with a pair of shears or scissors, cutting off the long locks of the Hebrew strong man Samson. An interesting picture—but wrong. So far as we know, Israelites did not use shears or scissors in those days. Delilah would have used a knife or razor. And as the book of Judges relates, Delilah only served to worm the secret of Samson's hair from him. One of the Philistine men actually did the shearing (Judges 16:19).

Wickedness in High Places

In Ephesians 6:12, Paul speaks of Christians doing battle against "wickedness in high places"—or so it reads in some translations. It is clear in the context that Paul is talking about the realm of the supernatural—specifically, war against the devil and his forces. Yet some people have quoted the section on "wickedness in high places" and used it to criticize big government and big business. The New King James Version, which has "wickedness in the heavenly places," is less misleading. (Of course, no one need rule out the possibility that big business and big government might indeed by influenced by wickedness!)

Unequally Yoked

In 2 Corinthians 6:14 Paul warned Christians, "Do not be unequally yoked together with unbelievers" (NKJV). Christians have correctly applied this to marriage, believing that Christians should not marry unbelievers. But over the centuries some readers have extracted another meaning: that people of different races, even if they are Christians, should not marry. This is most assuredly not the meaning that Paul intended.

Tongues Will Cease

In his famous "love chapter" (1 Corinthians 13), Paul notes that "tongues, they will cease" (verse 8). Some Christians who oppose speaking in tongues (glossolalia) cite this verse as Paul's indication that the practice will die out in time—that is, tongues was a phenomenon among the first Christians but is no longer needed. This is a wrong interpretation, for in the same verse Paul also notes that knowledge and prophecies will cease—but no one is willing to state that knowledge and prophecies no longer serve a purpose among Christians today.

Rain on the Just and the Unjust

In His famous Sermon on the Mount, Jesus observed that God "sendeth rain on the just and on the unjust" (Matthew 5:45). So many people miss the meaning: They take it to mean that all people, good and bad, receive their share of woes in life. In fact, in the dry land of Israel, which was always on the verge of a drought, rain was a good thing. The life-giving water was necessary for crops and for human existence. In the modern world we think of rain as what causes us to cancel picnics and sporting events, but Jesus' words on rain would have had a purely positive meaning for His first hearers.

Peter's Cursing

In the sad story of Peter denying that he knew Jesus, Mark's Gospel notes that Peter "began to curse and to swear" (Mark 14:71). Many readers assume that the overwrought, guilt-stricken Peter was using profanity. In fact, the "swearing" was literal swearing—he was swearing (though it was a lie) that he had no connection with Jesus.

An Ark, Not a Ship

Genesis gives us the dimensions of Noah's ark. Translated into modern measurements, the ark would have been around 437 feet long, 73 feet wide, and 44 feet deep. Artists have had fun depicting the ark, but they usually get it wrong. Based on the dimensions just given, the ark was a long, low barge that would have barely risen above the waterline. It was, as the name indicates, an ark—that is, a chest, not a ship in the usual sense. Unlike any normal ship or boat, it had no sail or rudder. Why would it? With the whole world flooded, there was nowhere to steer toward.

The Caduceus

Most people are familiar with the caduceus, the medical emblem showing two snakes twined around a pole. It is seen in doctors' offices, on ambulances, and elsewhere, and some people believe the symbol is based on the Old Testament story of Moses lifting up a bronze snake on a pole (see Numbers 21). In fact the caduceus has a Greek origin, not a Hebrew one. The staff with the serpents around it was the symbol of Asclepius, the Greek god of healing, so naturally it became associated with the medical profession.

Burying My Father

Matthew 8:21-22 mentions a would-be follower of Jesus who said to Him, "Lord, let me first go and bury my father." Jesus replied, "Follow me, and let the dead bury their own dead." This strikes some readers as rather unkind—after all, a dutiful son was making a simple request to bury his father, a request that Jesus should have respected, right? But scholars familiar with Middle Eastern culture interpret it differently: Most likely the man wasn't saying his father had just died. Rather, he was saying to Jesus, "I can't follow you until after my father is dead and buried." Obviously Jesus' message was more urgent than that. His reply to the man might have been His way of saying, "Cut the excuses. You're just trying to delay your commitment." Scholars say that even today Middle Easterners use "let me bury my father first" as a polite way of refusing a request.

Angels with Harps

Revelation 15:2 speaks of saints in heaven playing harps, and harps are mentioned many times in the Bible—but not in connection with angels. Despite harps being in heaven, and despite angels portrayed as praising God, the Bible never actually mentions angels with harps. Perhaps the common image comes from John Milton, whose great epic poem *Paradise Lost* describes angel harpists.

No Room in the Inn

Jesus was born in a stable because, as Luke's Gospel tells us, there was no room for His family in the inn in Bethlehem (Luke 2:7). We must not imagine that the inn was anything like a hotel or motel today. The inn in Bethlehem was most likely a large, walled enclosure with a roof to shelter people from the elements.

Elijah's Double Portion

The prophet Elisha was the protégé of the fiery prophet Elijah. In 2 Kings 2 we read the dramatic story of Elijah departing this earth in a fiery chariot. At their farewell, Elisha requested, "Let a double portion of thy spirit be upon me." Some readers interpret this in a greedy way: Elisha wanting to be twice as great as Elijah had been. But "double portion" had a definite meaning in ancient Israel: A man's firstborn son received a double portion of the inheritance. Elisha, the spiritual son of the great Elijah, was asking Elijah to treat him as (spiritually speaking) his firstborn and favorite son. Elisha was granted his request, and Elijah's mantle fell on him.

Jesus' Brothers?

You don't have to read too far in the New Testament to notice that *brother* is often used figuratively, much as we use it today. Jesus sometimes used it in the sense of "fellow man" and also as "friend," and in the book of Acts and the letters, it means "fellow Christian." However, in many cases, *brother* really does mean "biological brother." In the case of several passages that refer to Jesus' brothers, interpreters have disagreed over whether these were the children of Joseph and Mary or Joseph's children by a previous marriage. Matthew 1 relates the story of the virgin Mary giving birth to Jesus, who had no human father. Her husband Joseph "knew her not till she had brought forth her firstborn son"

(1:24). Here "knew" means "had sexual relations with." Later in the Gospels we learn that Jesus had at least four brothers (named James, Joseph, Simon, and Judas) and sisters also (Matthew 13:55-56). We can assume that after the birth of Jesus, Joseph and Mary had normal marital relations, and these brothers and sisters referred to in the Gospels were Jesus' younger siblings—or, more accurately, half-siblings, since Joseph was not Jesus' father.

This seems clear enough, yet an old, old tradition teaches that Mary and Joseph didn't have any children together and that the brothers and sisters referred to in the Gospels were Joseph's children from an earlier marriage (meaning that they were all older than Jesus). This idea isn't rooted in the Bible but in an old document called the Protevangelium of James, probably written sometime around 150. In this story, Mary is the daughter of Joachim and Anne, and at an early age she vows perpetual virginity. She is chosen by lot to marry the much older Joseph, a widower with several children, including James, who is supposedly the narrator of the story. Joseph respects Mary's vow of virginity. After the birth of Jesus, midwives inspect her and announce that her virginity is still intact.

The story is pure fiction, but since it claims to be the work of James, an eyewitness to the events, many people assumed it was true. It had a great influence, especially in art, where Joseph is almost always depicted as a gray-haired, middle-aged man, while Mary is young and fair. In the many pictures showing Mary, Joseph, and the infant Jesus fleeing to Egypt, the boy James is often leading the donkey Mary rides on.

The Catholic and Orthodox churches have insisted that Mary was indeed "ever virgin," and one modern Roman Catholic Bible commentary states that "The New Testament knows nothing of any children of Mary and Joseph." The Jerusalem Bible, a Catholic translation, renders Matthew 1:24-25 in this way: Joseph "took his wife to his home, and though he had not had intercourse with her, she gave birth to a son." A footnote admits that the literal translation is "he did not know her until the day she gave birth." The footnote adds that Mary's perpetual virginity is a certainty. Regarding the mention of Jesus' brothers in Matthew 13:55, the footnote in the Jerusalem Bible says they were "not Mary's children but near relations, cousins perhaps." This reflects the view of many Catholics that these so-called brothers were not even the children of Joseph. They were cousins who, for some reason, lived in the same household as Mary, Joseph, and Jesus.

Obviously this is a case of twisting the Bible to fit a belief. Catholics believe in the perpetual virginity of Mary, so when they read of Jesus' brothers, they conclude they can't be His real brothers because Mary never had sexual relations with Joseph. In fact, when the Protevangelium of James was first circulated, many people doubted it, including Pope Innocent I. Jerome, the famous scholar who translated the Bible into Latin in the 400s, also doubted the story. But it seemed to strike a chord with many people who found the idea of the "virgin mother" very appealing.

Protestants honor Mary, but not in the same way Catholics do, so they are more comfortable with the obvious meaning of the Bible: Mary, a virgin, gave birth to Jesus and afterward had normal relations with her husband and gave birth to several other children. Protestants also hark back to Luke 2:50 and Matthew 12:46-50, which indicate that Mary did not always understand or appreciate Jesus.

The Protevangelium of James was one of many "infancy Gospels" written long after the New Testament. These were the Christian fiction of their day, filling in the gaps of the Gospel with imaginative stories about Jesus' boyhood or the early lives of Mary and Joseph. They make for interesting reading, but they also contradict the clear meaning of the Bible, such as the obvious truth that Mary and Joseph had several children, the brothers and sisters of Jesus.

Pope Peter I

Was the apostle Peter the first pope? Roman Catholics certainly believe he was. The basis of this belief is Matthew 16:18, where Jesus says, "You are Peter, and on this rock I will build my church, and the gates of Hades will not overcome it" (NIV). Jesus had just asked His disciples who they thought He was, and Simon said, "You are the Christ, the son of the living God." Jesus then bestowed the nickname Cephas (in Aramaic) or Peter (in Greek), both words meaning "rock."

Reading the Gospels, you can't help but notice that Peter is the most prominent among Jesus' 12 disciples. You also notice that he is anything but rock solid. In fact, after Jesus' arrest, three times Peter denied knowing Him, just as Jesus had told him he would. After Jesus' resurrection, however, He gave Peter a commission: "Feed my sheep." Later, in the book of Acts, Peter has a prominent role, beginning with his bold sermon on the day of Pentecost. In Acts 15, however, at a council of the Christian leaders in Jerusalem, it is not Peter but James, Jesus' brother, who appears to be in charge. In Paul's letter to the Galatians, he mentions "James and Peter and John" as being "pillars" of the Jerusalem church. If Peter was, as the Catholics believe, the "prince of the apostles," we see no evidence of it in Acts or the letters of Paul. And Paul's long letter to the Romans makes no mention of Peter at all. Nor does Acts 28, where Paul finally goes to Rome himself.

However, a reliable old tradition says that Peter did go to Rome at some point and that he died there as a Christian martyr. The Bible's letter of 1 Peter claims to be written from Babylon, which was almost certainly a code name for the city of Rome. At a fairly early date Rome claimed to have the trophies of both Peter and Paul—"trophies" probably referring to their tombs. Rome was the largest city in the empire and soon had a large community of Christians. At some point the community designated a certain individual to be its head, or bishop. Eventually the bishops of

Rome began to refer to themselves as the successors of Peter and to Peter as the first bishop of Rome.

As more time passed, the bishops of Rome claimed to have more authority than any other bishops in the empire. This claim didn't go uncontested, but eventually most Christians in western Europe accepted the bishop of Rome as their spiritual head, with the title *pope*. Supposedly the pope had the "power of the keys," referring to Matthew 16, where Jesus spoke not only of the rock but also of giving the rock the keys of the kingdom of heaven. This is why the pope's official symbol shows two large keys.

Power and authority have a way of corrupting people. The popes of the Middle Ages and Renaissance led such scandalous lives that sensitive Christians became painfully aware that these rogues and scoundrels hardly deserved to be the spiritual heads over all Christians. The great Italian poet Dante was so outraged at the behavior of the pope (Boniface VIII) that in his famous poem *The Divine Comedy,* he pictured the wicked pope's soul already agonizing in hell. In the 1500s, the Protestant Reformation turned loose a flood of antipapal writings, with many of the Protestants claiming that the pope was more like an antichrist than a prince of the apostles. Naturally the Protestants totally rejected the pope's authority and still do.

One notable Protestant, English Bible translator William Tyndale, disagreed with the Catholic belief that Peter was head over the church. In his note on Matthew 16:18, Tyndale wrote that "Whosoever then thiswise confesseth of Christ, the same is called Peter. Then is every Christian man and woman Peter." This was the usual Protestant interpretation of the verse: The rock was not Peter himself but the statement that Jesus was the Christ, the Son of God. The Great Bible of 1539, the first English version approved by the king, took a slap at the pope's pretensions: On the Bible's title page, all 12 of the apostles were shown holding keys. This reflected the Protestants' belief that the power of the keys was given not just to Peter but to all the apostles.

This wasn't a new idea. Way back around the year 200, noted Bible scholars like Origen and Tertullian claimed that the Matthew 16 passage didn't make Peter the prince of the apostles and that the term *rock* applied to all the apostles—or, more broadly, to all who put their faith in Christ. The Orthodox Christians of Eastern Europe never accepted the pope as their spiritual head, which is one reason the Catholics and Orthodox separated centuries ago.

The Catholic belief that Peter received the keys of the kingdom is the root of all the jokes that picture Peter standing at the gate of heaven, either allowing or denying admittance. This is certainly a rather silly reading of the text in Matthew 16. File this under the category of pop religion.

On the Trumpet, Gabriel

Angels play an important role in the Bible, but their names generally go unspoken, with only two exceptions: Michael and Gabriel. Both of these appear in the visions of the book of Daniel, where Michael is referred to as a prince who is the protector of Israel (12:1). Gabriel is a cherished part of the Christmas story, since he announces to the virgin Mary that she will bear the Christ child (Luke 1). The brief letter of Jude refers to Michael as an archangel, one of two instances where this word occurs in the Bible. It probably refers to a ruling angel, which also fits with his title of "prince" from the book of Daniel. The last mention of Michael is in Revelation, where he leads the armies of heaven (angels, we assume) in battle against the powers of the dragon (Satan). This final image is the reason that artwork often depicts Michael clad in armor and standing triumphant over a beaten dragon.

Where did the idea of Gabriel—or any angel—blowing the trumpet come from? From the oldest book in the New Testament, Paul's first letter to the Thessalonians: "The Lord himself will come down from heaven, with a loud command, with the voice of the archangel and with the trumpet call of God" (4:16 NIV). Notice that the archangel is unnamed. Since the letter of Jude refers to Michael as an archangel, the logical conclusion is that Michael will blow the trumpet at the end of time. But pop religion isn't always logical. Perhaps Gabriel is seen as the judgment-day trumpeter because of his earlier role in announcing the conception of Jesus. At any rate, people now associate the blowing of the doomsday trumpet with Gabriel, as evident in such songs as Cole Porter's "Blow, Gabriel, Blow," in movie comedies such as *Gabriel over the White House* and *The Horn Blows at Midnight,* and in a thousand other cultural allusions.

Jesus the Peasant

People who like to criticize the Bible overlook one of its great virtues: Throughout its pages, it urges people to show compassion toward the poor. Both Testaments clearly show that God loves the poor and frowns on people who exploit or abuse them.

The New Testament demonstrates that Jesus loved the poor and was not averse to mingling with them. His harshest words were for the rich and self-satisfied, but He always showed compassion to the poor and outcast. But was Jesus Himself a poor man? People tend to assume He was, especially because one of the few facts people know about Him was that He was born in a stable. But Luke's Gospel explains why Jesus was born in a stable—it was the only place Mary and Joseph could find that would take them in that night. Joseph was a carpenter by trade, and we can assume Jesus was also. Historians tell us that carpenters weren't poor. They were definitely higher up the scale than farmers and day laborers. Jesus' hometown of Nazareth was near the bustling Gentile city of Sepphoris—Herod's pet project—so the family might have supplied furniture to this growing market. Jesus was almost certainly not poor but was more likely a member of what we might call the respectable working class.

According to Matthew 8:20, Jesus said, "Foxes have holes and birds of the air have nests, but the Son of Man has no place to lay his head" (NIV). The point of this saying is not that Jesus was from a poor family but that He had given up the comforts and security of home so He could preach salvation to the people.

The Most Misconstrued Story

The ultimate misquoted and misconstrued story in the Bible has to be John 8:2-11, the account of the woman caught in adultery. Everyone agrees it is a beautiful and touching demonstration of mercy and forgiveness. A woman is literally caught in the act of adultery. She is brought to Jesus, and the men who bring her (presumably they are Jesus' enemies) ask His opinion on the Old Testament law that mandates stoning for adulteresses. After a rather dramatic pause, during which He writes something on the ground, Jesus says His famous words: "If any one of you is without sin, let him be the first to throw a stone at her" (NIV). The people walk away one by one till only Jesus and the woman are left.

In the shortened, pop-culture version of this story, this is the end. Jesus has put these judgmental, mean-spirited people in their place. People not remotely familiar with the Bible can tolerate this Jesus, a Jesus who is extremely broadminded about sexual sin, a Jesus who modern people can appreciate. The story is often used to prove that the Jesus Christians claim to honor was more tolerant of sin than they are.

However, the actual story in the Bible doesn't end with the people walking away. More follows:

"Jesus straightened up and asked her, 'Woman, where are they? Has no one condemned you?'

" 'No one, sir,' she said.

" 'Then neither do I condemn you,' Jesus declared. 'Go now and leave your life of sin' " (8:10-11 NIV).

Or, in the more familiar version, "Go and sin no more." This puts the story in a new light. He is still full of mercy and compassion, but "go and sin no more" doesn't sound like the statement of a man who takes sexual sinning lightly. The woman is off the hook, but she is not given a license to continue in her sin.

The story apparently fascinates the public because it is included in almost every film about Jesus, including *The Passion of the Christ*. In most of these movies the scene ends as it does in the Bible, with Jesus saying "Go and sin no more." However, when silent-film director D.W. Griffith included the scene in his 1916 epic *Intolerance,* he omitted "Go and sin no more." This didn't surprise anyone, considering that Griffith was a notorious adulterer himself and that he included the scene in his movie because his main aim was to show that Jesus Christ was *not* intolerant, even if many Christians are. Decades later *The Last Temptation of Christ* followed the same pattern. Its sensitive, nonjudgmental Jesus didn't say, "Go and sin no more."

Judge Not (and No Jury Duty)

Here is one of Jesus' most quoted commandments from his Sermon on the Mount: "Do not judge, or you too will be judged" (Matthew 7:1 NIV). Perhaps it packs more of a wallop in the King James Version: "Judge not, that ye be not judged." Many Christians interpret this to mean that Christians should never serve as judges or as members of a jury. (One suspects this might serve as a ploy to get out of jury duty.) Surely this wasn't what Jesus intended. He wasn't speaking of judging in a legal context, but in our everyday, interpersonal relations. Moses, through God's authority, judged the people and helped settle disputes, and then he shared this job with others, so we can assume Jesus would approve of decent people with high morals serving as judges and members of juries.

In our age of political correctness, when being judgmental is unthinkable, Jesus' words seem to fit perfectly. But He couldn't have meant "judge not" as "don't have an opinion about anything." The probable meaning is that we should try not to criticize or condemn others, which is pretty clear in the following verse: "Why do you look at the speck of sawdust in your brother's eye and pay no attention to the plank in your own eye?" (7:3 NIV).

Murder, He Wrote

One of the best-known and most frequently quoted verses in the Bible is Exodus 20:13, "Thou shalt not kill." The Bible is full of passages that are difficult to interpret, but this one seems pretty basic and simple: no killing, period. People who oppose capital punishment like to quote the verse because it shows that God opposes any person taking the life of another.

Here's a bit of news: "Thou shalt not kill" is a bad translation. In fact, if you read past Exodus 20, you'll find plenty of laws in the Old Testament that mandate the death penalty for certain offenses. Is the Bible contradicting itself? Not in this case. The word translated "kill" in the King James Version actually means "murder." It doesn't rule out capital punishment, war, or even self-defense.

Most modern versions of the Bible have "you shall not murder," which is correct.

God Helps Those Who Help Themselves

If you have a Bible concordance or software, you can search

and search for the verse "God helps those who help themselves." Seek and ye shall not find because it isn't in the Bible! John F. Kennedy used the phrase in one of his speeches, and some people think he was the source of the quote. But Kennedy borrowed it (consciously or not) from American Founding Father Benjamin Franklin. Whether Franklin made up the quote himself or used one already in circulation is unclear.

No Gambling

If you're looking for a Bible verse that says "thou shalt not gamble," give up because you won't find it. However, many people do believe that gambling is immoral. They base their opinion on the one reference in the Bible to gambling: "Jesus said, 'Father, forgive them, for they do not know what they are doing.' And they divided up his clothes by casting lots" (Luke 23:34). The scene is the crucifixion. While Jesus hangs in agony on the cross, the callous Roman soldiers gamble over who will get His only worldly possessions, his clothing. The comparison of their inhumanity with Jesus' compassion is very striking. However, the fact that they gambled is hardly a basis for saying Christians shouldn't gamble.

Frankly, though, the Bible as a whole is opposed to gambling. The Bible praises hard work (Proverbs 10:4-5) and wise saving (Proverbs 6:6-8). It also opposes easy money or getting something for nothing (Proverbs 20:21), which is what gambling is all about. The rich who gamble could certainly use the wasted money for better things, such as helping the poor. And the poor who gamble would be much wiser to save or invest what little they have instead of throwing it away. In addition, gambling can become an addiction, and the Bible clearly counsels people to remain free of such control (Romans 6:16-23; Galatians 5:1,13). A person is not likely to be condemned by God just for buying a lottery ticket once in a while, but generally speaking, gambling is a bad thing for people, whatever their financial situation.

Poor Galileo

The Italian scientist Galileo is a hero to people who like to bash the Bible. In 1633 a church court condemned Galileo with these words: "The proposition that the sun is at the center of the world and does not move from its place is absurd and false and heretical, because it is expressly contrary to Holy Scripture." Galileo was a clear-thinking scientist who sought to find the truth, and when he found it, the church suppressed it.

But the court was wrong not only about science but also about the Bible. The Bible doesn't teach that the sun moves around the earth or that the earth is the center of the universe. In fact, the only hint that the sun moves is in the book of Joshua, where Joshua prays for the sun to stand still while Israel fights its enemies. His prayer was answered, though whether it was a miracle or perhaps a case of the men in the battle feeling that time had stood still is open to debate (Joshua 10:12-14). A few verses in the Bible refer to the sun rising and setting, but we say the same thing today, even though we know that it is the earth that is moving, not the sun. In the book of Job, we read of God moving the earth (9:6) and hanging it on nothing (26:7), which actually sounds like good science.

When Galileo was condemned as a heretic, the church really wasn't using the Bible as their source of ideas about the earth and the sun. Rather they were bowing to the authority of the man they called The Philosopher, Aristotle. He lived centuries earlier, and though he said many intelligent things, he taught that the sun and stars moved around the earth and that the earth did not move. Scientists called this the *geocentric* theory, which is opposed to the correct *heliocentric* theory—that the earth orbits around the sun and also rotates on its axis. The heliocentric theory was first proposed by the Polish scientist Copernicus, who died the year his theory was published. He was never condemned for his views, but Galileo was, and Galileo had to live under house arrest and agree not to publicize his views for the rest of his life.

Galileo, incidentally, was not anti-Bible. In fact, he stated that "the Holy Bible can never speak untruth—whenever its true meaning is understood." He was aware that the Bible really doesn't support the geocentric or heliocentric view. He was also aware that the Catholic Church at that stage in history had a blind devotion to a Greek philosopher who had lived centuries before Christ. Aristotle's outdated science, not the Bible, was the real cause of Galileo being condemned as a heretic.

The 4004 BC Error

One "proof" that the Bible is primitive and anti-science is that it seems to teach that the world was created in the year 4004 BC. This is an interesting idea, and one that many people believe—but it just isn't so. The Bible itself says nothing whatever about AD and BC because that system of dating wasn't invented until several centuries after the Bible was written. Dates in the Bible followed the usual pattern of ancient times: Writers began stories by stating, "In the tenth year of the reign of King Remo…" That was about as accurate as the ancient writers could get. You see this type of dating in Luke's Gospel: "In the fifteenth year of the reign of Tiberius Caesar—when Pontius Pilate was governor of Judea, Herod tetrarch of Galilee, his brother Philip tetrarch of Iturea and Traconitis, and Lysanias tetrarch of Abilene" (3:1 NIV).

So where did the 4004 BC date come from? Not from the Bible, but from the writings of James Ussher, an Irish minister who became archbishop of Armagh, meaning he was head of the church in Ireland. Ussher was a saintly man and also a scholar, and he wrote a book with the Latin title *Annales Veteris et Novi Testamenti (Chronicles of the Old and New Testaments)*. Ussher studied the Bible carefully and used the genealogies in it to work backward, dating all the key events in the Old Testament and coming to the conclusion that the universe had been created in 4004 BC—October 23, 4004, to be precise. Working from that date, Ussher could pin down the dates for most of the major events in the Old Testament. The great flood, for example, occurred in 2348 BC.

We might be quick to mock the man for being hopelessly naive. All but the most conservative Bible readers today know that the earth is much, much older than Ussher thought it was. But in one sense he was correct: The genealogies in the Bible lead back to the 4004 date. Remember that he lived a long, long time before the science of archaeology and before anyone knew the Bible doesn't list every generation in its genealogies. Also remember that the Jews of his day believed that the world had been created in 3761 BC. They too had based the date on their reading of the Old Testament. In the Middle Ages some Christian scholars calculated the date as 3962 BC. Note that all three years are similar—and all wrong, as we now know.

Ussher's book was published in the 1650s. He was widely respected as a scholar, so some Bibles began including the 4004 BC date in footnotes in the early 1700s. So let's be clear about this: The Bible does not say the universe was created in 4004 BC. Footnotes in some Bibles still have that bit of misinformation.

Naked Jesus?

The 1988 film *The Last Temptation of Christ* aroused a lot of controversy for a variety of reasons. It showed Jesus being married (more than once) and having serious doubts about His mission from God. It also showed Him naked on the cross—the camera positioned strategically so that the audience could see He was naked but without showing full frontal nudity. Was this historically accurate or just the producers' attempt to titillate and shock the audience?

Romans did crucify men nude as part of the public humiliation of crucifixion. The man not only was crucified in incredible pain but also was hung in a public place—usually by a well-traveled road. In addition to the physical suffering, he had to endure the taunts of whoever passed by, and people can be remarkably cruel in such situations.

However, Jesus was *not* crucified nude. Why? Because He was a Jew, and the Romans (who despised the Jews and found them very difficult to rule over) made certain concessions to the Jews, and one of these was allowing crucified Jews to at least wear a minimum of clothing—the loincloth, roughly the equivalent of underwear today. So the thousands of paintings of the crucified Jesus wearing a loincloth are correct, and *The Last Temptation of Christ* was wrong, although perhaps its scriptwriters made an innocent mistake of reading about crucified men being stripped naked and not realizing that Jews were given special privilege in this situation.

Lucifer and Satan

Strictly speaking, *Satan* isn't really a name. It's a title. It's the Hebrew word for an adversary, meaning that this character is the opponent of God—and all of God's creation, including humankind.

Satan is actually not very important in the Old Testament. An old tradition identified the crafty serpent in the garden of Eden as Satan in disguise, but the book of Genesis doesn't actually say that. Satan is named in the book of Job, where he isn't really the adversary so much as a sort of divine prosecutor who points out to God that Job is a virtuous man only because God rewards him with material blessings.

In the New Testament, Satan is much more important. He goes by several other names, notably the devil (meaning "accuser"), "the evil one" (Matthew 13:19), "prince of the power of the air" (Ephesians 2:2), and even "the god of this age" (2 Corinthians 4:4). Satan is a powerful character, and he and his multitude of demons tempt people to do evil things and cause them harm in other ways. Jesus makes it clear that one of His missions is to free people from the power of Satan and the demons. At the very beginning of His ministry, He Himself is tested by Satan, but He passes the temptation test with flying colors. In resisting temptation, Jesus does the reverse of what Adam and Eve did in the garden of Eden. Jesus also showed His great power by casting demons out of people who were possessed.

In an interesting passage in Luke, some followers report to Jesus that they had success in casting demons out from people. To this bit of glad news Jesus replies, "I saw Satan fall like lightning from heaven" (Luke 10:18). Meaning what, exactly? Jesus might have been commending the disciples in helping to thwart the power of Satan. He may also have been warning them that Satan fell through pride, and so could they.

What is the connection of Satan and the sin of pride? The Jews had an old tradition—not found in the Bible—that Satan and the demons had at one time been angels, that they became overly proud and rebelled against God, and that they were cast out of heaven. Out of spite, the fallen angels do whatever they can to harm God's creation.

A passage from one of the Hebrew prophets refers to a splendid being who falls because of pride. This is Isaiah 14:12-15: "How art thou fallen from heaven, O Lucifer, son of the morning! how art thou cut down to the ground, which didst weaken the nations! For thou hast said in thine heart, I will ascend into heaven, I will exalt my throne above the stars of God...I will be like the most High. Yet thou shalt be brought down to hell, to the sides of the pit." Now you see the connection between the names Lucifer and Satan. But in fact, Isaiah wasn't addressing this to Satan. He addressed the mighty king of Babylon. Even so, Christians have for centuries applied the Lucifer passage to Satan. Some have even speculated that Lucifer (which means "light bearer") was Satan's angelic name before he rebelled against God.

This is the only occurrence of the name Lucifer in the Bible. Most modern versions don't even have the name Lucifer, but rather "morning star," "Day Star," or the like. These are probably more correct, but the identifying of Lucifer with Satan is probably a permanent fixture in our mental landscape.

One other common blooper associated with Satan: Scripture speaks of only one devil but many demons. Some older versions like the King James refer to devils in the plural, but this isn't correct. There is only one devil (the Greek word is *diabolos,* from which we get our word *diabolical*), and he is the same as Satan. There are many *daimonia,* or demons, causing both mental and physical harm to human beings. Most modern versions use *demons* instead of *devils* for these beings.

Heaven, Hell, and the Third Option

Are heaven and hell the only options for us after death? Do we have a third option? According to the Roman Catholic church we do—purgatory. As the name suggests, it's a place of purging, or cleansing, for the person whose ultimate destination is heaven. The people in hell have no hope (which is part of what makes it hell), and the people in heaven are already in bliss. But those in purgatory are being prepared for heaven, though the prepping may take a while.

Why do Catholics believe in purgatory while other Christians do not? One reason is that Catholics accept the Apocrypha as divinely inspired. In the Apocrypha, 2 Maccabees 12:39-45 speaks of offering sacrifices and prayers on behalf of the dead. From this and from 1 Corinthians 15:29, Catholics drew the conclusion that people still alive on earth can do things to benefit those who have already died. They can't release people from hell, of course, and those already in heaven need no prayers or sacrifices, so the logical conclusion was that there is a place of cleansing and that the deeds of people still on earth can aid those who are there.

Purgatory is an idea that seems perfectly sensible to those who accept it but nonsensical to those who don't. The Catholic doctrine of purgatory was one reason that the Protestants at the time of the Reformation in the 1500s decided they no longer accepted the Apocrypha as part of the Bible—or at least that they would not make the Apocrypha the foundation for any belief.

All of Us Are (Not) God's Children

One of the most repeated prayers in the world, the Lord's Prayer, begins "Our Father..." The prayer is so familiar to us that we forget that when Jesus first spoke it, it was a bit shocking. The fact is, most religious Jews of His time did not think of God as Father. Jesus spoke often of God as His Father, even using the familiar word *Abba,* a term of endearment (roughly equivalent to "Dear Papa"). The first Christians believed that in some very special way, Jesus was the unique Son of this heavenly Father.

But did they believe all human beings were the sons and daughters of God? Definitely not. God, they thought, was the Maker of everyone—but not the Father. The key difference between Maker and Father was that being someone's child involved obedience. Jesus, of course, obeyed God totally. But most human beings are more or less disobedient—something we inherited from our rebellious ancestors, Adam and Eve. What the New Testament teaches is that any of us can be adopted into God's family: "To all who received him, to those who believed in his name, he gave the right to become children of God—children born not of natural descent, nor of human decision or a husband's will, but born of God" (John 1:12-13 NIV). Paul several times used the word *adopt* when referring to salvation. Christians can know that God has "predestined us into the adoption of children by Jesus Christ to himself, according to the good pleasure of his will" (Ephesians 1:5). As you can tell from those words, being sons and daughters of God is not a right but a privilege. If we love God as our Father, we have to obey. Paul urged Christians to "be imitators of God, therefore, as dearly loved children" (Ephesians 5:1 NIV). By "imitate" he didn't mean to rule the universe—he meant imitating the divine qualities of love, mercy, patience, and so forth.

St. James Bible?

The TV game show *Jeopardy* has some very bright contestants, but they occasionally give some really dumb answers. On one broadcast in 2006, a contestant referred to the "St. James Bible," which is wrong, of course. There is a King James Version of the Bible but no St. James Bible. This is a common mistake many people make. And for the record, the egotistical (and apparently bisexual) King James I was not even remotely a saint.

The Dating Game

Among bits of information that "everyone knows" is that we can't rely on the books of the New Testament because they were written long after the time of Jesus and the apostles. This idea has been floating around for centuries and is still being taught in many colleges and seminaries. However, the more we learn about the New Testament and the more we know about archaeology and history, the more the books of the New Testament appear to have been written very soon after the time of Jesus.

One surprising convert to this idea was English bishop John A.T. Robinson, who in the 1960s was the poster child for liberal Christianity. In the 1970s Bishop Robinson changed his mind about some things, including the late dating of the Gospels and epistles. In 1976 he published *Redating the New Testament*, which claims that everything in the New Testament was written before the year 70. Assuming Jesus was crucified sometime around the year 30, that would mean the writings were all dated within 40 years of Jesus. What is the significance of the year 70? That was the year the Romans destroyed the Jewish temple in Jerusalem, an event of immense importance for both Jews and Christians. Robinson thought that if the New Testament writers had lived to see the temple destroyed, they would certainly mention it or refer to it in their writings—but none do.

Robinson spends an entire book explaining why each book of the New Testament can be dated before the year 70. Obviously he didn't convince everyone, and skeptics about Christianity and the Bible prefer to stick with the liberal view that the New Testament was written long after Jesus and is not a reliable witness to what Jesus and the apostles actually did.

Aside from the issue of dating, Robinson responds to the accusation that some of the writing in the New Testament is too refined to be the work of working-class men like Peter and John. But Robinson says Jesus and the New Testament writers may in fact have spoken Greek as well as their native Aramaic. Church leaders like James or Peter may well have taken the trouble to acquire a reasonable command of literary Greek.

The book of Acts shows that the Jewish authorities marveled at how mere laymen like the apostles could speak so eloquently (Acts 4:13). In fact, the authorities were equally surprised at how both Jesus (John 7:15) and Paul (Acts 21:37) could speak with such authority.

Robinson also deals with the issue of people passing off their own writings under the names of the apostles. Skeptics doubt that the two letters with the name Peter attached to them were really written by the apostle Peter, that the Gospel of Matthew was really by the apostle Matthew, and so forth. Robinson admits lots of fake Gospels were floating around and also fictional stories about the deeds of the apostles. But he also notes that Christians weren't so easily duped by these forgeries. For example, a writing called the Acts of Paul and Thecla was a piece of fiction by a Christian minister who lost his post once authorities discovered he'd invented the stories. His intentions were good, but even so, the Christians didn't want him passing off fiction as history.

The Hill Called Calvary

Countless hymns, sermons, and poems refer to the place of Jesus' crucifixion as a hill. Strangely enough, the Gospels never refer to a hill. They only call it "a place called Golgotha (which means The Place of the Skull)." Luke's Gospel is the only one to refer to it by the Latin name *Calvary* (23:33 KJV). Archaeologists and Christian pilgrims have been debating for years just what site near the city of Jerusalem was Golgotha or Calvary. Several good guesses have emerged, but no one is certain. One complication is that we don't really know why the site was referred to as the Skull. Was it shaped like a skull, or were there skulls scattered about? Tourists often visit a site known as Gordon's Calvary, and it is a hill—but a low one. The Romans liked to make crucifixions as public as possible, often near well-traveled roads, and a hill would have been preferable to a flat place because more people could see the crosses. At any rate, even if Jesus was not crucified on a hill, we probably won't do away with some fine old hymns like *The Old Rugged Cross* with its opening words, "On a hill far away..."

FIVE

The Dreaded Essay Questions

Even in our secular age, some high schools and colleges teach courses with titles like The Bible as Literature. Based on some of the wacky (and very badly spelled) answers, either the teachers weren't doing their jobs or the students weren't paying attention. Maybe both. For obvious reasons, the schools, teachers, and students connected with the following writings will remain anonymous. (Note: We have retained the students' spelling and punctuation.)

Question: *Briefly describe the careers of the first two kings of Israel.*

The first king of Israle was named Soul. He was crowned by a man named Sam Ewell. Soul led the Isralights against their enemies, called the Fillystones. Soul's son was named Jonythun, he was the best friend of David, who slue the giant Gogliath with a slingshot, then he cut of Gogliath's head with the slingshot. Soul couldn't decide if he liked David or not, sometimes he did but sometimes tried to kill him, which was during the periods when he didn't like him. David could play the harp which made Soul feel good for a while but then he got depressed all over again and started throwing things so David hid out in the woods when Soul was having fits. David married Soul's daughter who was named Michael but she was really a girl but just had a man's name. David had an affair with a married woman named Bat-Sheva and he had her husband who was named Uriah killed in battle so he could marry Bat-Sheva. David had several other wives and conkewvines. David's son Solumon also had lots of conkewvines. The conkewvines were sort of like wives but were fun.

Question: *Briefly describe the career of Samson.*

Samsun was one of the judges of Izrael but he wasn't the kind of judge who wears black, he was a tough guy who fought hard, he killed lots of enemy solders with the jowlbone of a donkey. Then he carried off the city gates of a town called Gaga. Samsun met his downfal when he met the wicked woman named Duliluh, she was very crafty and got him to divulgicate the secret of his great strength, which was his long hair. Duliluh cut off his long hair and he became normal and weak, then his enemies the Philistites poked out his eyes and made him work in a mill like an animal but then Samsun's strength came back and he killed many of the Philistites by tearing down the temple of their god Dago.

Question: *Summarize the two books of Chronicles.*

The two books of Cronicles are about the kings of Isrel but a lot of the books are just old family trees that aren't really very intersting to read about unless maybe you were one of the people in the tree. The first book of Kronicles tells all about King David and how he brought Noah's ark into Jerusalem and fought lots of other countries, then at the end of the book David dies, so his life is over. Then Second Khronicles talks about Solomon building a temple for God, Solomon also is visited by the queen of Sheeba and impresses her big time. I don't remember much else about Second Kronicles because I missed class twice in one week, once because of the flue and once because I had stayed up late the night before in an internet chatroom.

Question: *Summarize the book of Acts.*

The book of Acts is about the early Christians after Jesus left. The twelve disciples choose a replacement for the wicked Judas who had killed himself then there is a big thing called Pintacost where the Holy Spirit falls on people and they speak in tongues which sounds unusual. Some of the apossels go to prison but are released by an angle. A very nice man named Steven is stoned, but not in a bad way, they actually threw stones at him and he died and so he is supposed to be the first Christian mortar. But most of Acts is about Paul who is a really rough persecutor of Christians but he has a vision on the road to Dumascuss and sees Jesus and this changes him all around. He travels around a lot and does a lot of cruising, these are called his missionary journeys, he winds up in Rome. Paul is a great preacher and converts a lot of people and makes others real mad at him.

Question: *Summarize the first five books of the Old Testament.*

The first five books of the Bible are called the Tora, they were written by Moses even though he wasn't born when the world was created. The first book is Genises which is the story of the world being made in six days but maybe not real normal type days but who knows. There is a story about Adam and Eev and how they were tempted by the talking snake, then things went all wrong when Adam and Eev had kids, the first one was named Cane and he killed his brother Able and ran away and got married but we dont know where the wife came from since there weren't any women except his mom. There is the story about Noah and the ark where the world gets flooded out and everyone dies except the ones who survive it, then Noah celebrates by getting drunk afterward. There is a tower called Babble where people get all tongue-tied. Abaraham is an old man who is told by God he will have a son and become the father of a big nation but after he has the son, God tells him to sacrifice the son but at the last minute God saves the son. The story about Sodomy and Gomoro is about two really bad towns that God destroys with fire and flintstones. When Lott's wife turns and looks back on the burning towns, she turns into a pillow of salt.

Question: *Summarize the book of Psalms.*

Palms is a long book of poems about different things like complaning to God or being grateful or things like that. It is the longest book in the whole Bible. Most people have never read the whole thing. Some of the Palms are supposed to be written by the king of Isrel named David but he didn't write them all because he didn't have that much time. Palms is one of those books they put in those little books the Gidians give out for free.

Question: *Summarize the book of Exodus.*

The book of Exodis is about Moses and the faro of Ejypt. Moses saw that his people were oppressed by the Ejyptians and that faro wasn't going to set them free so God sent twelve plaigs on the Ejyptians but faro had a hard hart and wouldn't free them so the plaigs kept coming and finally there was a plaig of slaying the firstborn and faro had had enough so the people were freed. But then he went after them in the desert with his chariots and the people were scared big time because they were at the Red Sea and couldn't walk on water but God parted the Sea and they went over but the Ejyptians drowned. Then all the ones who didn't drown camped out at a mountain called Sinite and Moses went up on it and talked to God who gave him tablets but not the kind you swallow these were like blocks of rock with things God wrote on them, these were the Ten Commandments. Moses come down from Sinite with the commandments and got all stressed because while he was up with God the people made a gold idle out of a calf and were having a really wild party around the idle. There was a good movie about this with Charleton Hestin, they show it every year around Ester time. I don't remember all Ten Commandments but I know one of them is Thou shall not kill and another is Thou shall not steel. You said we wouldn't have to memorize them all for this test and I didn't.

Question: *Summarize the books of the Minor Prophets.*

The Minor Prophets were twelve prophets who didn't write any long books but this makes their books a lot easier to read. One of the Minor Prophets was Jonah the one who was swallowed by a whale who spit him out on dry land, then later Jonah wrote the story all down after he dried out. He told the people of Ninivah to repent and they did but that made him mad. There was one named Amos who told people to behave right and there was one named Hosayuh who married a woman named Gomer which the class all thought was funny and anyway she fooled around a lot and cheated. The prophet named Joel had a vision of a plage of lotus which is some kind of bug that eats things. We liked Obedia because it was only one chapter long. The book about Mica told people to beat their plow shares into pruning sheers and there won't be any more wars. The last book was Maleki which said that Elijuh was supposed to return to earth.

Question: *Briefly describe the differences between the four Gospels.*

The differences between the four Gospels are like this. Mark's is short so people can read it easier. It doesn't have an ending because he didn't finish it. Matthew's has the thing in the Christmas pagent with the gold and frankisinse and mur and the three kings riding on camels. People read it a lot in December. John's Gospel is the one they are always holding up at football games, John 3:16, but they never do explain why they do that. The other one is Luke, he has that story about the prodigal son the one that throws all his money away on parties and women then goes home and says he's real sorry and his dad is happy to have him back so they killed a flattened calf but the prodigal son's brother is bummed out by the whole thing.

Question: *Summarize the career of King Solomon.*

Solomon was a great king because he built a temple that had a lot of gold and cool stuff and he also built a palace to live in, it had everything in it even though they didn't have electricity back then or batteries. Also he was really wise and knew everything and could solve problems and puzzles. Once they brought him a baby that had two different mothers but only one was real and Solomon told them to cut the baby in half at the wasteline but the one who was the real mother told them that was not the right way to cut a baby so somehow Solomon figured out she was the real mom and he gave the baby to her without cutting it. The other woman who was a fake didn't get anything. God got real mad at Solomon because he built temples to make all his wives happy, he really was into temple building but God only wanted one temple so anyway Solomon got told that the country would split in half but it would be after he died so he probably didn't care much. There was a woman named Queen Lasheeva who came from way off and she was impressed with Solomon after she'd heard so many stories about how smart he was, when she finally saw the real thing she was absolutely speachless.

Question: *Summarize the life of Elijah.*

Elijah was a profit in Isreal. He was hairy and lived out in the dessert and did not like for people to worship the foreign god Bail. His enemy was the queen, named Jessebell. Elijah had a show-down with the Bail profits on top of Mount Caramel where fire came down from the sky to prove that Bail wasn't a real god, then the Bail profits were all killed but Jessebell scared Elijah anyway and he ran off to hide but God took care of him by bringing food to him by using cravens. Elijah performed miracles and he didn't even die, he was take into heaven in a chariot of fire like in the movie, and he threw down his mantle and it landed on his friend Elishah who was also a profit.

Question: *Summarize the book of Esther.*

The book of Ester tells about people living in the land of Persia where the king was named Ahazewayrus. He gave big parties and ordered his wife named Vashti to come out and display her beauty but she wouldn't so he decided to create a new queen and pick from all the foxy girls. One of them was a Jewish girl named Had-dasema, later she changed her name to Ester so he wouldn't know she was Jewish. There was a nasty character named Heyman, he hated the Jews and plotted to kill them all but Ester and her cousin Mortaguy thought this was a bad thing so they told the king of Persia about the plot and so they saved all the Juws. Then they made a big holiday out of it and called it Purim, Jews still cellebrate Purim today. Oh, and one other thing, Heyman had planned to hang Mortaguy on a really high gallows, but Heyman ended up hanging by the gallows instead.

Question: *Describe the famous incident of Caesarea Philippi.*

Caesarea Philippi was a Roman woman related to Julius Caesar, and her last name was Philippi. I think she had something to do with Caesar persecuting the Christians but I'm not sure. I haven't been getting much sleep lately because my roommate drinks a lot and has girls over.

[Note: Caesarea Philippi was the locale where the disciple Peter made the statement that Jesus was "the Christ, the Son of the living God" (Matthew 16:13-20). It is considered a turning point in the career of Jesus, since His disciples now perceived He was more than just a teacher and healer.]

Question: *Summarize the book of Nehemiah.*

Nehemiah was a servant in Persiah, and he was a eunuch, and we all know what that means. He served liquor to the Persiahite king. He was all upset because he heard things were going really bad back in Jerusalem. He cried and the king got upset and so Nehemiah went to Jerusalim to do things and make things happen. They built the walls which probably meant bringing in lots of concrete and stuff and hiring a contractor. There were guys named Levites, I think they had something to do with clothing. There was a guy named Ezrah in there somewhere too, I didn't really understand that because I think there was another book about him. Anyway it had a happy ending but I didn't really get why someone wrote a book about building walls, I did not find it inspiring a bit. I think in the future you should let people skip this one and read something more intresting. The Bible maps in the back are kinda cool, maybe you could give us a quiz on the maps.

Question: *Discuss the concept of a Messiah.*

Messiah is a thing that people sing around Christmass time. A

French guy named Handle wrote it I think, my mom took me once to a big concert hall to hear it, there was a big group of singers and there was two men and two women and they'd sing by themselves sometimes and they sang okay I guess but it got boring, I think mom said the words were from the Bible but it didn't sound like it to me, plus they'd repeat themselves a lot when they sang and the Bible doesn't do that. I figured they had forgot some of the words and just kept repeating themselves to fill up the time and so they wouldn't be imbarassed. Anyway it was real real long and then at the end they did this Halliluyah Chorus where everybody stands up which was good cause we were tired of sitting, my feet were asleep. They don't ever sell food or drinks at these kind of places, I wonder why. I have a friend Kyle who reads science fiction books, he read something called Dune Messiah which was weird, I tried to read it but I don't think it had a thing to do with the Bible or that thing they sing at Christmas. This is a strange question, I don't remember talking about it in class at all, maybe this was the day the ambulance went by outside and we all ran to the windows to see what was going on and we saw there was a wreck on the street so we forgot about class totally. It is hard to concentrate at times. I am not a religion major anyway.

Question: *Describe as many of the plagues on Egypt as you can.*

I don't know if these have to be in orrder so I will just jump in and start with the ones I remember. All the firstborns were killed by the angel of death. This part was in the movie with Charlten Hester. Oh and the river which I guess is the Nile river got all bloody but our science teacher said it wasn't really blood but something else. Anyway God sent hell which fell on all the crops so there wasn't enough food. Then there was locus I'm not really sure what that was but it was some kinda bug that ate things and made mess. Then there was whole lotsa frogs which I guess was bad cause some people especialy girls are creeped out by frogs plus they croke at night and you can't sleep. Then God parted the Red sea but that was not a plague on the Isrelites, they were glad cause they could walk on dry land but it was a plague on the Egyptains because they drowned when the tide came back in. And also there was the pillar of fire which burned the Egyptians. That's only seven. Were there more than seven? Oh one more, the people got broils on their skin and that was bad.

Question: *Briefly summarize three of Jesus' parables.*

The parable of the sewer is about a farmer who scatters lots of seeds around and they fall on different things so some of the seeds grow and some don't. Some birds ate seeds too. I forget what the birds were suposed to mean, but they symbolized something else.

There was a shepurd who had a hundred sheep and one ran away into the hills so the shepurd went looking for him cause it was his favorite sheep. So Jesus was saying that God looks out for his favorite sheeps.

The other parable was the Golden Rule, which says you do things to people like they do to you.

Question: *What three types of writing do you find in the New Testament? Describe each type briefly.*

There were the Gosples that tell about Jesus and how he was born in a manager and was baptized in a river, then he gathered his disciples and went around doing exorcisms and healing sick people and he preached too. Also he got into trouble and was crucified but then came back in three days.

The epistels were letters written by Christins to tell other Christins what to do and what do think. Most of the epistels were by Paul, I don't remember his last name or if he had one.

The last type is my favarite which is Revolation where the Beast takes over the world and he has 666 written on him somewhere. This is about the end of the world and the ante Christ and the four horsemen. This book spooks a lot of people because they don't understand it.

Tripping Up the Translators

If you've ever tried translating English into, say, Spanish or French, you know it can be tricky. Translating ancient Hebrew, Aramaic, and Greek, the languages of the Bible, is even trickier. Over the centuries, translators have watched their hair turn gray as they did their best to understand the ancient texts and render them in understandable and accurate translations. Even when they got it mostly right, as in the well-loved King James Version, the English language itself changed, so that what made perfect sense in one century can seem puzzling and comical later on.

Unicorns, Satyrs, and Dragons, Oh My!

If you wanted to mock the Bible, you could start by snickering at the fact that it mentions mythical beasts as if they really existed. First, consider the satyrs. In Greek mythology, satyrs were wild beings that were half-man, half-goat—goats from the waist down, human above, except their faces were goatlike. They were thought of as living in the wilderness and being extremely lustful creatures (which is why the word *satyr* is sometimes applied to a lecherous man).

These creatures never existed, of course—and yet the King James Version seems to assume they do. For example: "Wild beasts of the desert shall lie there; and their houses shall be full of doleful creatures; and owls shall dwell there, and satyrs shall dance there" (Isaiah 13:21). "The wild beasts of the desert shall also meet with the wild beasts of the island, and the satyr shall cry to his fellow" (Isaiah 34:14). Satyrs? Really?

The translators involved in the King James Version and earlier versions had an inadequate knowledge of Hebrew. They were wise enough to know that the Hebrew word referred to some kind of shaggy creature of the wild. And they were naive enough about the rest of the globe that, for all they knew, satyrs really did exist somewhere. Modern versions are probably correct in using *wild goat* instead of *satyr*. So the King James Version is at least half-right. (Incidentally, in the very first translation of the Old Testament into English, William Tyndale's, he used the term *field-devils*.)

A much more appealing legendary creature, the unicorn, also appears in the King James Version. The actual Hebrew word, found in Numbers 23:22; Job 39:9; and Psalm 92:10 (which reads, "My horn shalt thou exalt like the horn of an unicorn"), was *re'em*. When the text was translated into Greek, the word used was *monoceros*—"one-horned," which is also the meaning of the Latin word *unicornis*. The authors of the ancient Hebrew text knew what this beast was, but frankly, we don't. One candidate is the rhinoceros, with a prominent horn on its nose, and another is the extinct aurochs or wild ox. Some modern translations have *rhinoceros*, some have *wild ox*. None has *unicorn*, for the obvious reason that we know for sure that unicorns don't exist. (Who knows? Maybe unicorns did exist at one time.)

The King James Version's references to unicorns had an effect on Christian art and symbolism. In the Middle Ages and Renaissance, the unicorn is a pure white horselike beast with a horn coming from its forehead, sometimes shown purifying a lake or river with its horn. In the symbolism of the period, the unicorn was a symbol of Christ, a unique being with the power of healing. Our distant ancestors thought there was only one unicorn in the entire world—which is a bit odd, since the King James Version mentions unicorns in the plural. The unicorn also appears in many paintings of the animals parading into Noah's ark.

One more mythical creature: the dragon. The fearsome red dragon in the book of Revelation appears in a vision of the end of time, so we can assume the author of Revelation intended to use the symbol of an actual dragon. However, some other dragons appear in the Old Testament, as in "Their wine is the poison of dragons, and the cruel venom of asps" (Deuteronomy 32:33). "I am a brother to dragons, and a companion to owls" (Job 30:29). "Praise the LORD from the earth, ye dragons, and all deeps" (Psalm 148:7). In the King James Version, *dragons* was the translation for two words, *tannim* and *tannin*. Frankly, we're even less certain about what those words mean than we are about satyrs and unicorns. So modern versions have a wide range of options: whale, wolf, sea monster, sea creature, serpent, and even jackal. Whatever the dragons were, they were scary beasts, and that's about as much as we can be sure of.

Friend or Foe, Pharaoh?

Translations of 2 Kings 23:29 show that we're learning more about Hebrew. In the King James Version, it reads, "Pharaoh-nechoh king of Egypt went up against the king of Assyria to the river Euphrates." The word "against" is all wrong here. No one was the wiser until the 1920s, when a scholar trained in the ancient Assyrian language translated an inscription that spoke of an Egyptian army coming to the aid of Assyria. Pharaoh Necho wasn't going *against* Assyria, but rather *to* it, for the purpose of aiding the Assyrian army. The New International Version has a more accurate reading: "Pharaoh Neco king of Egypt went up to the Euphrates River to help the king of Assyria."

Not in the East

You've read it, and no doubt you've heard it spoken aloud at numerous church Christmas pageants: "Where is he that is born King of the Jews? for we have seen his star in the east, and are come to worship him" (Matthew 2:2). Being a little wiser in the Greek language than the King James Version scholars were, we now know that the wise men referred not to a star "in the east" but rather to a star "when it rose."

Men in Girdles

The King James Version seems to indicate that most men wore girdles—Israel's high priest had a girdle (Exodus 28:4,8), the prophet Elijah had a girdle of leather (2 Kings 1:8), the prophet Jeremiah had one of linen (13:1), John the Baptist had one (Matthew 3:4), so did the apostle Paul (Acts 21:11), and even Jesus Christ had a golden one (Revelation 1:13) Girdles, really? Well, yes, if you understand that when the King James Version was published, *girdle* had the same meaning that *belt* does today. In those days, a girdle was anything that encircled the body— "girded it," that is. Girdles in biblical times were not intended to flatten bulging bellies! Most modern translations use *belt* or, in some passages, *loincloth*.

"Church" or Something Else?

In most English versions of the Bible, the word *church* appears several times. In Matthew's Gospel, Jesus Himself uses the word twice, first when Simon, one of His 12 apostles, states that Jesus is the Son of God. Jesus replies, "You are Peter, and on this rock I will build my church, and the gates of Hades will not overcome it" (Matthew 16:18 NIV). Later in the Gospel, Jesus refers to His followers settling disputes among themselves, and He recommends telling it "to the church" (Matthew 18:17). Later, in Acts, the epistles, and Revelation, the word *church* occurs many times.

What did it mean? First, our English Bibles use "church" to translate the Greek word *ekklesia,* which meant something like "assembly" or "congregation." It definitely did not refer to any kind of building, since the early Christians met in homes, and several centuries would pass before actual church buildings were constructed. It also did not refer to any kind of institution or bureaucracy. The churches in the New Testament were local fellowships of Christians that had very little organizational structure but that shared a common faith.

In the 1520s, English scholar William Tyndale began making the first translation of the Greek New Testament into English. When he came to the word *ekklesia* in the text, he chose not to use the word *church,* because he knew that in his own time the word referred to either a building or to the very corrupt, materialistic organization of bishops, priests, monks, and nuns; to the Inquisition; and to other extrabiblical practices. So *church* was the last word that came to mind when he read about the *ekklesia* in the Bible. He used the word *congregation,* which is a good fit. The Catholic church's bureaucrats were, of course, horrified at what they thought was a mistranslation. As far as they were concerned, their own organization was exactly what the New Testament meant by *ekklesia.* Tyndale could not get the church authorities to approve his translation, so he had to move from England and have his English Bible smuggled back into his homeland. Eventually Tyndale was executed as a heretic.

When the English church finally got around to approving a

Bible for everyone to use, Tyndale's version of the New Testament was the basis of it. The so-called Great Bible, published in 1539, was the first English Bible approved by the king (Henry VIII), and it followed Tyndale in using *congregation* instead of *church.* However, most later versions used *church,* including the long-lived King James Version, whose revisers were specifically ordered by the king to keep "the old ecclesiastical words," specifically, "church." A Baptist minister named Adolphus Worrell published a New Testament translation in Philadelphia in 1904, and in it he translated *ekklesia* as *assembly.*

Bishops or Something Else?

As noted in the last entry, translator William Tyndale knew that the Greek New Testament's word *ekklesia* was best translated as *congregation,* not *church.* His choice of words got him into trouble with the church authorities, and so did his translation of the Greek word *episkopos.* The word literally means "overseer" (*epi,* "over," *skop,* "see"). The word could be translated *bishop,* but Tyndale knew most of the bishops of his day were materialistic and very unspiritual men, nothing like the Christian leaders described in the New Testament. So he used *overseer* instead of *bishop.* However, in later versions of the English Bible (including the King James Version), church authorities insisted that *bishop* was correct. Most English Bibles use *bishop,* but some do use the more accurate *overseer.*

Pastors and Priests

In Catholic, Orthodox, Episcopal, and some other churches, pastors are called *priests,* a word that is derived from the New Testament's Greek word *presbuteros,* meaning "elder." Christian pastors had been called priests for centuries, but a huge change came with the Protestant Reformation, when most Protestant churches ceased calling their pastors *priests* and began using *pastors, ministers, elders,* and other terms. Which was more correct?

By definition, a priest is a sort of mediator between man and a god. Israel had its priests, who officiated at sacrifices and other rituals. The Jewish priests in the New Testament don't come off looking too good because they constantly opposed Jesus and orchestrated His crucifixion. The letter to the Hebrews states that the old priesthood is no longer valid because Christians have a high priest who lives forever, Jesus Christ. He is both the mediator and the sacrifice, so earthly priests are no longer needed.

The New Testament uses several different words to refer to Christian leaders: *episkopoi* ("overseers" or "bishops"), *presbuteroi* ("elders"), *diakonoi* ("deacons" or "helpers"). None of these words have anything to do with the idea of a priest offering up sacrifices. So, with all respect to churches that call their ministers priests, the practice isn't based on the New Testament. As time passed, Christian worship began to focus on the Holy Communion service, and church authorities taught that each Communion was a kind of reenactment of the sacrifice of Jesus on the cross. The church began teaching that the bread and wine used in Communion actually became the body and blood of Christ, enhancing the role of the priest.

When William Tyndale first translated the Bible into English, he was absolutely certain that the word *presbuteros* should not be translated *priest.* He first translated it as *senior* and in later revisions used *elder,* and both words are what the Greek word means.

For a long time the Catholic church and other churches that have priests maintained that the church's rituals, even the hand gestures used by priests, were part of an oral tradition of Jesus' own, though not found in the Bible. Needless to say, this idea hasn't convinced everyone.

Cods and Pods

In the famous parable of the prodigal son in Luke 15, we are told that the son, after he had squandered all his money, was reduced to tending pigs and that he would gladly have eaten the *keration* that the pigs ate. This referred to the fruit of the locust tree. The King James Version has *husks,* while most modern versions have *pods.* The quirkiest word used has to be William Tyndale's *cods.*

Bethlehem's Coast

Literature buffs like to snicker at William Shakespeare's mention of the "coast of Bohemia," for the country of Bohemia has no coast. Some similar readings are found in the King James Version—for example, the "coasts" of Bethlehem (Matthew 2:16), even though Bethlehem is nowhere near a sea. Here's a simple explanation: For the King James translators, *coast* could mean "district" or "the adjoining region."

Naked...or Almost

Be careful when you encounter the word *naked* in an English Bible. It may mean "stark naked," but not usually. In both Greek and Hebrew, the word that we translated as *naked* could mean "stark naked" but also "almost naked" or "inadequately clothed." If you showed up at a formal dinner wearing a swimsuit, you wouldn't be technically naked, but you would certainly get some disapproving stares and snickers from the other guests. That is the basic idea behind most passages of the Bible referring to nakedness: the person is wearing less than he should. So translations use *naked* because *naked or nearly so* is pretty clumsy wording.

The first mention of nakedness is in the garden of Eden, of course, where Adam and Eve "were both naked...and were not ashamed" (Genesis 2:25). After they disobey God and eat the forbidden fruit, they suddenly realize they are naked, and they cover themselves with fig leaves. We can safely assume that *naked* in this context really does mean "stark naked" because the story provides an explanation of why human beings wear clothing. The next mention of nakedness involves the saintly Noah, who, alas, gets drunk on wine and lies naked in his tent (Genesis 9). Naked, or almost? We don't really know, except that two of his sons were so embarrassed, they walked backward and draped a cloth over their father.

Later in the Old Testament, two different prophets went naked, making themselves living symbols of shame and lamentation. Isaiah (20:2) and Micah (1:8) probably were not totally nude but more likely were clad in their loincloths—the equivalent of being in their underwear. In ancient cultures, such a state was not considered sexually titillating. On the contrary, going without one's normal clothing implied poverty and wretchedness. The richer you were, the more clothes you wore—and vice versa. Even though the two prophets probably weren't totally nude, their appearance was enough to get people's attention, which was the whole idea.

The New Testament has a couple of cases of nakedness. In Mark's Gospel, a young man with a linen cloth around his body is present at Jesus' arrest, and when the guards attempt to seize him, he "ran away naked" (14:51-52 NIV). In John 21:7, the apostle Peter is naked while busy at his work of fishing. In both these cases, the men were probably clad in their loincloths, not totally nude. Jesus also mentions nakedness in His famous parable of the sheep and goats, where the righteous people (the sheep) are compassionate enough to clothe the naked stranger—which refers to people lacking adequate clothing to protect them from the elements (Matthew 25).

Hell...but Not Always

You'll find the word *hell* 31 times in the King James Version

Old Testament. But here's a curious thing: In every case the translation is wrong. The actual Hebrew word is *Sheol,* which refers to the realm of the dead, where all people went whether they were good or bad. Sheol wasn't really hell but certainly wasn't heaven either. It was a sort of gloomy place that wasn't nearly as desirable as life on earth. In fact, the ancient Hebrews did not seem to have a fully developed belief in the afterlife. Several times in the King James Version, Sheol was translated metaphorically as *the grave* or *the pit.*

The word *hell* does not appear in most modern translations of the Old Testament. *Sheol* is translated "the grave" or "the realm of death," or sometimes it isn't translated at all.

The story is different in the New Testament, where Jesus and His contemporaries definitely did believe in both hell and heaven after death. The Greek word translated "hell" was *Gehenna,* a word rooted in the place called Ge-Hinnom, a sort of a garbage dump near Jerusalem that was kept perpetually burning. It was associated with the horrible practice of child sacrifice, and to devout Jews it symbolized the never-ending fire of the wicked after death. Another Greek word translated "hell" was *Tartarus,* found only in 2 Peter 2:4. The Christians borrowed the name from Greek mythology, where Tartarus was a place of punishment for the wickedest sinners.

One other word borrowed from Greek mythology is *Hades,* which occurs eight times in the New Testament. The ancient Greeks thought of Hades much the same as the Hebrews thought of Sheol: the realm of the dead, but not heaven and not hell—although a few verses in the New Testament do seem to indicate that Hades is a place of punishment. Hades was also the name of the Greek god of the dead, and four times in the book of Revelation Hades is named as kind of a personification of the power of death. At the end of time, both death and Hades are destroyed in the lake of fire (Revelation 20). The King James Version used "hell" to translate *Hades,* but most modern versions are more correct in using either Hades or "the depths."

One more thing: The ancient statement of faith called the Apostles' Creed states that after Jesus was "crucified, dead, and buried," He "descended into hell." The word actually used in the original Greek version of the creed was *Hades*—that is, after dying, Jesus descended into the realm of death, not to a burning place of punishment.

Solomon's Outlandish Wives

We generally use the word *outlandish* to refer to something odd or shocking. It didn't mean that four centuries ago, however. Consider the King James Version of Nehemiah 13:26: "Among many nations was there no king like him [Solomon], who was beloved of his God, and God made him king over all Israel: nevertheless even him did outlandish women cause to sin." Is this a reference to some odd women who led Solomon into sin? No. When the King James Version was written, *outlandish* simply meant "from another land"—or, as most modern versions have it, "foreign."

Jot and Tittle

According to Jesus, not "one jot or one tittle" of the Old Testament Law shall pass away until all has been fulfilled (Matthew 5:18). So the King James Version reads. The jot was the *yodh,* the smallest letter in the Hebrew alphabet. A tittle was a small horn-shaped Hebrew accent mark. Jesus was saying that the tiniest particle of the Law was still valid. Most people now have no idea what jots and tittles were, so contemporary versions have readings like this one from the New International Version: "Not the smallest letter, not the least stroke of a pen, will by any means disappear from the Law until everything is accomplished."

Candles

Wax candles didn't exist in the biblical world. Yet *candle* and *candlestick* appear in many Bibles. The item called a candlestick in the King James Version, the Hebrew *menorah,* was in fact a lamp stand, with the light coming from burning oil. The same is true for the candle and candlestick in Jesus' Sermon on the Mount (Matthew 5:15). Jesus was referring to the typical oil lamp of His time, not to candles and candlesticks as we know them.

Sodding Pottage

Consider the King James Version's reading of Genesis 25:29: "And Jacob sod pottage: and Esau came from the field, and he was faint." Crystal clear? Perhaps it is more so in the New King James Version: "Now Jacob cooked a stew; and Esau came in from the field, and he was weary."

A Change of Bowels

In the 1600s, the word "bowels" didn't mean just intestines but could generically mean "inward parts," and metaphorically, it could include a person's emotions. That might help you understand the King James Version's rendering of 2 Corinthians 6:12: "Ye are not straitened in us, but ye are straitened in your own bowels." The New King James Version might be clearer still: "You are not restricted by us, but you are restricted by your own affections."

Meat or Food?

An old proverb says that "one man's meat is another man's poison." In that proverb—and in old versions of the Bible—*meat* meant "food," not necessarily the flesh of animals. In the King James Version, an offering of grain is referred to as the "meat offering" (Leviticus 14:10).

Cherishing David

In 1 Kings 1, we read that old King David needed warmth, so a young virgin was sought to "cherish" him. So the King James Version reads. Curiously, *cherish* in the 1600s meant "to keep warm" and had no emotional meaning. Later versions have reworded the verse appropriately.

Ageless Eagles

According to Psalm 103:5, God renews the vigor of His people so that their "youth is renewed like the eagle's." The Church of England's official version, called the Bishops' Bible and published in 1568, has this note for the verse: "An egle of all birdes liveth a long tyme without all kind of feebleness, dying never of age, but of famine." The author of Psalm 103 and the Bishops' Bible scholars were somewhat more keen on theology than on their knowledge of birds.

Corny Scripture?

The word *corn* has different meanings, depending on which side of the Atlantic you are on. In England, it means "grain" and can refer to wheat, barley, rye, or other grasses. In America, we use it to refer to the native plant the Indians already cultivated, the familiar "eared" plant called maize or Indian corn. The King James Version of 1611 used the word *corn,* but in a silly blooper (which is also evidence of the hold that the KJV has on readers), later American versions continued to use *corn* even though the translators knew better. American Bibles, if they are to be accurate, ought to use the word *grain* because that is what the original Hebrew and Greek referred to. They certainly weren't referring to the plant that Americans call corn because that plant grew only in America when the Bible was written.

Glass

When the Bible uses the word *glass,* it usually means "mirror," as in Paul's famous statement on seeing "through a glass, darkly," which in most modern versions reads "mirror" (1 Corinthians 13:12). In times past, a mirror was often called a looking glass, or sometimes just a glass. Mirrors in Bible times were not actually glass but were highly polished metals. When the word *glass* occurs in Job 37:18 and Revelation 21:18, it may actually mean a bright, transparent mineral such as quartz. We know that the ancient Egyptians made actual glass, but this glass, the material we are familiar with today, is not mentioned in the Bible.

Mansions in Heaven

In the King James Version, John 14:2 reads, "In my Father's house are many mansions." Mansions, as in big impressive houses? No, definitely not. We owe "mansions" to William Tyndale, who used the word for the first English translation in the 1520s. In fact, Tyndale borrowed the word *mansiones* from the old Latin Bible. It meant something like "dwelling places," which is the phrase many modern translations use. Some simply have "rooms," which is accurate enough.

Help Meet or Helpmate?

"And the LORD God said, It is not good that the man should be alone; I will make him an help meet for him." So reads Genesis 2:18 in the King James Version. What is "an help meet"? The KJV used "meet" in the old sense, meaning that the helper was to be suitable or appropriate. God intended that Adam would have a suitable helper. Over the centuries, *help meet* evolved into *helpmate,* which is not accurate, though the idea is a pleasant one. The New King James Version reads "a helper comparable to him," and the New International Version has "a helper suitable for him."

Parbar Westward

First Chronicles 26:18 may qualify as the most bizarre verse in the King James Version: "At Parbar westward, four at the causeway, and two at Parbar." Happily, our knowledge of Hebrew has advanced since the King James Version debuted in 1611. The New International Version makes much more sense: "As for the court to the west, there were four at the road and two at the court itself."

Appearance of Evil

The apostle Paul told Christians to "abstain from all appearance of evil" (1 Thessalonians 5:22)—a perfectly valid Christian idea but not really a good translation of the Greek. People assume this means "don't do anything that appears evil," which is fine, but the original Greek meant something more like "avoid every kind of evil" (NIV).

Debts or Trespasses?

One verse from the Lord's Prayer has proved difficult to translate. Consider Matthew 6:12 in the King James Version: "And forgive us our debts, as we forgive our debtors." Some later versions have "trespasses" instead of "debts," and some contemporary versions have "sins" or "wrongs." Strictly speaking, "debts" is a literal translation of the Greek. But some translators point out that beyond the Greek lie the Aramaic words (and ideas) Jesus Himself would have used, and though the Gospel uses the Greek words for "debts" and "debtors," the idea is really closer to "sins" and "those who sin against us."

Business but Spiritual

Romans 12:11 says to be "not slothful in business." Countless sermons have been preached on this, encouraging people to work hard and providing a hook to businessmen, letting them know that Christianity has a concern for the world of business. But in fact the word *business* ought to be *zeal,* as it is in most modern versions. The NIV has "never lacking in zeal," which is pretty accurate.

Another Man's Wealth

"Let no man seek his own, but every man another's wealth" (1 Corinthians 10:24). Doesn't sound very Christian, does it? When the King James translators were writing, *wealth* actually meant "welfare" or "well-being"—and with that idea, the verse sounds very Christian. Also, in that period, *wealthy* did not mean rich but contented (see Psalm 66:12; Jeremiah 49:31).

Virtue and Virtuous

We use the word *virtuous* to describe someone who is moral or righteous. In 1611, the year the King James Version was published, it could mean that, but it usually meant something more like powerful or competent. In Proverbs 31, the praise of the virtuous woman might be more correctly praise of the competent woman. And consider the account of the woman who touched the hem of Jesus' garment: "And Jesus, immediately knowing in himself that virtue had gone out of him, turned him about in the press, and said, Who touched my clothes?" (Mark 5:30).

Feebleminded and Fainthearted

We use *feebleminded* to mean stupid or mentally slow. It meant something else to the King James translators, something like what is found in the New King James Version at 1 Thessalonians 5:14: "comfort the fainthearted."

Quick...and Also Alive

The Apostles' Creed states that Jesus will "come to judge the quick and the dead." The word *quick* is used in the old sense, the same as in the King James Version: It meant alive. Not once in that version does it mean rapid. (See Numbers 16:30; Psalm 119:25; John 5:21; Hebrews 4:12; 1 Peter 3:18.)

Champaign, Campaign...

Certain words all have the same root, as do campaign, camp, champagne, campus, and others. All these come from the Latin *campus,* meaning a plain or field. Knowing this, the King James reading of Deuteronomy 11:30 makes some sense: "in the land of the Canaanites, which dwell in the champaign over against Gilgal." Most modern versions have *plain* instead of *champaign.*

Cousin John

Bible readers have long assumed that Jesus and John the Baptist were cousins. This is based on Luke 1:36, which speaks of Mary, Jesus' mother, and Elizabeth, John the Baptist's mother, as cousins. In fact, as newer translations indicate, *cousin* in the King James is probably more accurately translated as *relative* or *kinswoman,* which could mean distant cousins. Jesus and John were in some way related by blood, although they were second cousins at best and probably more distant than that.

The Galatians Contradiction

Many readers look for contradictions in the Bible, and certainly Galatians 6 seems to have one. In the King James Version, verse 2 has "bear ye one another's burdens," while verse 5 has "every man shall bear his own burden." Hmmm. The problem is that two

different Greek words are both translated with the English *burden.*
Verse 2 has *baryos,* meaning a heavy or burdensome weight, while
verse 5 has *phortion,* meaning simply "something carried," not necessarily heavy or burdensome. So the two verses don't contradict
at all. We should each try to carry our own normal loads (verse 5),
but we should help each other with the heavier ones (verse 2).

Bible Bugs

Miles Coverdale's 1535 Bible was the first full Bible in English.
It included Tyndale's entire New Testament and about half of
his Old Testament. Coverdale himself translated the rest of the
Old Testament, though he didn't work from the original Hebrew
as Tyndale did. Coverdale's Bible has sometimes been called the
Bug Bible because of his wording of Psalm 91:5: "Thou shalt not
need to be afraid for any bugs by night." Bugs? No, he didn't
mean insects. Coverdale had learned from some scholars that the
Hebrew word used here meant something like a horrible thing
or a monster—what we might call a bugbear or bogeyman. His
contemporaries in the 1500s didn't generally apply the word *bug*
to insects. Incidentally, the King James Version of 1611 has the
verse this way: "Thou shalt not be afraid for the terror by night."
A little better than *bugs,* yes?

The Bug Bible has also been called the "Treacle Bible" because
of Coverdale's translation of Jeremiah 8:22: "Is there no treacle in
Gilead?" The King James Version has the more familiar, "Is there
no balm in Gilead?"

Coverdale's was the first full English Bible, so the names of
all the books of the Bible hadn't been set in stone just yet, and
Coverdale could assign them whatever name seemed appropriate.
The book that came to be called Obadiah, he called Abdy. Our
Zephaniah was his Sophony. And most amusing of all, our Song
of Solomon was his Salaman's Balettes. (*Balettes* was something
close to *ballads.*)

The Skin of My Teeth

The phrase "the skin of my teeth" is so familiar that many people have no idea it is from the Bible. Job 19:20 says, "I am escaped with the skin of my teeth." Some later updatings of the King James Version have *by* instead of *with*. Either way, it has become part of our language, and playwright Thornton Wilder used *The Skin of Our Teeth* as the title of his popular Pulitzer Prize–winning play.

But (sigh) the phrase isn't quite right. We now have a more advanced knowledge of Hebrew than the King James scholars did. So Job 19:20 is more accurate as "I gnaw my underlip with my teeth," as a 1989 Bible has it. More accurate, yes, but the old phrase still has a nice ring to it.

God Speaking Latin

The first officially approved English Bible ever printed is known as the Great Bible, which was printed in 1539 when Henry VIII was king. In his younger days, Henry was staunchly opposed to any translations into English (which is why the great William Tyndale had to live outside England and smuggle his translation back in). Henry had a change of heart as he aged, and he approved a Bible that, ironically, was largely a revision of what Tyndale had done. On the title page of the Great Bible (so called because it was a large volume), the words "The Bible in English" are easy to see. But on the same page, God is shown speaking words from the Bible...in Latin. Henry was still old-fashioned enough to think of Latin as the language of the church. Apparently the designers of the title page wanted the new Bible to appeal to everyone— including people as old-fashioned as the king was.

Tyndale's Good Friday

William Tyndale translated his New Testament for people

who had never had the Bible in English before. Occasionally he made an error, and in a few cases he deliberately edited. Here's one example: Matthew 27:62 speaks of the chief priests coming to Pilate the day after Jesus' crucifixion. The Greek here literally means "the day of Preparation." Tyndale knew that this phrase would have no meaning at all to readers unless he explained it in a footnote. Instead of using a footnote, he simply referred to the day of Jesus' crucifixion as "Good Friday"—a wise choice because all churchgoers, even if they'd never read a word of the Bible, knew that Good Friday was the annual holy day in memory of Jesus' crucifixion. (Tyndale's actual spelling was "good frydaye.")

Tyndale made another such intentional error: In Acts 20:6 he has "we sailed away from Philippi after the Easter holy days." (His spelling: "ester holydayes.") The name *Easter* wasn't in use when the New Testament was written, and the actual Greek means "the days of Unleavened Bread," referring to the Jewish holy season of Passover, which occurs near Easter on the calendar. Tyndale knew that *Easter* was technically wrong, but his readers (who had probably never met a Jew and didn't know much about their customs) would have no clue what "days of Unleavened Bread" meant.

And one more intentional holy day error of Tyndale: In 1 Corinthians 16:8, Paul says he will stay in Ephesus until Pentecost. Instead of Pentecost, Tyndale refers to Whitsuntide (in his spelling, "whitsontyde"). The English church in Tyndale's day was unfamiliar with the name *Pentecost* (which all churches use today) but quite familiar with the name *Whitsunday* for the same day. (In case you were wondering, *Whitsunday* is from "white Sunday"; newly baptized people wore white robes to church at this time.) In another place in the New Testament, however, Tyndale translated Pentecost as "the fiftieth day"—which is what Pentecost literally means.

A few more Tyndale tidbits: In Acts 14 the gates of the town of Lystra are referred to as the "churche porche," and elsewhere a centurion is referred to as an "under-captain."

The Nautical Dilemma

One translation task that caused many scholars' hair to turn gray involved the nautical narrative in Acts 27–28, where the apostle Paul is shipped off to Rome for his trial before the emperor. When the early English versions were being done in the 1500s and 1600s, knowledge of biblical Greek was limited regarding ships and sailing. We know a lot more now than our ancestors did.

Consider Acts 27:16-17 in the New International Version: "We were hardly able to make the lifeboat secure. When the men had hoisted it aboard, they passed ropes under the ship itself to hold it together." Now, Miles Coverdale's version of 1539: "We coulde scarce get a bote. Which they toke up and used helpe, and bounde it under harde to the shippe." Clear enough? The 1611 King James Version wasn't much of an improvement: "We had much work to come by the boat: which when they had taken up, they used helps, undergirding the ship."

Human Angels?

Angels appear throughout the Bible, sometimes appearing not quite human but often appearing human. Regardless of their appearance, we generally think of them as supernatural beings sent to do God's bidding. But many of the angels in the Bible may have been normal humans doing God's will. The Hebrew word *malakh* and the Greek word *angelos* both refer simply to a messenger, not necessarily a nonhuman being. Whether a particular messenger was human or otherwise depends on the context.

Nowhere is deciding whether an angel was human or not more difficult than in the first three chapters of Revelation. Here Christ addresses seven different churches, with each message beginning "To the angel in _____, write..." When William Tyndale first translated the Greek into English, he used *messenger* instead of *angel*. His footnote on these verses is interesting: "Messenger is the preacher of the congregation." Later in Revelation he has an even more detailed note: "Angel is a Greek word and signifieth a messenger. And all the angels are called messengers, because they are sent from God to man on message: even so prophets, preachers, and the prelates of the church are called angels, because their office is to bring the message of God unto the people. The good angels here in this book are the true bishops and preacher, and the evil angels are the heretics and false preachers which ever falsify God's word." A handful of modern translations follow Tyndale and use "messenger" in Revelation 1–3. Which is more correct? Perhaps only God knows.

A Bible with Only Three Christians

The New Testament refers many times to Christians—but rarely by that name. Most of the time, Christians are referred to as brothers (or, in the more gender-neutral versions, brothers and sisters). The actual word *Christian* appears a grand total of three times: twice in Acts (11:26; 26:28) and once in 1 Peter 4:16.

You might not guess that from several modern translations of the Bible, which use *Christians* in many of the cases where the older versions used the more correct *brothers*. This is a case of a forgivable blooper. The translators of these versions (such as the NLT) knew that *brothers* was more correct than *Christians,* but they avoided inserting a footnote saying, "*Brothers* here refers to fellow Christians." Also, *Christians* has the advantage of being gender-neutral.

Moses with Horns?

One of the most famous works of art in the world is Michelangelo's marble statue of Moses, showing him as an old but muscular man holding the stone tablets inscribed with the Ten Commandments. He also has two small horns on top of his head. Why? Did the sculptor think Moses stayed so long on the mountain that he turned into a mountain goat?

Blame it on the Latin version of the Bible. Exodus 34:29-33 (NIV) says, "When Moses came down from Mount Sinai with the two tablets of the Testimony in his hands, he was not aware that his face was radiant because he had spoken with the LORD. When Aaron and all the Israelites saw Moses, his face was radiant, and they were afraid to come near him... When Moses finished speaking to them, he put a veil over his face." Moses had encountered God on the mountain and had received the Ten Commandments from Him. He had been gone 40 days, and the Israelites feared something had happened to him. When they finally saw him again, he was not only alive but literally glowing. Note that this modern version uses the word *radiant,* which is correct. But the old Latin Bible that Michelangelo was familiar with used a rather clumsy translation from the Hebrew, stating that Moses had horns. Had Michelangelo and other artists known the real meaning of the Hebrew, they would have depicted Moses with a kind of halo around his head. Instead, the famous statue— and many other artworks showing Moses—show him with horns on his head.

Fetching the Compass

Acts 28:13 relates that Paul and his companions "fetched a compass," yet we know for a fact that navigational compasses did not exist in those days. (No GPS devices either!) This is the fault of the King James Version. The actual meaning of Acts 28:13 is clear in the New King James: "We circled round."

Drink Ye All of It

At the Last Supper, Jesus spoke of the cup of wine He was holding and told His disciples, "Drink ye all of it" (Matthew

26:27). Some people have taken this to mean that when churches have Communion service, they must consume all the wine (or juice). But in fact, the word *all* in the verse is connected with *ye,* not with *it* (the wine). The New King James more accurately reflects the Greek: "Drink from it, all of you."

A Lawyer Joke

We live in a lawsuit-prone culture, where lawyers seem to be a necessary evil. But most people consider some lawyers as more evil than necessary, which is why scads of lawyer jokes are floating around. Sometimes people point to the New Testament and say that Jesus Himself directed some very harsh words at lawyers. Here's an example: "Woe unto you also, ye lawyers! for ye lade men with burdens grievous to be borne, and ye yourselves touch not the burdens with one of your fingers...Woe unto you, lawyers! for ye have taken away the key of knowledge: ye entered not in yourselves, and them that were entering in ye hindered" (Luke 11:46,52). Strong words—but they were not directed at the kind of lawyers we have in our society. The lawyers in the King James Version were experts in the Law of Moses, which governed the lives of Jews. Jesus was lashing out at them because they had the habit of nitpicking about the Law and making daily life for Jews an unbearable burden of petty regulations. Annoying as these experts were, they were not similar to the lawyers of our time. Most modern translations have *scribes* (not much of an improvement over *lawyer*) or *teachers of the law* (much better).

All Glorious Within

Sermons have been preached on Psalm 45:13: "The king's daughter is all glorious within." And what a wonderful and very Christian idea: a woman that is beautiful inwardly, spiritually. But this is not what Psalm 45:13 actually means. The New King

James is more accurate: "The royal daughter is all glorious within the palace."

Quoting the Competition

The Geneva Bible of 1560 was the most popular English Bible until the King James Version of 1611 became the big seller. Most of the men who worked on the KJV probably had been using the Geneva for their own personal use. This shows up in the KJV's preface, where, amazingly, the Bible verses actually quoted are not from the KJV itself but from the Geneva.

By the way, King James himself hated the Geneva Bible, so it is ironic that so many verses from it went unchanged into the King James Version. However, the egotistical king got what he wanted: The new version would replace the Geneva in time (though it was slow in doing so), and the most popular English Bible ever would bear his name.

Where There Is No Vision

Proverbs 29:18 reads, "Where there is no vision, the people perish." That verse has been quoted and preached on countless times, and most people would accept it as true: Where a culture lacks a vision for itself, the people wither spiritually. However, the way we use *vision* is not quite what the author of Proverbs had in mind. He meant something more like an oracle from a prophet or a revelation (as the New King James Version correctly reads).

Married Apostles?

When William Tyndale's New Testament was smuggled into England in 1526, readers were in for some surprises because the Bible had never been available in English. One big surprise was that the apostle Peter was married—which hinted that perhaps all the apostles were married. More explicitly, 1 Corinthians 9:5 mentions the apostles and the brothers of Jesus having wives. The English had been long accustomed to the idea that priests had to be celibate, so this was a shock. In time the English church did away with its requirement that ministers be celibate, thanks to a greater acquaintance with the foundation of Christian practice, the Bible. At least one English clergyman claimed that this new English Bible was heretical because it was corrupt enough to claim the apostles were married men!

Columbus in the Bible?

Psalm 45:9 refers to the "gold of Ophir." No one has a clue where Ophir was, but the Bishops' Bible, published in 1568, went out on a limb and provided this footnote: "Ophir is thought to be the island in the west coast, of late found by Christopher Columbo; from whence at this day is brought most fine gold." Well, the footnote was partly right: gold was being found in some of the countries Columbus had visited. But since the Atlantic Ocean was an uncrossable barrier until Columbus made his famous trip in 1492, we can safely assume that wherever Ophir was, it was not in America.

Lusty Zeus in the Bible

Most of the early English Bibles were illustrated, sometimes lavishly so. The Bishops' Bible published in 1568 was apparently a "rush job," and some of its illustrations were not of Bible characters but of people from Greek and Roman mythology. The printer picked some illustrations from a printing of the Roman poet Ovid's *Metamorphoses*. So in the Bishops' Bible, the letter to the Hebrews begins with a huge initial letter showing, strangely enough, the god Zeus (appearing in the form of a swan), who, in the myth, impregnates the woman Leda.

Gardiner, the Latin Buff

After the Great Bible was published in 1539 with the approval of King Henry VIII, many people were elated to have the Bible in their own language—and legally. Not everyone was, however. Some of the more conservative ministers still clung to the old idea that the only real Bible was the Latin version. One of the leaders of these reactionaries was the powerful bishop of Winchester, Stephen Gardiner. He realized the people weren't going to give up their English Bibles, but he wanted the English Bible to retain some of the old Latin phrases that were familiar in the worship service. Gardiner drew up a list of 132 of these phrases. Had his list been followed, we would have had the voice of God at Jesus' baptism saying, "This is my dilect son in whom complacui." But doesn't it sound better to say, "This is my beloved son, in whom I am well pleased"? Gardiner also wanted to retain such Latinisms as *commilito, lites, panis propositionis, didragma, ejicere, increpair,* and *zizania*—fondly remembered by some Latin scholars maybe, but the laity had no problem dumping these words that they never understood anyway.

Biblical Organ

The King James Version mentions the organ as a musical instrument (Genesis 4:21; Job 21:12; Psalm 150:4). This is most definitely not the large instrument with several keyboards that we know today. Newer translations refer to flutes and pipes, and this is probably more accurate. (Technically these are all wind instruments, since pipe organs produce sounds by pushing air through the pipes.)

Denarius

The common coin in New Testament days was the Roman denarius, called a penny in the King James Version but usually a denarius in newer translations. It was silver and resembled the American dime. A denarius was, in those days, about a day's wages. Just as our modern coins feature the heads of famous statesmen, so the Roman denarius had a man's head—always the head of the reigning emperor, as seen in the story of Jesus and the question of paying taxes (Matthew 22:19). The coin mentioned there would have had the image of either Tiberius or Augustus.

Worshipping Scarecrows

The prophet Jeremiah mocked people who worshipped idols: "Like a scarecrow in a melon patch, their idols cannot speak; they must be carried because they cannot walk. Do not fear them; they can do no harm nor can they do any good" (Jeremiah 10:5 NIV). Put another way: the false gods aren't real gods at all, having no power to act any more than a scarecrow does. Incidentally, while most Bible versions now have *scarecrow,* the King James Version had *palm tree,* which is most likely wrong.

After God's Own Heart

For several hundred years, English-speaking people have been reading and hearing sermons about King David being a "man after his [God's] own heart," the phrase used in 1 Samuel 13:14 and Acts 13:22. It is a phrase that easily sticks in the memory, and it seems appropriate for David because he does indeed seem to be desirous of God's affection and doing things to win God's love. Unfortunately, with all respect to the many translators and preachers who have used the phrase, it is wrong. The Hebrew word used in 1 Samuel is *leb,* usually translated *heart,* but referring neither to the bodily organ called the heart nor to the seat of the emotions. In fact, *leb* meant something more like "center"—either literal (as in the center of a forest) or figurative (as in the center of the person, meaning the mind, will, or soul).

The Hebrews didn't know quite as much about human anatomy as we do, and the knowledge that the brain was the center of mental processes was centuries in the future. We tend to connect the brain with the mind and the heart with the emotions, but they did not. In fact, when they were speaking of the emotions, affections, and passions, they were more inclined to talk of the bowels than the heart, which is why some old versions like the King James seem so quaint and amusing with their talk of bowels. In Colossians 3:12, Paul tells Christians to "put on...bowels of mercies." In the 1600s and today, we figuratively refer to bodily organs that in fact are not the centers of the emotions.

But back to David. When the Bible refers to him as a "man after God's own *leb*," it really means something like God's own mind or God's own will. And here's another shocker. The word *after* here is misleading because the Hebrew word used in 1 Samuel actually means something like "according to" or "corresponding to." God is in fact referring to David as "a man who is in accord with my mind" or "my plan." (The Good News Bible is reasonably accurate in 1 Samuel with "the kind of man the Lord wants.") But it will probably be a long, long time before translators or preachers ever put aside the familiar "man after God's own heart" and use the more accurate "man in accord with God's mind." This is an example of why a literal translation of the Bible can actually be misleading.

Stumbling Hands and Caper-berries

One of the slowest and least successful revision projects ever was the English Revised Version, a long-needed and long-awaited editing of the King James Version. Amazing individuals like Martin Luther and William Tyndale could produce a fresh translation from Greek and Hebrew in a matter of months, but 65 English scholars took much longer to revise an existing version.

Was it worth the wait? Not totally. The English Revised Version New Testament, published in 1881, had such ridiculous wordings as having Jesus say, "If thy right hand causeth thee to stumble" (Matthew 5:30).

Consider the King James wording of Ecclesiastes 12:5: "Desire shall fail." The English Revised Version corrected and improved it with this wording: "the caper-berry shall fail." Better? Wisely, the New International Version has "desire no longer is stirred," and the New King James Version has "desire fails."

One oddity of the English Revised Version was that it actually *added* some outdated words to the Bible, such as *howbeit, haply,* and *behooved.* It even added the suffix *-ward* in some places, making *to us* into *to us-ward,* which looks just plain silly (and sounds even sillier when read aloud). Totally bewildering archaic words like *amerced* were thrown in (it means to punish by imposing a fine). It even coined some words that seemed foolish, such as translating the Greek monetary word *denarion* as *denary,* when most English versions wisely used the word *penny.* In the Sermon on the Mount, Jesus refers to "footstool of his feet," where the King James had the simple (and correct) "footstool." And for no good reason, the English Revised Version retained such archaic words as these: *sith, holpen, bewray, strowed, hough, marish,* and *pourtray.*

Such curiosities as these bothered the many Americans who were hoping for a new and usable updating of the Bible. However, the English scholars weren't keen on making Americans equal partners in this version. When the English Revised Version New Testament was published in 1881, Americans bought copies, but disappointment set in quickly, with people on both sides of the Atlantic scratching their heads over words that seemed even more outdated than those in the King James. So in 1901 a New York company published the American Standard Version, which dumped most of the quirky words of the English Revised Version and also made thousands of helpful changes in the King James.

(For some odd reason, it still retained some quaint words like *besom* and *scall*.) Later the American Standard Version would serve as the basis for the Revised Standard Version.

Overcome or Understood?

All languages have words with double meanings, and sometimes Bible translators can't be sure whether the authors intended a double meaning. The classic case is John 1:5, which in the New King James Version reads, "And the light shines in the darkness, and the darkness did not comprehend it." The Greek word translated "comprehend" here is *katelaben,* which could also mean to overpower. Thus various modern translations have something like *comprehend* or *understand,* while others tilt toward the other meaning and have *overpower* or *overcome.* Usually a footnote explains that either meaning is possible. The New English Bible of 1970 came up with an attractive alternative: *mastered,* which itself has the double meaning of understanding and overcoming (as in "I finally mastered algebra"). The New English Translation, available on the Internet, also uses *mastered.*

Translating *Cherubim*

A Hebrew word that gives translators fits is *cherubim,* plural of *cherub,* and referring to majestic winged creatures (or angels)— definitely not the cute, chubby babies we call cherubs. The *-im* on the word indicates it is plural, although most modern readers don't know that, and using the plural *cherubs* isn't appropriate (the fat baby problem again), although several translations do so. Today's English Version has *living creatures,* which doesn't communicate much—but then, neither does *cherubim* or *cherubs.* This is one of many cases where the Bible reader definitely needs an explanatory footnote.

Pericope Adulterae

This is the name that Bible scholars use to refer to John 7:53–8:11, the story of the woman caught in adultery. The story puzzles many scholars, not because they don't believe it is authentic but because the oldest Greek manuscripts of the New Testament have it in different locations. Those who study Greek closely agree that it doesn't seem to fit in John's Gospel, for its wording makes it read more like Matthew, Mark, and Luke. Read John 7, ending at verse 52, then start reading again at John 8:12. The text seems to flow perfectly, doesn't it? Scholars have also noticed that 7:53 through 8:11 are an interruption, but nobody knows just where the inserted material really belongs.

Doulos

Here's a Greek word translators argue about: Do we translate it *servant* or *slave?* Strictly speaking, it means a slave, and many translations have it that way. The difference is meaningful, for the ancient world recognized a definite difference in status between a servant and a slave. Other Greek words also mean a servant, and one wonders if translators simply don't like to use *slave,* even in such phrases as *slave of Jesus Christ.*

Call Him/Her June

In the last chapter of his letter to the Romans, the apostle Paul does a shout-out to some of the Christians in Rome. One of these is named Junias—or Junia, depending on which version you're reading. Here's Romans 16:7: "Salute Andronicus and Junia, my kinsmen, and my fellow prisoners, who are of note among the apostles, who also were in Christ before me." The New International Version has "Junias," as do several others. If this person's name was Junias, he was probably a man, but if Junia, she was a woman. You might ask the obvious question: Is it important? The really important thing is that Paul was commending this person, who apparently was also in prison for his (or her) faith. However, Paul's mention of Junia(s) being "of note among the apostles" is tantalizing. We aren't sure if he meant that Adronicus and Junia(s) were considered apostles themselves or were regarded highly by the apostles. If Junia, female, was an apostle, that means there were women apostles—an interesting notion and very appealing to feminist scholars. Adronicus and Junia may have been husband and wife, like Paul's friends Prisca and Aquila, mentioned earlier in the letter.

This puzzle may never be solved.

Isaac, Izhak, and Isahac

Bible translators face a problem when translating names from the Hebrew and Greek: Do they use the familiar English form of the name (if one exists), or do they literally translate the name as it appears in the original? Some examples: the Greek text of Acts has *Stephanos,* but we usually use the familiar name *Stephen,* just as we use *Jesus* instead of the Greek name *Iesous.* Some early translations into English tried too hard to follow the Hebrew and Greek. For example, they used *Izhak* or *Isahac* instead of the familiar name *Isaac.* The King James Version was the first to try to use the familiar names instead of the sometimes bizarre-sounding Greek and Hebrew names.

Corrupt Greek and Hebrew

In the long history of Christianity, this is one of the strangest things: the Catholic church's official banning of Bible translations from the original Greek and Hebrew. Around the year 400, the great scholar Jerome produced his famous Latin translation of the Bible based on the Hebrew and Greek. Jerome's Latin Bible, known as the Vulgate, became so loved by the church hierarchy that they believed it to be divinely inspired. In the 1500s, Martin Luther and other Protestants insisted on going back to the basics— producing translations based on the original Hebrew and Greek. William Tyndale asked a pertinent question: "St. Jerome translated the Bible into his mother tongue. Why may not we also?"

But the Catholic officials said no—no Bibles were to be translated from these "new" languages of Greek and Hebrew but only from Jerome's Vulgate. This is supremely ironic because Jerome himself had used the Greek and Hebrew. Catholic officials said the Hebrew text, even if it was older than the Latin (which it was), had been corrupted by the Jews. In fact, the Jews were absolutely obsessive about making precise copies of their ancient holy books (the ones we call the Old Testament).

When some English Catholics did get around to making their own English New Testament in 1582, they insisted on translating from Latin, stating that it was "truer than the vulgar Greek text." The title page of this version read: "The New Testament of Jesus Christ, translated faithfully into English, out of the authentical Latin." The preface states that this version "is not only better than all other Latin translations, but than the Greek text itself in those places where they disagree." The preface applauds the fact that in times past the Bible could not be understood by "every husbandman, artificer, prentice, boys, girls, mistress, maid, man." As you might imagine, this Catholic version was not intended for the laity to read, but for the priests and bishops only.

A full Catholic Bible was published in 1610 (one year earlier than the King James Version), and in its preface it stated that the Old Testament's Hebrew text was not used because it had been corrupted by the Jews. Based on the Latin text, this Catholic Old Testament gave such oddities as Psalm 58:9: "Before your thorns did understand the old brier, as living son in wrath he swallowed them." It's a bit clearer in the King James Version: "Before your pots can feel the thorns, he shall take them away as with a whirlwind, both living, and in his wrath."

Fast-forward a few centuries: Not until the mid-1900s did the Catholic church finally allow Catholic Bibles to be translated from the Greek and Hebrew. Sadly, in the intervening centuries, many faithful people, such as the great English translator William Tyndale, had been burned as heretics for daring to base their translations on the Greek and Hebrew instead of on the Latin Vulgate.

Conquinations and Other Oddities

English Catholics were generally horrified at the new English Bibles being produced in the 1500s because the translators were all heretics (Protestants, that is) using the original Greek and Hebrew texts instead of the Catholic-approved Latin. However, the Catholics realized that they had to do their own English versions, or the laity might start reading the heretic versions. The first Catholic-approved English New Testament was published in Rheims, France, in 1582, and imported into England. Everyone now agrees that it was one of the worst English Bibles ever and nearly unreadable. In fact, some people joked that the laity were as stumped by it as they were by the Latin Bible.

Here are just a few tidbits, with the corresponding verses from the King James:

- 1 Corinthians 5:7: "that you may be a new paste as you are Azymes."

  KJV: "that ye may be a new lump, as ye are unleavened."
- Ephesians 3:6: "concorporat and comparticipant."

  KJV: "of the same body, and partakers."

- Hebrew 13:1: "Let the charity of the fraternity abide in you."

    KJV: "Let brotherly love continue."

- 2 Peter 2:13: "conquinations and spots, flowing in delacies."

    KJV: "Spots they are and blemishes, sporting themselves."

- Hebrews 13:16: "Beneficence and communication do not forget, for with such hosts God is promerited."

    KJV: "To do good and to communicate forget not: for with such sacrifices God is well pleased."

- Romans 6:13: "Exhibit yourselves to God as of dead men, alive."

    KJV: "Yield yourselves unto God, as those that are alive from the dead."

- Romans 9:28: "consummating a word, and abridging it in equitie; because a word abridged shall our Lord make upon the earth."

    KJV: "Finish the work, and cut it short in righteousness: because a short work will the Lord make upon the earth."

Granted, the King James wording is a bit hard for us today, but it is crystal clear compared with the disastrous Rheims version of 1582.

An Updated Catholic Bible

In 1610, the Catholics' Rheims New Testament was joined with a translation of the Old Testament completed in Douay, France, and for a long time the Douay-Rheims version of 1610 was the only English Bible Catholics were permitted to use. The Douay-Rheims was a poor translation because it was based on the

Latin text and because it sometimes didn't bother to translate the
Latin words. Some quotable tidbits from it: "If thou be a prevari-
cator of the law, thy circumcision is become prepuce" (Romans
2:25). "Thou hast fatted my head with oil, and my chalice ine-
briating how goodlie it is" (Psalm 23:5). "He exinanited himself
(Philippians 2:7). "Let us cleanse our selves from al inquinatio
of the flesh and spirit" (2 Corinthians 7:1). "Contristrate not the
holy Spirit of God" (Ephesians 4:30). The Douay-Rheims version
had the habit of using a long Latin word when a shorter and
simpler English word would have worked better—for example,
"veritie" for truth, "benignity" for kindness, and the laughable
"longanimity" for patience. In Acts, instead of "northeast wind" it
has "a wind that is called Euro Aquilo."

A revision of Douay-Rheims, published in 1749, was a breath
of fresh air for English-speaking Catholics. The revising was
done by the priest Richard Challoner. The Challoner revision
was the standard for Catholics until the mid-1900s. It made
some needed changes, such as, in Philippians 2:7, saying that
Jesus emptied himself instead of the Douay-Rheims wording,
"exinanited himself." The "azymes" of Luke 22:1 was changed to
"unleavened bread." The "scenopegia" of John 7:2 was changed
to "Feast of Tabernacles." However, some of the old quirks
remained, notably that John 19:14 still had "the parsceve of the
pasch" instead of the "Passover Eve" of Protestant Bibles. On
the brighter side, Challoner deleted many of the Douay-Rheims
Bible's anti-Protestant footnotes.

Repent or Do Penance?

The Roman Catholic church regards penance as one of its seven
sacraments. When men like William Tyndale began translating
the Greek New Testament in the 1500s, they accurately translated the Greek word *metanoia* as *repent*. The Catholics' Latin

Bible used a word that meant to do penance, which is definitely not the same as to repent—after all, a person can repent without doing penance, which means a person can bypass the church and its rituals. Catholics were horrified by this, and the first Catholic Bible in English, the Douay-Rheims Bible, used *do penance* instead of *repent.*

In 1764, Matthew Carey of Philadelphia published a revised Douay-Rheims Bible and actually used the word *repent* in it—adding a footnote saying that repentance actually meant "penitential exercises."

Wesley and His Bowels

We use the word *bowels* to refer literally to the intestines, but in times past, *bowels* could also refer figuratively to the human center of pity, compassion, or courage. People in the 1500s and 1600s sometimes used *bowels* figuratively in the same way we use *heart* today. For example, consider Jeremiah 4:19: "My bowels, my bowels! I am pained at my very heart; my heart maketh a noise in me." And Lamentations 1:20: "Behold, O LORD; for I am in distress: my bowels are troubled." The use of *bowels* wasn't a blooper when the early English Bibles were printed; most people understood *bowels* in the figurative sense. No modern versions use this word in the old way, of course.

In the 1700s, English minister John Wesley, founder of the Methodist movement, realized that the King James Version was hard for many of his followers to understand, given the changes in the language. So in 1755 Wesley published an edited version, changing words here and there and also adding footnotes. It was a "modernized" version, but in one instance, Wesley made a verse sound more dated than the King James Version. This was in Luke 15:20, part of Jesus' parable of the prodigal son. In the King James Version, we read that the father "saw him, and had compassion." In John Wesley's retro version, the father "saw him, and his bowels yearned."

Y or U?

You might be aware that many of our English words originally came from Greek—such as *psychic, synthesis, sympathy, pylon, dynamic,* and many others. Here's a bit of alphabetic trivia: All those words are spelled and pronounced incorrectly. Greek did not have a letter *y* at all. It did have the letter upsilon, which was the vowel *u*. A capital upsilon had exactly the same form as our letter *Y,* and when Greek words were printed in our English alphabet, the printers wrongly used a *y,* whether it was capital or lowercase. In other words, the Greek word we use often, *synthesis,* would actually have been spelled and pronounced *sunthesis,* and *martyr* is correctly *martur.*

Printers have never been consistent about this. For example, the letter upsilon is found in the common name *Paul* (in Greek, *Paulos*), but no one ever spelled the name as *Payl.* Yet at the end of the letter to the Romans, a *y* is used in the names of Tryphaena and Tryphosa, who would correctly be Truphaena and Truphosa. Stachys would correctly be Stachus, Olympas would be Olumpas, and so on. The same is true for place names—Cyprus should actually be Cupros.

Incidentally, the many Greek names that end with *-us* in our English Bibles actually ended with *-os* in Greek, so Cornelius was really Cornelios, and Festus was Festos.

New and
(Not!) Improved

As the most read book in the world, the Bible has been published in countless editions. Many of these are faithful attempts to translate the original Hebrew and Greek texts accurately. But some are the products of good intentions gone astray. And some are...well, just plain weird.

The PC Effect

Like most Bible versions, the Revised Standard Version was updated late in the twentieth century, especially in regard to sexist language. The New Revised Standard Version, published in 1989, generally changed "man" and "men" when they referred to human beings in general. This nod to political correctness did not go far enough for some people, so in 1995 *The New Testament and Psalms: An Inclusive Version* was published. The familiar New Testament phrase *kingdom of God* was said to be offensive because it was patriarchal, so it was changed to *dominion of God*. Even more radical, and a definite departure from the Greek text, was that *Father* was changed to *Father-Mother* when referring to God, so that Jesus says, "I am in the Father-Mother, and the Father-Mother is in me."

Being inclusive apparently involves more than just eliminating sexist language. As a nod to the increased sensitivity toward Jews, the word *Jews* in John's Gospel (which occurs many times) was changed to *religious authorities. Darkness* as a metaphor for ignorance was considered offensive to blacks, so the term *night* was used. The many references to God's right hand were changed to *mighty hand* (apparently so as not to offend left-handed people). *Obey your parents* was considered too strong for these sensitive translators, so they softened it to *heed your parents.*

As you might expect, all this heightened sensitivity makes for a clunky translation. Consider John 5:26-27 in the New International Version: "For as the Father has life in himself, so he has granted the Son to have life in himself. And he has given him authority to judge because he is the Son of Man." Now the Inclusive Version: "For just as God has life in Godself, so God has granted the same thing to the Child, and has given the Child authority to execute judgment, because of being the Human One."

The preface to this version states that it was published to "provide direction and sustenance to those who long for justice." The *Wall Street Journal* wrote a mocking review, noting that in the genealogies of Jesus, which name the male ancestors but not many of the female, the new version included both parents' names if the mother's name was known. Slaves are now called "enslaved people," and parents guide children but do not discipline them. God as Lord and King is now Ruler and Sovereign. Satan is also gender-neutral. The *Journal* noted that "the contemporary equivalent of pondering how many angels can fit on the head of a pin is to calculate the number of gender-offensive words in the Bible."

On the other side of the denominational aisle, a Roman Catholic group called Priests for Equality published its own *Inclusive*

New Testament in 1994. In a preface, they state that their new version is "a re-imagining of the holy scriptures and our relationship to them." They even acknowledged that in some parts of the Bible "the point of the passage was so encrusted that to remove the sexist language would necessitate removing the text itself." Consider their treatment of John 8:3, which the New International Version has this way: "The teachers of the law and the Pharisees brought in a woman caught in adultery." Here's the inclusive rendering: "A couple had been caught in the act of adultery, though the scribes and the Pharisees brought only the woman." Now consider a New Testament passage that always riles radical feminists, Colossians 3:18-19. First, the NIV: "Wives, submit to your husbands, as is fitting in the Lord. Husbands, love your wives and do not be harsh with them." Now, the inclusive: "You who are in committed relationships, be submissive to each other. This is your duty in Christ Jesus. Partners joined by God, love each other. Avoid any bitterness between you."

An inclusive Old Testament was published in 2001.

Radical to the Max

Every Bible translation ever made has its bloopers, but a 2004 version is *all blooper*. In fact, reading this one makes a person wonder if some conservative Christian put this book together as a kind of spoof of how ridiculous liberals can be. But alas, John Henson's *Good as New: A Radical Retelling of the Scriptures,* published in England, is for real.

One element that has brought this version so much attention is its distortion of the New Testament's two main passages that condemn homosexual behavior. One of these, Romans 1:26-27, reads this way in the New International Version: "Because of this, God gave them over to shameful lusts. Even their women exchanged natural relations for unnatural ones. In the same way the men also abandoned natural relations with women and were inflamed with lust for one another. Men committed indecent acts with other men, and received in themselves the due penalty for their perversion." Now, the radical retelling: "God let them go on to pursue their selfish desires. Women use their charms to further their own ends. Men, instead of being friends, ruthlessly exploit one another." The *Times* (London) half-flippantly reviewed the book and noted that "St. Paul's notorious condemnations of gay sex are deleted and Christians are told to go out and have more sex." John Henson, the version's editor, claimed that he did not delete Paul's words, but that his version was "less homophobically translated," that the older versions were "slanted," and that Paul's words were "notoriously and shamefully used by the church in times past."

Distorting the writers' words was not the only serious change. This version doesn't even include all the New Testament: 1 and 2 Timothy, Titus, 2 Peter, 2 and 3 John, Jude, and Revelation are all missing. And amazingly, the book includes the Gospel of Thomas, the same phony Gospel that the Jesus Seminar chose to include in its book *The Five Gospels.* But the Gospel of Thomas contains the very sexist statement that "every woman who will make herself male will enter the kingdom of heaven." *Good as New* twists this into "every woman who insists on equality with men is fit to be a citizen in God's New World."

Typical of liberal versions, this one does not refer to God as Father but as All Loving God. Jesus is not the Son of Man but rather the Complete Person, and He is not Son of God but is God's Likeness. Feeling that the word *Pharisee* meant nothing to modern readers (even though a footnote could explain it easily enough), this version uses "one of the strict set." The Holy Spirit is consistently referred to as *she*—at Jesus' baptism, "she was like a pigeon flying down and perching on him." Following the baptism—or "dipping," as this version has it—Jesus is not tempted by Satan but by His own inner thoughts. The entire temptation takes place in His mind.

One oddity that is actually pretty accurate: John the Baptist is referred to as John the Dipper, which reflects the original Greek word, which means to immerse. (Many "immersion versions" of the Bible have been produced by people who insist that baptism in the New Testament was always done by immersion.) On the other hand, the wise men or magi of Matthew 2 are "members of an eastern religion who studied the stars." The part about studying the stars is accurate enough, but "members of an eastern religion" sounds as if they could have been Buddhists, Hindus, or Confucianists. Instead of an angel communicating with Joseph, he hears "someone sent from God." Elsewhere angels are called "God's helpers." Instead of disciples, Jesus has 12 friends.

The editor, John Henson, is a retired Baptist minister and an active member of ONE, described on the publisher's website as "a network of radical Christians and over twenty organizations in the United Kingdom. In different ways they work to renew the church from within." Radical or not, the book was given the seal of approval by none other than Rowan Williams, archbishop of Canterbury, head of the Church of England. In fact, he wrote a forward for the book, praising it as "fully earthed." It remains to be seen whether the poor attendance in the Church of England will be increased or decreased by this radical and fully earthed version of the New Testament.

The Jesus Seminar's Five Gospels

Because Christianity is composed of thousands of different denominations and groups, no individual or official body can speak for all Christians. This is certainly true for the infamous Jesus Seminar, a group of liberal academics who have taken on the task of reading the New Testament and deciding which parts are real and which aren't. Of course, individuals (Thomas Jefferson, for example) have been doing this for centuries—the old process of throwing out the parts of the Bible we happen not to like. But in our media age, the Jesus Seminar has apparently relished playing the role of Christian skeptics, claiming to be Christian but extremely doubtful if much of the Bible is really true.

Beginning in the 1980s, the participants used colored balls to vote on whether a verse from the New Testament is "certainly authentic," "might be authentic," or is "definitely not authentic." The Seminar has, needless to say, found a lot of "definitely not authentic" passages in the Gospels. In 1996 the Seminar's so-called scholars claimed that the four Gospels were "notoriously unreliable," and the Seminar threw out the nativity, the Sermon on the Mount, and the resurrection.

To no one's surprise, the group decided to publish its own "authentic" version of the Gospels—that is, the four Gospels, printed in different colors to mark which parts are real (not many) and which aren't (quite a few). In 1993 the group published *The Five Gospels: The Search for the Authentic Words of Jesus*. Yes, five— the group chose to include the so-called Gospel of Thomas, a Gnostic writing long ago rejected as not authentically Christian. The Jesus Seminar claims that it contains more authentic sayings of Jesus than the Gospel of John.

In this translation, red type indicates authentic sayings of Jesus, pink indicates that Jesus probably said something similar, gray indicates words that Jesus did not say but that the idea is close to His own, and black indicates words that Jesus definitely did not say. Later writers or editors used these words to put their own ideas in the mouth of Jesus. The text doesn't include much red or pink but does have lots of black and gray. (In the Lord's Prayer, for example, the only words in red are "Our Father." So they consider this prayer, one of the most familiar and most repeated prayers in the world, not to be the authentic words of Jesus.) In fact, the book's preface states that "eighty-two percent of the words ascribed to Jesus in the Gospels were not actually spoken by him." Interestingly, in the case of the Gospel story of Jesus and the woman about to be stoned for adultery, the book says that the editors put it in the special category of "things they wish Jesus had said and done."

If this doesn't jar the sensibilities of many Christians (and it definitely does), the translation itself certainly will. It is also called the Scholars Version, but it is, to put it mildly, a very loose translation. Consider Matthew 23:13, where Jesus denounces the Pharisees. The New International Version reads like this: "Woe to you, teachers of the law and Pharisees, you hypocrites! You shut the kingdom of heaven in men's faces. You yourselves do not enter, nor will you let those enter who are trying to." Now, the Scholars Version: "You scholars and Pharisees, you impostors! Damn you! You slam the door of Heaven's domain in people's faces. You yourself don't enter, and you block the way of those trying to enter." Note that, as a bow to political correctness, the old sexist term "kingdom of heaven" is replaced by "Heaven's domain." In the Beatitudes from the Sermon on the Mount, the text dumps the familiar "Blessed are they..." for "Congratulations to..."

Robert Funk, whose name is usually listed first on the Jesus Seminar's title page, is a former Texas revival preacher and now a devoted liberal who has made it clear he does not believe in the divinity or resurrection of Jesus or in a personal God. Funk and the other editors of *The Five Gospels* ostentatiously dedicated the book to Galileo, Thomas Jefferson, and David Friedrich Strauss—three high-profile rebels against the authority of the Bible.

Every few years the Jesus Seminar publishes one of these books to the delight of liberals and to the chagrin of conservatives.

The Cheeky Cheke Bible

Ever heard of the twelve frosents? Probably not, but in John Cheke's 1550 translation of the New Testament, Jesus had 12 frosents, not apostles. Cheke had been a professor of Greek at Cambridge University and was tutor to the boy king Edward VI, son of the famous Henry VIII. Although he obviously had a deep affection for and understanding of Greek, he thought a truly English Bible ought to dispense with as many words of Greek and Latin origin as possible. So in his version, an apostle is a frosent (one sent forth, that is), a resurrection is either an uprising or a gainrising, a lunatic is moond, wise men are wizards, and a centurion is a hundreder. He really went out on a limb with using *Welshmen* instead of *foreigners* and using *head bishop* instead of *high priest.* Obviously none of his oddities ever made it into a popular Bible. He served as the prototype of the too-smart scholar whose knowledge of ancient languages is good but whose feeling for English is very poor.

The RSV's Virginity Problem

The Revised Standard Version of the Bible, published in 1952, must rank as one of the great publishing successes of all time. The first printing was a million copies, which would have made a pile 24 miles high if they were stacked together. A thousand tons of paper were used, two thousand gallons of ink. On September 30, 1952, more than three thousand churches in the United States held services celebrating the new Bible. The project's heads presented a copy to a grinning President Harry Truman. The British were as pleased with the new version as the Americans were. For many people it seemed ideal: retaining as much of the King James Version as possible but modernizing the vocabulary where it seemed appropriate. It seemed an ideal Bible for public worship and for private study.

The RSV eliminated all the archaic words of the KJV and the American Standard Version of 1901. It also changed the ASV's name for God, Jehovah, to LORD (note the small caps).

As popular as the RSV was, however, its wording of two important verses caused many conservative Christians to hold more firmly to their faithful KJVs. One of these was Isaiah 7:14, which in the KJV was the familiar "a virgin shall conceive, and bear a son." The RSV changed "virgin" to "young woman," for the Hebrew word *almah* used in Isaiah does mean young woman, not necessarily a virgin. Matthew's Gospel quotes Isaiah 7:14 as a prophecy of the virgin birth of Jesus. Matthew, in Greek, uses the word *parthenos,* meaning "virgin." Arguing against the meaning of *almah* is difficult, but many readers felt that the RSV's rendering of Isaiah 7:14 was a deliberate slap at a key article of belief—Jesus being born of a virgin. The RSV revisers may have been right in making the change but wrong in not anticipating the effect that changing "virgin" to "young woman" would have on many readers. In a sense this was one of the greatest bloopers in the history of Bible translation because the change caused a huge percentage of American churchgoers to prefer the KJV—and in time, to give their allegiance to some new evangelical versions. It is interesting to speculate what might have happened if the RSV had left "virgin" in Isaiah 7:14 and inserted a footnote saying that the Hebrew word *almah* could also be translated "young woman." The RSV conceivably could have become *the* Bible of the twentieth century as the KJV had been in past centuries.

The other troublesome change in the RSV was at the familiar John 3:16. In the KJV, we have "God so loved the world that he gave his only begotten Son." RSV drops the word "begotten." This troubled many readers because the New Testament teaches that all Christians are God's sons and daughters—by adoption, to use the term that Paul uses. The KJV's "begotten" made it clear that Jesus is God's Son in a unique way, that His sonship is different from that of the adopted children. The tricky word in the Greek text is *monogene,* which literally refers to an only child. Jesus is *huion ton monogene,* literally, "the son, an only child."

That wording obviously doesn't work well in English. The KJV's "only begotten son" communicated that Christ was begotten, not adopted—although using *begotten* in reference to God is odd because God does not beget children in the same way that the promiscuous gods of Greek mythology were always begetting children by human women. In short, there really is no satisfactory way to translate *huion ton monogene* into English. *Only son* isn't quite right, and neither is *unique son,* which is found in some versions. And *only begotten son* is good but not perfect. But at any rate, conservative Christians took offense at *begotten* being dropped from one of the most familiar verses in all the Bible. The change, along with the change at Isaiah 7:14 and a handful of more minor changes, drove some conservative evangelicals into the "King James only" camp and, in the 1970s, led them to make their own translations.

Here's a historical tidbit worth remembering: William Tyndale, the first man to ever translate the New Testament from Greek into English, wrote "his only son."

The Jehovah Bible and the Yahweh Bible

Many Bible readers know that in the Hebrew Old Testament, the name of God is "YHWH" (that's right—no vowels), usually written as "Yahweh" or in the past as "Jehovah." But almost all English Bibles have chosen to translate the Hebrew "YHWH" as "the LORD" (note the small caps in "LORD"). One notable departure from this was the American Standard Version, issued in 1901 and intended as a revision of the King James Version. Because the ASV used "Jehovah" instead of "the LORD," some people referred to it as the Jehovah Bible.

There is also a Yahweh Bible—the Jerusalem Bible, first published in the 1960s. The translators chose not to use "the LORD" but to use the Hebrew name itself, "Yahweh." Not all readers have been pleased with this, though in a sense the Yahweh Bible is true to its Hebrew roots. The fact is that after several centuries of English-speaking people referring to God as either God or the Lord, the chances are slim that people will think of God as Yahweh.

Fact is, "Yahweh" is almost impossible to translate. In Exodus 3, Yahweh appears to Moses in the burning bush, and Moses asks his name. God replies, "I Am Who I Am"—which is roughly equivalent to saying "I won't tell you my name." In ancient time the Jews had such reverence for the divine name of Yahweh that, when reading the Bible aloud, they would not say "Yahweh" but would substitute *Adonai,* the Hebrew word for "Lord." When the Old Testament was translated into Greek, the translation used the Greek word *Kurios*—"Lord." In other words, the name "Yahweh" didn't make it into the Greek version. The habit of using "Lord" as a substitute for "Yahweh" passed into English and most other languages. As already noted, "LORD" with the small caps is "Yahweh," while "Lord" without small caps is "Adonai."

Before the Jerusalem Bible used the name "Yahweh," a few Bible versions attempted to translate the name. The Scottish translator James Moffatt, for example, used "the Eternal," and other versions have used "the Everlasting" (both words mean the same thing, of course). Perhaps God is less concerned about language precision than we are.

The Bloodless Bible

One very popular modern version is the American Bible Society's Good News Bible, also called Today's English Version. Its New Testament was published in 1966, the full Bible in 1976. It is an entirely new translation, not a revision in the King James tradition. Like any version, it has its supporters and its foes. One criticism of its New Testament is that where the Greek text refers to the blood of Christ, the Good News Bible uses "sacrificial death" of Christ—not entirely wrong, but not quite right, either. Considering all the hymns, poems, and devotional writings that refer to the blood of Christ (not to mention, more recently, the film *The Passion of the Christ,* showing just what was involved in the shedding of Jesus' blood), changing "blood" to "sacrificial death" seems a bit...well, wimpish. After the New Testament was published, some of its critics referred to it sneeringly as the bloodless Bible.

In one particular verse the Good News Bible seems a bit timid. John 14:1 has Jesus saying, "Let not your hearts be troubled; ye believe in God, believe also in me." In the Good News rendering, He says "Do not be worried and upset." Critics have pointed out that "worried and upset" is pretty tame compared to having troubled hearts. We get worried and upset about forgetting to pay the phone bill, but troubled hearts are much more serious.

Latinizing to Impress

Not many people study Latin anymore, but in times past a knowledge of Latin was the sign of a truly educated person. Unfortunately, a few people who fancied themselves to be good in Latin chose to translate the Bible into English—using as many words of Latin origin as they could. For example, in London in 1754, an elderly fruit seller published his very odd version of the Bible. Consider this selection from Genesis 1: "AELOHIM, beginning, created lucide and illucide matter. And the illucide, void of co-adjunct cohesion, was unmodified, and distinguishableness was nowhere upon the face of Chaos. And the Ruach of AELOHIM emanated over the periphery of the fluctuation." The translator apparently was aware that *Elohim* (which he misspelled) was the Hebrew word for God and that *Ruach* was the word usually translated Spirit. Needless to say, this ultra-snobbish (and unreadable) translation was not a bestseller.

Which James Are We Talking About?

The King James Version of the Bible was named for James I, king of England. In 1971 a firm headquartered in Byron Center, Michigan, published the King James II Version of the Bible. The title was intended to communicate that this was a modernized and improved version of the faithful KJV, but a few book buyers snickered at the title, since it seemed to refer to King James II, the grandson of James I.

Woodruff the Weird

In 1852, Hezekiah Woodruff of New York state published *An Exposition of the New Testament, or New Covenant of Our Sovereign Savior.* Calling it an exposition was odd because it had no notes. Woodruff retitled the books of the Bible with names like The Good News of Salvation According to Matthew, The Doings of the Commissioners (Acts), and The Letter of Paul (a Commissioner) to the Romans. He used *commissioner* instead of *apostle, the Anointed* instead of *Christ, Sovereign* instead of *Lord, pupils* instead of *disciples.* Here are some of his translation oddities: "Happy are they who hunger and thirst for correctness, for they shall be satisfied" (Matthew 5:6). "His pupils came to him and awoke him, and said to him, 'Sovereign, save us or we die'" (Matthew 8:25). "Whosoever shall divorce his wife, except on account of lustful conduct before marriage, not apparent till after marriage, exposes her to commit adultery" (Matthew 5:32). "Inimical and adulatory people wish for a token, but there shall be no token exhibited to them except the token of the prophet Jonah" (Matthew 12:39). No wonder people were happy to stick with the King James Version.

Check Your Calendars

In 1928, George LeFevre of Pennsylvania translated and printed the New Testament. In its notes he stated that Jesus was crucified on Wednesday because He was in the tomb exactly three days and three nights—overlooking the fact that this would have Jesus in the tomb for four nights. His notes also stated that the wine Jesus made at Cana was just grape juice.

Jonah in the Belly of the Barge?

The book of Jonah is a story that many people find (pardon the pun) hard to swallow. Could a man really be swallowed by a whale and survive? At least one man, a sailor on a whaling vessel, did so. However, some Bible translators have found the Jonah story so outlandish that they concluded that the Hebrew text didn't refer to a whale but to something else. An 1818 Bible by John Bellamy, published in London, has this on the title page: *The Holy Bible, newly and wildly translated from the Original Hebrew, with notes critical and explanatory and Ridiculous!* Bellamy claimed to be the only man to translate any part of the Bible from Hebrew since AD 128 (which wasn't even remotely true). Jonah 1:17 read, "Now Jehovah had prepared a great barge to remove Jonah, and Jonah was in the belly of the barge three days and three nights."

Toning Down the Psalms

Psalms is undoubtedly the most read and perhaps most loved book of the Bible. It is also the longest, and the 150 individual psalms run the gamut of religious emotion, including praise, gratitude, doubt, guilt, and fear. Some of them are also extremely vengeful, calling down God's wrath on evil men. These psalms of vengeance are known as the imprecatory psalms, and Christians have struggled with these because their vengeful tone doesn't harmonize with Jesus' words about loving and forgiving one's enemies. On occasion, translators and editors have attempted to soften the tone of these songs of vengeance. In 1795, Samuel Seabury, the first Episcopal bishop in the United States, published *Morning and Evening Prayer with the Psalter.* He softened the harsh imprecatory psalms by changing the imperative tense to the future tense. For example, Psalm 5:10 reads, "Destroy thou them, O God, let them fall by their own counsels, cast them out in the multitude of their transgressions." Here's Seabury's version: "Thou wilt destroy them, O God; they shall perish through their own imaginations; thou wilt cast them out in the multitude of their ungodliness."

Phonetic and Just Plain Odd

In 1848, attorney Jonathan Morgan of Portland, Maine, published his translation of the Greek New Testament. One of his oddities was phonetic spelling of words like synagog, thru, like, bro't, tung, and thot. He also got a little weird with his translation: "And he out-cast the spirits with his word" (Matthew 8:16). "The angel said unto them, Fear not, for behold, I gospelize unto you great joy" (Luke 2:10). "Why are you troubled, and why do dialogs arise in your hearts?" (Luke 24:38).

Andrew Comstock designed a "purfekt alfabet" for his phonetic New Testament, published in 1848 in "Filadelfia." The Longley brothers also published a "fonetik" New Testament in 1855 in "Sinsinati." An interesting concept with good intentions, but none of these caught on with the public.

Loaning out the Bible

In 1924, Dubois H. Loux, a Presbyterian minister in Michigan, published what he called "a Labor Determinative Version" of Matthew's Gospel. Loux believed that charging interest on loans was not Christian, so he edited some sayings of Jesus this way: "Give to him that asks you, and from him that would obtain a loan without interest, turn not you away" (Matthew 5:42). "Love your enemies to bring about utmost good, and create good, and lend without interest, despairing of no man" (Matthew 5:44).

Wet or Only Damp?

In 1850, Spencer Cone and W.H. Wyckoff published *The Commonly Received Version of the New Testament, with Several Hundred Emendations.* (*Emendations* means changes, by the way.) This was the King James Version with some updating, but the most noticeable change was that the New Testament word *baptize* was changed to *immerse*—which sounds like a blooper, but in fact is quite correct. In fact, several "immersion versions" were published in the 1800s, all of them by Christians who firmly believed that the only valid way to baptize was by immersion. Technically these versions are correct, although reading *immersion* instead of *baptism* is kind of jarring: "And he saith unto them, Ye shall drink indeed of my cup, and be immersed with the immersion that I am immersed with" (Matthew 20:23). "John did immerse in the wilderness, and preach the immersion of repentance for the remission of sins" (Mark 1:4).

Hanson's Edited New Testament

In 1885, John Wesley Hanson published his own edited version of the English Revised Version. It had several distinctives: for one thing, it was an "immersion version," meaning that it used the word *immerse* instead of *baptize.* For another, Hanson merged the four Gospels into one continuous narrative (he was neither the first nor last to do this). Hanson also arranged the New Testament books in what he thought was their chronological order. (The idea was resurrected a hundred years later. You can now choose from a few chronological Bibles, though not Hanson's version.)

Oh, and here's one more unique trait: Hanson was a universalist—that is, he believed everyone would eventually be saved—and he wrote notes for the New Testament reflecting his universalist beliefs.

What Happened to the Old?

An American minister saddled with the name Leicester Ambrose Sawyer was a Presbyterian who eventually called himself a Christian rationalist. In 1891 he published *The Bible, Analyzed, Translated, and Accompanied with Critical Studies.* In fact, it was only the New Testament, and was in chronological order— 1 Thessalonians was first, and it ended with the Gospels, Acts, and Revelation. He did not believe Jesus was divine and in time came to believe that the only genuine parts of the New Testament were five of Paul's letters.

Divide and Confuse

Some intelligent people have thought so highly of their own intellects that they tended to tear down faith rather than help it grow. One example was Reverend William Wallace Martin, who in 1930 published his *Epistles of the New Testament,* translated from Greek. In his version, Romans is divided into two letters, one by Paul and the other by Apollos. Hebrews is divided into three, one by Paul, one by Apollos, and one by Barnabas. Other epistles are also strangely divided. In 1928 he had published his translation of the Psalms, separated into 125 prayers, 122 collects, and 47 praises. In 1929 he published Job, separating it into two versions, the Judean and the Ephraimean.

Really Long Days

Are the days of Genesis 1 really 24-hour days, or are they

something else? Science has helped erode most people's belief that God made the world in six literal days. Ferrar Fenton, a wealthy Englishman, published a new Bible translation in 1903, trying to harmonize Genesis with the new science. Thus in Genesis 1 the days are called *periods*. Scholars mocked it, so in a later edition he used *age* instead of *period*. He was consistent, for the Ten Commandments say, "For in six ages the Ever-living made the heavens and the earth, but rested at the seventh age. Therefore the Ever-living blessed the seventh age and hallowed it." Note his translation of 2 Corinthians 5:2: "We groan in this, longing to be endowed with out little cottage from heaven." Fenton's preface claimed, "I am the only man who ever applied real mental and literary criticism to the Sacred Scriptures."

Break Out the Microscope

Not so long ago, brides sometimes carried Bibles at their weddings, so some printers produced attractively bound Bibles that were meant to be worn, not read. This is probably the explanation behind a tiny Bible printed in Baltimore in 1812, given as a wedding present to a Mr. and Mrs. Phinehas Eastman. This Bible was printed in a type size called diamond—so tiny as to be unreadable for most people.

Liberal and Very Weird

Over the centuries, including our own, people have attempted to publish easy-to-understand translations of the Bible. This is a noble goal, and certainly it was the goal of the great William Tyndale in the early 1500s. However, some translators have attempted to make the Bible more classy and elegant. One of the most laughable of these was done by Edward Harwood (1729–1795), a well-educated Scottish minister and also a respected Greek scholar. Regrettably, Harwood made a truly bad translation of the New Testament and included this on its title page: "A

Liberal Translation of the New Testament; being an attempt to translate the Sacred Writings with the same freedom, spirit, and elegance with which other English translations from the Greek classics have lately been executed."

Did he succeed? Judge from this rendition of the parable of the prodigal son: "A Gentleman of a splendid and opulent fortune had two sons. One day the younger approached his father and begged him in the most importunate and soothing terms to make a partition of his effects betwixt himself and his elder brother. The indulgent father, overcome by his blandishments, immediately divided all his fortunes betwixt them. A few days after, the young brother converted all the estates that had been thus assigned him into ready money..."

In this New Testament, Jesus' words "Blessed are the merciful, for they shall obtain mercy" (Matthew 5:7) become "Happy are those who are truly compassionate and charitable—that benevolence which they express towards their fellow creatures shall be abundantly recompensed to them." Instead of "Blessed are they which hunger and thirst for righteousness" (Matthew 5:6), Harwood has "Happy are those whose minds are inflamed with a sacred ardour to attain universal virtue—their enlarged and generous desires shall be satisfied." The Lord's Prayer begins, "O Thou great governor and parent of universal nature—who manifestest thy glory to the blessed inhabitants of heaven—may all thy rational creatures in all parts of thy boundless dominion be happy in the knowledge of thy existence and providence, and celebrate thy perfections in a manner most worthy thy nature and perfective of their own" (Matthew 6:9). Paul's famous "love chapter," 1 Corinthians 13, reads this way:

> Benevolence is unruffled, is benign. Benevolence cherishes no ambitious desires. Benevolence is not ostentatious, is not inflated with insolence. It preserves a consistent decorum, is not enslaved to sordid interest, is not transported with furious passion, indulges no

malevolent design. It conceives no delight from the perpetuation of wickedness, but is first to applaud truth and virtue. It throws a veil of candour over all things, is disposed to believe all things, views all things in the most favourable light, supports all things with serene composure. Benevolence shall continue to shine with undiminished lustre when all prophetic powers shall be no more, when the ability of speaking various languages shall be withdrawn, and when all supernatural endowments shall be annihilated.

The reviewers who called it ridiculous were quite correct. Yet Harwood insisted his version was for the "intelligent Christian" and people of "polite taste" and that the words he chose were the ones the Bible authors themselves would have chosen had they been living in 1768. Harwood was trying to mimic the style of popular English novelists like Samuel Richardson—and making a laughable book in the process. He actually saw himself as a kind of evangelist to intellectuals and aristocrats, but they found his translation amusing, not inspiring. No one would guess from Harwood's New Testament that the Gospels and epistles had been written by fishermen, tentmakers, and tax collectors, or that the Son of God was a carpenter. Harwood stated that William Tyndale's translation (much of it retained in the King James Version) was "bald and barbarous and vulgar"—yet Tyndale's is still clear and readable, while Harwood's is just plain silly. He seemed to think the more syllables a word had, and the more Latin-based and Greek-based words were included, the better.

Hieroglyphics for the Kiddies

One of the oddest Bibles ever printed was the Curious Hieroglyphic Bible. It was published in England in 1784 and was popular in both England and America. In this version, which used the King James text, some words are replaced with small illustrations, such as a picture of a door instead of the actual word *door*. Apparently some families thought the illustrations would help make children interested in the Scriptures.

A Bible with No Eternity

The eccentric American preacher Abner Kneeland started out as a conservative Christian but later became a universalist. He had a colorful life, even spending time in jail for the crime of blasphemy. He also published a New Testament with the Greek and English in parallel columns. As a universalist, Kneeland didn't believe in hell—in fact, his New Testament gives the impression he didn't believe in eternal life at all. In most English Bibles the Greek words *aion* and *aionion* are usually translated "eternity" and "eternal." In Kneeland's 1822 version, he chose to translate them as "age" and "for an age."

The Agitated Bible

In 1833, a South Carolina man with the unlikely name of Rodolphus Dickinson published his *Minute Revision and Professed Translation of the New Testament*. It was an attempt to do what dictionary maker Noah Webster was doing at the same time: to update, improve, and Americanize the popular King James Version. Webster's problem was that he made such minor changes in the KJV that people didn't see any real need to pay money for his version. Considering that Webster knew both Greek and Hebrew (and several other languages as well), it is disappointing that he did not draw on his knowledge to make a really thorough revision of the KJV.

Dickinson's version made more radical changes—but alas, not good ones. In Luke 1, when the pregnant Mary meets with her pregnant relative Elizabeth, we learn that "the embryo was joyfully agitated," and Elizabeth says, "Blessed is your incipient offspring." Later, Mary exclaims that God has "precipitated potentates from their thrones" and has "satisfied the necessitous with benefits, but the affluent he has dismissed destitute." Ephesians 1:3-14 is rendered in 54 words in the KJV, but Dickinson's version uses 268 words. Dickinson even changed some of the books' titles—for example, he retitled Acts as Apostolic Transactions. His was another failed attempt to make the straightforward New Testament text sound highbrow.

Corrected by the Spirits

Spiritualism—the practice of trying to communicate with the dead—was popular in America in the late 1800s. In 1861, Leonard Thorn published *The New Testament, as Revised and Corrected by the Spirits.* According to Thorn, Jesus and His apostles came in spirit and revised and corrected the New Testament. The spirits apparently liked to shorten things, for this revised edition has only seven chapters in Romans and only three in Revelation, and it is entirely missing Hebrews. Thorn also added an appendix for his fellow spiritualists.

One Spirit or Several?

Several versions of the Bible have been published by and for spiritualists (people who attempt to communicate with the dead—even though the Bible itself forbids doing so in Deuteronomy 18:10-11). In 1937, Johannes Greber, a former Catholic priest who became a spiritualist, published his New Testament with several "corrections" given by spirits. Consider his translation of John 4:24: "God is a spirit, and those who worship Him must therefore be under the guidance of a spirit of God and of

the divine truth when they come to do Him homage." (Here's
the wording of John 4:24 in the King James Version: "God is a
Spirit, and they that worship him must worship him in spirit and
in truth.")

Vegetarian Christians

Among the more curious versions of the Bible ever published
was the one by American vegetarian advocate Olive Pell. Her
version of the Bible, published in 1852, "cleaned up" the King
James Version, not only by taking out all the sex and violence (a
major deletion) but also by removing all references to eating meat.
Miss Pell believed that true believers would (like herself) frown
on anything but pure vegetarianism.

The No-Testament Bible

The Jehovah's Witnesses published their own New World
Translation of the Bible. Curiously, this version has no Old Tes-
tament or New Testament. Rather, the Bible is divided into the
"Hebrew-Aramaic Scriptures" (that is, the Old Testament) and the
"Christian Greek Scriptures" (the New, of course).

A few other tidbits about the New World Translation: The
word *church* (it's *ekklesia* in the Greek) is not used, but instead,
congregation. As might be expected from a group that calls itself
Jehovah's Witnesses, the name of God ("Yahweh," which is translated "the LORD" in most English versions) is "Jehovah." Likewise
in the New Testament, when "Lord" (Greek *kyrios*) refers to God,
the New World Translation uses "Jehovah" instead of "Lord."
The cross is a "torture stake" (Matthew 10:38, 27:32) on which
Jesus was "impaled" instead of crucified (Luke 23:21). A footnote
beneath the text explains that, yes, Jesus was nailed to a piece of
wood, but it was an upright pole, not a cross.

Pop Culture
Gone Astray

If you want an education in the Bible, you're not likely to get it from popular culture. Names and incidents from the Bible are embedded in our minds, but people don't necessarily know much about the biblical people referred to in movies and songs. Some of these pop-culture Bible bloopers are laughable; some are insulting to the Bible and religion.

Arc, Ark, What's the Difference?

In 2005, *Harper's* magazine ran an article on Christianity. The article revealed that 12 percent of Americans polled believed that Joan of Arc was the wife of...Noah! Since Joan lived in the 1400s, this is a case not only of biblical illiteracy but also of historical illiteracy.

Dan Brown and the Bible

You have undoubtedly heard of *The Da Vinci Code*, the best-selling novel by Dan Brown. The book is a murder mystery set in the present, but the main characters are "history detectives" who know a lot about Jesus and Mary Magdalene—or to be more accurate, know a lot about a fable about them. In Brown's novel, Mary Magdalene is not just a devoted follower of Jesus but His wife, and she bore Him a daughter named Sarah. Jesus never knew of Sarah because He was crucified (but not resurrected) before the birth. Mary left Palestine and fled to France, where she gave birth to Sarah, who became the ancestor of the Merovingian family of French kings. In other words, the kings of France were descended from none other than Jesus Himself, the Son of God.

Brown's novel is fiction, of course, but because some folks have so little knowledge of or respect for the Bible, many readers have mistakenly assumed that Brown was drawing on actual history. Their minds were already prepared to accept such fiction because plays and movies like *Jesus Christ Superstar* and *The Last Temptation of Christ* depict Mary as being in love with Jesus, and in the case of *Last Temptation,* married to Him. These and other works of fiction about Jesus get attention because they feed people's taste for conspiracy theories—that is, people like to believe that Christians long ago decided to cover up the real truth about Jesus. They may have heard some so-called expert state that Jesus must have been married because *every* Jewish man in Jesus' time married. That isn't the case, of course. Celibacy was rare among Jewish men at that time, but there were some cases, including John the Baptist and Paul the apostle. Brown's book (also made into a movie) has not only sold hugely but also spawned an onslaught of books—some written by Christians, some not—pointing out its errors.

In *The Da Vinci Code,* the sleuths claim to draw on the Gospel of Philip for the material about Jesus and Mary Magdalene being married and producing a child. The Gospel of Philip is one of many false Gospels written in ancient times, usually in the name of one of Jesus' apostles to add credibility. In *The Da Vinci Code,* we are told that the Gospel of Philip was among the very old manuscripts called the Dead Sea Scrolls, but this is nonsense because no Gospels or other Christian writings were among the Dead Sea

Scrolls. The novel states that Jesus' marriage to Mary Magdalene was reported in many of the Gospels that did not become part of the New Testament, but that isn't so. No Gospel, whether in the New Testament or not, reports such a marriage. The Gospel of Philip is a weird hodgepodge of parables and sayings of Jesus with very little data about Jesus' life story. It does say that Mary Magdalene was a companion of Jesus, but *The Da Vinci Code* claims this really meant she was His wife. The novel also errs in saying the Gospel of Philip was written in Aramaic because it was actually written in Coptic, the ancient language of Egypt. It also errs in claiming that the Gospel of Philip states that Jesus and Mary Magdalene used to kiss each other frequently on the mouth, which is a misreading of that Gospel. The actual manuscript of the Gospel is in poor condition with some gaps in it, and Dan Brown chose to fill in some of the gaps.

Mary Magdalene is, of course, a very minor character in the New Testament. Her main claim to fame is that she is the first person to see the risen Jesus (Mark 16:9; John 20:1). Other than that, and the fact that the Gospels say that Jesus had driven seven demons out of her (Luke 8:2), we know little else, although tradition depicts her as a reformed prostitute (see page 108 for more about that misconception).

The Sheba Story Greatly Revised

The story of Solomon and the queen of Sheba has been a gold mine for movie producers, not so much because of the actual story in the Bible (which is extremely brief) but because of the old legend that Solomon and the queen actually conceived a child. In fact, the ruling family of Ethiopia long believed that its kings were the descendants of Solomon and the queen.

One of the early attempts to film the legend was the 1921 movie *The Queen of Sheba*. After the queen's visit to Solomon, she bears his child, and when the child reaches age four, she sends him to visit his father. Solomon's brother Adonijah fears that Solomon will make the boy his heir, so he plans a revolt against Solomon, a revolt that is crushed thanks to the aid of the queen. The film wanders a long, long way from 1 Kings 10:1-13.

The Misunderstood Adulterer

An amazing thing happened in 1951. The most profitable movie of the year was a biblical one: *David and Bathsheba.* Whether people went to see the film because it was based on the Bible or because it starred two of the most attractive actors in Hollywood is debatable. The movie presented the world's most famous story of adultery but put enough spin on it that we sympathize with David and Bathsheba instead of condemning them. David's shrewish wife Michal constantly nags him, and Bathsheba's husband (Uriah the Hittite) is a soldier who lusts for battle more than for his wife. In seven months of her marriage—an *arranged* marriage—she has seen her husband only six days. The Bible makes no excuses for David's behavior, but the film certainly does. The Bible says that David sent Uriah into the thickest of the fighting knowing he would be killed (2 Samuel 11:14-17), but in the film Uriah himself asks to be sent there. After David and Bathsheba marry, famine strikes the land, apparently as God's judgment on the adulterers. This part of the story is entirely fictional. So is the threatened rebellion against David's authority. Obviously the film took great liberties with the Bible's story of David. It did, however, stick to the Bible in one specific area: The ark of the covenant in the film was made to the exact specifications found in the Bible.

Salome the Sweet

For a character who is not even named in the Bible, Salome

has been the subject of numerous films, plays, and novels as well as a notable opera. In the New Testament she is called simply "the daughter of Herodias" (Matthew 14:6), though we know from historians that her name was Salome. (A *good* Salome is mentioned in the Gospels, so perhaps the Gospel authors chose not to mention the name of the bad Salome.) The Gospels relate that at a birthday party for Herod, her stepfather, Salome danced so wonderfully that Herod offered her whatever she desired. Prompted by her mother, she asked for the head of John the Baptist on a platter (Matthew 14:6-8). John had boldly denounced the marriage of Herod to his own sister-in-law, and Herod had him in prison (Mark 6:17-18). The dirty deed was done as Salome asked (Matthew 14:10-11). That is all the information the Bible gives us.

The 1953 film *Salome* featured screen siren Rita Hayworth in the title role. She is radically different from the Salome of the Bible. Her famous "Dance of the Seven Veils" is an attempt to *save* John the Baptist, and she is horrified when he is executed by her mother's order. At the end of the movie, she and her true love, a Roman soldier, are shown listening attentively to Jesus' preaching. Her change of heart isn't totally impossible, but it is extremely unlikely. The movie gets other biblical details wrong: It names Jerusalem, not Caesarea, as the residence of the Roman governor, and it shows Pontius Pilate being sent to Judea years after he was already installed. This cavalier attitude toward history was typical of films of this period.

Moses the Eloquent

The 1956 Cecil B. DeMille epic *The Ten Commandments* is one of the great biblical movies—great, but not perfect. On the whole the script stuck pretty close to the Moses saga in Exodus, and DeMille was fanatical about getting details of costuming and architecture right. The movie added some unnecessary romantic subplots, but most notably it presents Moses as being extremely charismatic and a superb speaker—even though Exodus 4:10-16 clearly shows that Moses is slow of speech and requires his brother Aaron as a spokesman.

The Exotic Sheba yet Again

The 1959 movie *Solomon and Sheba* was yet another attempt to film—and seriously distort—the Bible's brief story of the queen of Sheba paying a visit to the wise and wealthy Solomon. The studio paired two very attractive stars (Yul Brynner and Gina Lollobrigida), and as in other films about Solomon and the queen, the two have a romantic fling. In the Bible, the queen pays Solomon a visit because she has heard of his amazing wisdom, but in the film she intends to destroy him politically. She eventually converts to the religion of Israel, something the Bible would have mentioned had it actually occurred. The political rivalry of the brothers Solomon and Adonijah is reported in the Bible, but the film's version of the story is radically different from what is found in 1 Kings.

The Semibiblical Esther

Joan Collins as the virtuous Jewish girl Esther in the Bible? That may sound like a blooper in casting, but in fact the young Joan did well in the role in the 1960 movie *Esther and the King*. However, the film played fast and loose with the story in the Bible. In the Bible, the king of Persia orders his wife, Vashti, to appear at a banquet and "display her beauty" to his cohorts. She refuses, which leads the king to search for a new wife (which eventually will be Esther). In the film version, Vashti is incredibly promiscuous, and she crashes the king's banquet and performs a lewd dance, leading the king to cast her aside. The king speaks of having to deal with the "upstart Alexander of Macedon," meaning

Alexander the Great, but Persia's feud with Alexander happens decades after the time of the book of Esther. The Bible says that Esther and Mordecai are cousins, but in the film they are niece and uncle.

"Freely" Indeed!

The 1960 film *David and Goliath* opens with a disclaimer: "Freely adapted from the Bible." Yes, *very* freely. The movie was one of many cheaply and poorly made historical epics cranked out of Italy in the 1950s and '60s. The film refers to the Persian empire even though that empire did not even exist in the time of David. Saul, king of Israel, is portrayed as a tyrant, which is not true of the Saul in the Bible. Saul is shown standing on the steps of the temple in Jerusalem even though Israel had no temple at that time and Saul's court was not in Jerusalem. The soldier Abner tries to kill David with a spear, but Saul kills Abner with an arrow first—a totally fictional incident. Actually the most unbiblical aspect of the movie is that Saul, described as very handsome in the Bible, is played by a very fat and prematurely aged Orson Welles, who could hardly qualify as handsome. The film could not even correctly spell the name of Saul's daughter Michal— "Michael" is listed in the film credits. Ironically, for all its biblical bloopers, the movie was one of the few biblical movies actually shot in Israel.

Spaghetti Epics

Dozens of cheaply made sword-and-sandal movies were filmed in Italy in the 1960s. Some were biblical, and some only used the name of some biblical person in order to draw the audience. Some of these featured a character named Samson who generally had nothing in common with the Samson of the Bible except his strength.

The Teenage Jesus

The 1961 film *King of Kings* was mocked by some critics who called it *I Was a Teenage Jesus,* perhaps thinking that actor Jeffrey Hunter was too young for the role. In fact, Hunter was 30 at the time, which agrees with what the Bible says about the age of Jesus (Luke 3:23). Overall the script stuck pretty close to the Gospels, but it threw in some fictional elements, such as Jesus going to visit John the Baptist in prison. And interestingly, Jesus' trial before the Jewish council is not shown, probably because the producers didn't wish to be accused of anti-Semitism. This omission is unfortunate because an important part of the Gospels' message is that Jesus was condemned by the religious leaders of His own people.

Sodom Without the Sodomy

A few movies have been made about the wicked cities of Sodom and Gomorrah, but in the past it wasn't even possible to show (or even hint at) the most famous sin of Sodom, homosexuality. The ridiculous 1962 film *Sodom and Gomorrah* made it appear that the real sins of the two cities were slavery and greed. There are hints of sexual vice in general but not about homosexuality in particular. Genesis 14:2 refers to Bera, the king of Sodom, but in the movie Bera is a queen. Lot, the nephew of Abraham, is put in prison in Sodom but released by two angels, who inform him that wicked Sodom is about to be destroyed. The biblical incident of the men of Sodom surrounding Lot's house and demanding that the two angels be brought out for sexual pleasure is not shown, of course. And instead of Sodom being destroyed by "fire and brimstone," as in Genesis, it suffers a terrible earthquake, with fire coming up from beneath the ground. At least the movie does end on a biblical note: Lot's wife looks back on the destroyed Sodom and is turned into a pillar of salt (Genesis 19:26).

Satan, the Perfect Villain

The 1965 film *The Greatest Story Ever Told* might qualify as the most biblical movie ever made because the script is saturated with words taken straight from the Gospels. In fact, it opens with the appropriate words from John 1:1: "In the beginning was the Word, and the Word was with God, and the Word was God." Strangely, though, this very long movie (more than three hours) omits important things, such as the dove and the voice from heaven at Jesus' baptism. While teaching in Jerusalem, Jesus tells the crowd that the three greatest things are faith, hope, and love—words Paul wrote in 1 Corinthians 13. Technically this is a blooper, although we can certainly imagine Jesus agreeing with Paul's sentiments.

The most irritating thing about the film is that it does exactly what *King of Kings* did in 1961: It refuses to blame the religious leaders for Jesus' death. In this film, the leaders don't shout for Jesus to be crucified; Satan does (in human guise). The film places the blame on Pilate and Satan, not the Jews.

Perhaps the worst blooper of all is one that was true of all movies about Jesus: He does not seem to be in much pain on the cross. In 2004, *The Passion of the Christ* would communicate just how horrible crucifixion was. Watching all earlier movies about Jesus, we get the impression He was in no more pain than if His shoes were too tight.

The Almost-Perfect Miniseries

The 1977 TV miniseries *Jesus of Nazareth* was a real crowd-pleaser, and it solved the old problem of how to tell the story of Jesus and do justice to it. The answer: Instead of making one feature-length movie, broadcast two parts on different nights. Despite all the good things about this TV epic, it had a few bloopers. For example, there is no temptation scene after Jesus' baptism, even though Christians have always considered this a crucial part of the gospel message. Also, the film distorts one Bible passage that makes Jesus' mother, Mary, look bad: In the Gospels, Jesus' mother and brothers seek Him out, leading Jesus to point out that whoever are His followers are His true family. In the movie, a man goes to visit Mary and kisses the hem of her robe, saying, "You are His mother." Mary says, "Anyone who obeys our Father in heaven is His brother, His sister, His mother." (The director, Franco Zeffirelli, was letting his Catholic bias show.)

Sugarcoating Adultery Again

King David, released in 1985, was a colossal failure, even though David was played by handsome star Richard Gere. For people familiar with the Bible, one of the oddities of the film is that it tries to play down David's role as a mighty warrior. On a more detailed level, it has some minor bloopers, such as David not killing Goliath until after two stones were already fired even though the Bible says the first stone felled the giant (1 Samuel 17:49). The film shows Michal, daughter of Saul, disliking David from the day they marry, yet the Bible makes it clear that Michal was at first deeply in love with David (1 Samuel 18:20). And, as in the 1951 movie *David and Bathsheba,* the story of David's adultery is distorted: In this film, Bathsheba laments that after five years of marriage, Uriah has had no relations with her. Again, this is an attempt to condone an adultery that the Bible very heartily condemns.

The movie's ties to the Bible get even looser toward the end. The aged David, confined to bed, designates Solomon his heir. He reminds Solomon that God speaks to man through the heart, not through the prophets. His last words are, "I am waiting, Lord, hide your face no more." These are a far cry from the last words recorded in 2 Samuel 23, which state that a reverent king is like the sun shining, and that God will bless all his descendants because of His eternal covenant with David. First Kings 2 records David's last instructions to Solomon, which include telling him to obey all the Lord's commands written in the Law of Moses. But the movie depicted David as never having been happy with the Law of Moses, seeing it as strict and merciless.

Perfectly Biblical But...

The Gospel of John, released late in 2003, can surely claim to be the most biblical movie ever made. Every word from the Gospel is either spoken or acted out in the film. However, one error of judgment appears at the very beginning:

> The Gospel of John was written two generations after the crucifixion of Jesus Christ. It is set in a time when the Roman empire controlled Jerusalem. Although crucifixion was the preferred Roman method of punishment, it was not one sanctioned by Jewish law. Jesus and all His early followers were Jewish. The Gospel reflects a period of unprecedented polemic and antagonism between the emerging church and the religious establishment of the Jewish people. This film is a faithful presentation of that Gospel.

It appears the producers wished to defuse any accusations of a Jesus film being anti-Semitic. However, the claim that John's Gospel was written "two generations" after Jesus is open to debate, and most scholars now believe it was probably written within 30 years of the events it describes.

Deep, Deep Controversy

At the beginning of *The Last Temptation of Christ,* released in 1988, the audience is told that this movie is a "fictional exploration" and is not based on the Gospels. Well, fair enough. But the main characters and the plot are all taken from the Gospels, so we can't help comparing it to the Bible. And where the Bible is concerned, *Last Temptation* is almost "all blooper." For example, in the film the woman caught in adultery is Mary Magdalene (which is wrong), and after the people walk away and leave her unstoned, Jesus does not say "Go and sin no more" (which is also wrong). Jesus bites into an apple and tosses a seed on the ground, and a tree in full fruit appears—exactly the kind of showy, pointless miracle that Jesus did *not* do. But perhaps the most offensive (and incorrect) aspect of the movie is that the apostle Paul is such a murderous fanatic that he kills the risen Lazarus—and later in the movie tells Jesus that the new religion of Christianity has no need for Jesus at all.

Miscasting Satan

The 2004 movie *The Passion of the Christ* was hugely popular, but people found much to nitpick. It was criticized for being too violent—as if a real crucifixion was something like a slap on the wrist. It was also criticized for having a woman play the role of Satan—although Satan in the film actually appears androgynous (which most people thought added to the otherworldly, creepy quality). Some people also complained about the dapper, "hip" Satan in the 2001 TV movie *Jesus*. The truth is, the Bible doesn't tell us what Satan looked like.

One blooper in *The Passion* is that the woman about to be stoned for adultery is Mary Magdalene—which almost certainly was not the case. This is an error it shared with a much more controversial film, *The Last Temptation of Christ*.

Perhaps the most notable blooper in *Passion* is the depiction of Pilate as a decent, compassionate man, practically forced to crucify Jesus. What we know of Pilate from the Bible—and from historians—is that he was anything but compassionate and he certainly despised the Jews that he ruled over. If he showed compassion—or at least fairness—toward Jesus, it was probably more out of spite for the Jewish leaders than for any warm feeling toward Jesus. In the movie, though, Pilate's decency is more than outweighed by the brutality of the other Romans, the brutal soldiers that flog and then crucify Jesus, delighting in what they do.

Many Protestants criticized the film for being too Catholic, meaning it made Jesus' mother, Mary, too important a character. John's Gospel only says that Mary was present at the crucifixion, and we can safely assume she was as distraught as she appears in the movie. One doesn't have to be a Catholic to be touched by maternal love.

Moses Without a Childhood

Director Cecil B. DeMille is remembered for his lavish 1956 epic *The Ten Commandments,* but in fact that classic film was a remake of his film with the same title released in 1923. The old version was, of course, silent and black-and-white. It is actually a fine film in many ways, but for some odd reason it totally omits the story of Moses being hidden away by his mother and being reared in the Egyptian court. The film also introduces his brother Aaron to the pharaoh as "priest of Israel," which is an error because Aaron wasn't made the high priest of Israel until after the Israelites had left Egypt. Later in the film, Moses' sister Miriam leads the rebellious Israelites in worshipping the golden calf idol even though the Bible makes no mention of her in this incident.

DeMille's Rich and Famous Magdalene

One of the most successful biblical films every made was Cecil B. DeMille's 1927 *The King of Kings,* telling the story of Christ.

It has the distinction of being one of the few Hollywood movies that missionaries have used to tell the Gospel story. (Being a silent film, it lent itself to having the title cards done in foreign languages.) The film's script was by DeMille's assistant (also his mistress) Jeanie Macpherson, who took the story and the title cards straight from the Bible. However, she chose to open the film with a totally fiction scene: Mary Magdalene is a high-class courtesan, living lavishly but angry that one of her male admirers, Judas, is neglecting her to follow after some wandering teacher from Nazareth. Mary goes to meet this Jesus, riding in a chariot drawn by zebras. None of this folderol is in the Bible, of course, but it certainly does grab the audience's attention.

Later in the movie, Jesus casts out seven demons from Mary, a biblical incident that films have rarely shown. The story of Jesus' temptation is out of sequence, occurring at the point in the story that the crowd tries to make Jesus their king (John 6:15). However, the temptation does make sense at this point in the story because Jesus is being tempted to be the political Messiah the Jews had hoped for.

When Jesus is on the cross, the curtain in the temple is torn in two. Seeing this, the evil high priest Caiaphas falls to his knees and prays, "Lord God Jehovah, visit not thy wrath on thy people Israel—I alone am guilty!" This prayer is not in the Bible, and from what we know of Caiaphas, he was not likely to have felt guilt over Jesus' death. But by including this fictional scene, DeMille was trying to defuse critics who would accuse him of blaming Jesus' death on all the Jews.

Noah and the Flood (and Some Added Drama)

In 1929 Warner Brothers released its biblical epic *Noah's Ark*, based on the Genesis story—and with some major nonbiblical additions. The scriptwriters apparently felt that because the world was very wicked in Noah's time, the film needed to show just how wicked it was. In the film, Noah's son Japheth is blinded by the pagans and chained to a mill, and his future wife Miriam is about to be sacrificed by the wicked pagans. (The scriptwriter must have borrowed the blinding and chaining from the story of Samson in Judges.) Then a great wind blows the temple doors open and announces Noah. A ring of fire protects the ark against pagan troops. When Noah hears God's warning about the flood, he encounters God in a burning bush and sees the words in a flaming book on a mountainside. (Here the writer was apparently borrowing from the Moses saga.)

The Fish Fry Heaven

The 1936 movie *The Green Pastures* had the distinction of being the only biblical film made in the United States in the 1930s. Saying it was based on the Bible is a bit of a stretch; it was actually based on a stage play of the same name, which in turn was based on Roark Bradford's stories *Ol' Man Adam and His Chillun*. Bradford had written down the Bible stories as related by black workers on his father's farm. The stories take some great liberties with the Old Testament, showing God as a bearded man in a frock coat, heralded by the angel Gabriel, who announces, "Gangway for the Lord God Jehovah." Heaven is presented as an eternal fish fry, pleasant people spending a relaxing day together. The stories of Adam, Noah, and Moses are acted out, with some comic additions. The last story in the film concerns a character name Hezdrel who is not in the Bible at all.

Samson and the Guilty Delilah

Released late in 1949, Cecil B. DeMille's film *Samson and Delilah* was followed by a successful series of lavish biblical epics in the 1950s. DeMille based the film on the Samson story in Judges but added material from a novel titled *Judge and Fool.* In that book and in the film, Delilah is the younger sister of Samson's Philistine bride. In Judges, Samson rejects this younger sister (who is not named). Spurned by Samson, the Delilah of the film has a reason for wanting to destroy Samson. She is the hate-filled cast-off woman. However, toward the end of the film she repents of her wickedness and goes to visit the blinded Samson in prison.

Steve Reeves and the Spaghetti Epics

If you're a fan of really bad movies, you probably know the name Steve Reeves, the Mr. Universe featured in some cheaply made movies of the 1950s and '60s. Since the target audience for these sword-and-sandal films was the under-18 crowd, the producers could take great liberties with the stories they pilfered from the Bible, ancient mythology, and folklore. Reeves got his start playing the Greek mythological muscleman Hercules, but he also played another strongman named Goliath, though this character had no resemblance at all to the Philistine giant of the Bible. Apparently the producers figured that kids had a general idea that Goliath was a big strong guy they had heard of somewhere.

Another biblical name that was tacked on to some pretty tacky movies was Samson. Several movies have been made about this Old Testament strong man, but the movies we're talking about here were some cheaply made Italian and Mexican films of the early 1960s—camp classics like *Samson Versus the Vampire Women, Samson in the Wax Museum,* and *Samson and the Seven Miracles of the World.* Some of the films threw Samson together with Hercules and other mythological figures. In the 1964 *Hercules, Samson, and Ulysses,* the two wandering Greek heroes aid Samson in fighting the Philistines in Israel—hardly the Samson story told in Judges. A very nonbiblical Samson also was featured in the 1968 rubbish *Samson and the Lost Treasure of the Aztecs.* The producers of these spaghetti epics must have figured Samson was a good name for any muscle man of an earlier time. Pity the poor teachers and preachers who had to undo the mental damage done by these silly films!

When noted producer and director Cecil B. DeMille was casting his 1949 film *Samson and Delilah* (based on the Bible, incidentally), his first choice for Samson was the amazingly muscled Steve Reeves, who definitely had a more Samsonish body than the man who got the role, Victor Mature. So Reeves the unbiblical Samson of some cheapie movies was almost the biblical Samson in a Hollywood epic.

Carrie's Weirdo Mom

Stephen King's horror novel *Carrie* tells the story of a shy and persecuted teenage girl who endures not only the snubs and insults of her catty classmates but also the constant scolding of her religious mother. In the book and in the popular 1976 movie based on it, Carrie's mom is shown several times reading and quoting from a book that appears to be the Bible. It isn't. Her rantings about "Eve was weak" and "the raven was sin" and other loony statements are nowhere in the Bible. King hasn't shown himself too friendly to Christianity, so he engaged in some religion bashing by having the wacky mother spouting ridiculous misquotes.

Quoting Ezekiel (Not!)

In the holdup scene at the end of the very violent film *Pulp Fiction,* one of the characters quotes a long verse from the book of Ezekiel, citing it as 25:17. Readers have looked in vain for the quote in Ezekiel, but it simply isn't there or anywhere else in the Bible. The quote was pure fiction, fabricated by the scriptwriters.

Becoming an Angel

The idea that people become angels after they die is in no way rooted in the Bible, but the idea is pretty entrenched in pop culture. In the 1960s, the Smothers Brothers starred in a short-lived situation comedy in which Tommy Smothers played a deceased man who walked the earth as an angel (no wings) and often spoke to his heavenly supervisor named Ralph. Amusing, but not biblical.

However, to be fair, one passage in the Bible does give a hint that a person who died might have an angel stand-in who looks just like him. We see this in Acts 12, where the apostle Peter is miraculously released from prison. He goes to his friends, who have assumed he was executed. He knocks on the door, and when the servant girl Rhoda hears his voice, she reports to Peter's friends that he is alive, and their reply is "It is his angel!"

Even so, the Bible quotes many people who said things that weren't true.

Don't Trust Those Museum Guides

In his fine book *The Bible in English,* British scholar David Daniell tells of a visit to New York City's Metropolitan Musem of Art. A group of teenagers was being given a tour by a museum guide, and the group paused to gaze at a painting by the Italian Renaissance master Raphael. The apostle Paul was one of the figures in the painting, and the guide explained that Paul was holding a sword "because he had been a soldier." This isn't even remotely true.

Paul is often shown in artwork holding a sword because in one of his epistles he described the "whole armor of God" that a

Christian wears in the world. This armor includes "the sword of the Spirit, which is the Word of God" (Ephesians 6:17). In many artworks, the sword is even inscribed with the Latin words *Spiritus Gladius*—"sword of the Spirit." The poor teens on this particular tour not only didn't learn this important bit of information about the great apostle but also were given the misinformation that he was a soldier.

Blast Those Printers!

Psalm 119:161 reads, "Princes have persecuted me without cause." Sometime in the 1600s a printer who was not doing his job properly produced a Bible that had the verse as "Printers have persecuted me without cause." Chalk it up to human error: No Bible ever rolled off the printing press totally free from printing mistakes. This chapter contains some amusing examples of persecution by printers.

The Murderers' Bible

Printers' errors can make for amusing Bibles. Consider an edition of the Bible published in England in 1795. Mark 7:27 should read "Let the children first be filled," but this misprinted version read, "Let the children first be killed." This misprinted Bible (which is eagerly sought by book collectors) has been referred to as the Murderers' Bible.

Gender Confusion

The first printing of the King James Version in 1611 had a bit of gender confusion in Ruth 3:15. Some of the Bibles printed had

"She went into the city," while others had "He went into the city." Thus book collectors talk about the "He Bibles" and "She Bibles."

The Wicked Bible

Possibly the most famous printing error ever was the omission of the word "not" from the commandment "Thou shalt not commit adultery" (Exodus 20:14). This occurred in a 1631 printing done by the King's Printer, Robert Barker. The pressmen at the firm were fined 300 English pounds, and even worse, the whole print run had to be recalled and destroyed, a severe financial drain on poor Barker. Since most of the Bibles were destroyed, only a handful still exist, prized by rare book collectors and known as the Wicked Bible or the Adulterers' Bible.

No Success with Women

One of the earliest Bibles printed in America was the work of a Quaker, Isaac Collins. He printed the King James Version in 1791, and naturally he omitted the KJV's dedication to the king of England. The Bible had one curious error: Isaiah 53:3 should read, "He is despised and rejected of men; a man of sorrows, and acquainted with grief." The Collins printing had "rejected of women."

Proofreader Desperately Needed

From 1676 to 1711, a Mrs. Anderson had the exclusive right to print Bibles for Scotland. One of her many critics said that "nothing came from her press but the most illegible and incorrect Bibles and books that ever were printed in any one place in the world." An example from a 1705 Bible: "Whyshoulditbethough tathingincredible wt you, yt God should raise the dead?" (Acts 26:8). Despite her firm's ineptitude, she had several people fined for violating her exclusive right.

What, No Spell-Checker?

Unlike modern publishers, the earliest printers didn't care much about correct spelling. The first printed Bibles were full of "bloopers"—at least by our standard that a word always ought to be spelled the same way. On one page of William Tyndale's 1525 New Testament, he has the word *righteousness* spelled five different ways. Tyndale's rendering of *Jerusalem* was sometimes *Ierusalem*, sometimes *Hierusalem*. In Acts, he referred to Stephen and also Steven. No one much cared as long they knew what word he was aiming for. People weren't even that fussy about their own names. William Shakespeare apparently spelled his own last name in different ways, as indicated by a handful of signatures.

A Really Old, Old Bible

One of the most unattractive Bibles ever printed was done in Lunenberg, Massachusetts, in 1825. Not only were the printing and binding really sloppy, but the date of publication was wrong: the title page shows the date as 825.

Deserving a Break

The Lord's Prayer taught by Jesus contains the familiar plea "Give us this day our daily bread." A large family Bible printed in Philadelphia in 1875 had "Give us this day our daily break."

Seeing Ears

A Methodist evangelist named Hiram Kisrow was intrigued with the Hebrew language. In 1852, he had a printer produce several hundred copies of his *Bible Corrected According to the True Hebrew Text*. This was simply the King James Version, the main difference being that where the KJV has "the LORD," Kisrow changed it to the Hebrew name *Yahweh*. However, Kisrow and the printer overlooked this minor error in the New Testament: "Ear hath not seen, nor eye heard, neither have entered into the heart of man, the things which God hath prepared for them that love him" (1 Corinthians 2:9). Apparently someone's ears didn't see well enough to give the Bible a decent proofreading.

Nauseated God

Maybe you've heard this joke: The dyslexic agnostic asked, "Does dog really exist?" Maybe that same dyslexic was responsible for a Bible that was printed in Chicago in the 1880s with this rendering of Proverbs 26:11: "As a god returneth to his vomit, so a fool returneth to his folly." That should be *dog*, not *god*.

Pan Pals

Ever tried writing with a pan? Or a pin? A Bible printed in Boston in 1892 had some sort of pen shortage, as seen in these verses: "The sin of Judah is written with a pan of iron, and with the point of a diamond" (Jeremiah 17:1). "I had many things to write, but I will not with ink and pin write unto thee" (3 John 13).

Algonquin Errors

One very admirable man of America's colonial era was John Eliot (1604–1690), who served as a missionary among the Algonquin Indians and translated the Bible into their language—the first Bible printed on American soil, in fact. However, Eliot's Indian translation, published in 1661, was not exactly flawless. At 2 Kings 2:23, it mistranslated "go up, thou bald head" as "go up, thou ball head." The Indian word refers to a ball used for play. Jesus' parable of the ten virgins became the parable of the ten young men, as the interpreter did not understand these were

women, not men. Apparently the Indians thought of chastity as a
male virtue, not a feminine one. Their language had no word for
salt, so verses like "Ye are the salt of the earth" (Matthew 5:13)
posed problems. Interestingly, Eliot's interpreter was an Indian
named James Printer.

Pretty, Heavy, and Occasionally Wrong

One of the great successes in American book publishing was
the Illuminated Bible, published by Harper and Brothers of New
York in 1843. Weighing 14 pounds, it had a fine leather binding
with metal clasps, pages with gilded edges, and fine illustrations—
more than 1600 of them, in fact. It also overflowed with notes,
study helps, and, of course, a section for creating a family tree. It
was a classic example of a "parlor Bible," probably serving more as
a decoration than as a book for actual study and spiritual growth.
It sold more than 75,000 copies, which for that period of history
was amazing. But, like any Bible ever published, it wasn't perfect.
In Judges 16:17, Samson tells Delilah that if his head is sheared,
"I shall become weak, and be like any mother man." The correct
word is *other*, not *mother*.

Bottled-Up Anger

In Deuteronomy 2:9, Moses tells the Israelites, "And the Lord
said unto me, Distress not the Moabites, neither contend with
them in battle." A 1912 Bible printed in Philadelphia ends the
verse with "content with them in bottle."

King of the Buffet

According to Psalm 29:10, "The LORD sitteth upon the flood;
yea, the LORD sitteth King for ever." An ornate, leatherbound
book of Psalms printed in London in 1837 had it as "The Lord

sitteth upon the food." The same book was missing an *l* in these other verses as well: "The sorrows of death compassed me, and the foods of ungodly men made me afraid" (18:4). "He turned the sea into dry land: they went through the food on foot: there did we rejoice in him" (66:6).

TEN

Reveling in Revelation

In some ways Revelation is one of the best books of the Bible because it gives us a dramatic vision of God and His people triumphing over evil at the end of time. Unfortunately, the book has so many puzzling symbols that people have been arguing for 2000 years about how to interpret them. Just what is the correct interpretation? No one knows. But we do know that many people have been famously incorrect in using the book to predict the end of time. No wonder that in times past, church authorities feared letting laypeople read Revelation and get some kooky ideas in their heads. It's happened many, many times...

Singular, Not Plural

Some people not only misunderstand the book of Revelation, they can't even get its name right. For the record, it's *Revelation,* singular, not *Revelations,* plural. (The book's title in the original Greek is *apokalypsis,* meaning "a revelation.") On an October 2006 broadcast, the popular quiz show *Who Wants to Be a Millionaire?* known to be fanatical about checking and double-checking the information in its questions, had *Revelations* as the name of a book of the Bible.

No Antichrist Here

Here's a shocker: the word *Antichrist* does not even appear in the book of Revelation. In fact, the only occurrences of the word are in 1 John (three times) and 2 John (once). This is odd because many people who have never actually read Revelation have a vague idea that the book has something to do with the number 666 and the Antichrist. Traditionally, though, Christians have believed that the Beast in Revelation is the same evil figure as the Antichrist in the two letters of John.

The Omen Number

One of the hit movies of the 1970s was *The Omen,* a horror movie telling of the birth and childhood of the Antichrist of Revelation. In this film, the Antichrist child actually had the telltale numbers 666 as a kind of birthmark on his scalp—as if the Antichrist would be dumb enough to give away its identity with such an obvious sign! The movie and its various clones did have the effect of making people who had never opened a Bible familiar with 666 as the number of the Beast from Revelation. When the movie was remade years later, it opened on June 6, 2006—that is, 6-6-06. It was not as successful as the original, so maybe the frightening 666 no longer has the impact it once had.

666, Cough

The Tonight Show with Jay Leno sometimes features a segment called "99-Cent Shopping Spree," where Leno shows the audience some odd and badly labeled products, usually made abroad. One of these was the "666 Cough Preparation." Leno noted that the foreign packagers don't seem too familiar with Christian terminology. The audience found it delightful, especially when Leno's band played the theme music from the diabolical movie *The Omen.*

Hal Lindsey and the End

The New York Times, no friend of Christianity or the Bible, described Hal Lindsey as the bestselling author of the 1970s. He certainly had a string of successes, beginning with *The Late Great Planet Earth,* which sold 20 million copies worldwide. People were fascinated by Lindsey's prediction of the fulfillment of the Bible's prophecies of the end times. Lindsey followed up with *The Liberation of Planet Earth,* a study of what the Bible says about human sin, and *Satan Is Alive and Well on Planet Earth.* Like hundreds of authors before him, Lindsey was wrong in his predictions about the end times.

The Montanists

The region of Phrygia (modern-day Turkey) had a long and colorful history as a breeding ground for odd religions. Followers of the goddess Cybele indulged in a wild form of worship that often resembled an orgy, which was also true of followers of the wine god Dionysus. Centuries later, ecstatic Muslims known as the whirling dervishes flourished in Phrygia. In between, sometime around the year 156, a man named Montanus attracted a group of followers. He claimed not to be starting a new religion but to be taking Christianity back to the Bible. He claimed to have the gift of speaking in tongues—a gift definitely mentioned in the New Testament but that church authorities had come to frown on. Montanus spoke out against formality and dryness in Christian worship. He also spoke out against people claiming to be Christians but not practicing what they preach. So far, so good. However, he went beyond the Bible in teaching that believers must be celibate and that Christians must fast rigorously. He urged his followers to eat dry foods only. If a person committed any serious sin after being baptized, he or she could not be forgiven.

Two of Montanus' aides were Priscilla and Maximilla, both

believed to be prophets, although Maximilla had the unfortunate habit of prophesying disasters that did not occur. Montanus and many of his followers claimed to be guided by the Holy Spirit, who gave them the gifts of tongues, prophecy, and other charismatic gifts. The Montanists loved the Gospel of John, and they took seriously John 14:12: "Anyone who has faith in me will do what I have been doing. He will do even greater things than these" (NIV). They believed that the New Jerusalem predicted in Revelation 21 would come into being in their native Phrygia.

The Montanists scandalized many Christians, although one very prominent Christian theologian, Tertullian, was associated with the movement for a while. (Tertullian coined the word *Trinity,* by the way.) In fact, the movement attracted many sincere Christians who saw the Montanists as more moral than many nominal Christians were. Both Montanists and other Christians suffered persecution under the Roman emperor Severus, and the Montanists generally had a higher rate of martyrdom—that is, fewer of them renounced their beliefs under threat of being killed. This willingness to die for their faith impressed many Christians and helped the movement spread. The Montanists were also avid missionaries, and their beliefs spread over the Roman empire until the fifth century, when the Emperor Justinian was mostly successful in suppressing the movement. But in fact it died of natural causes—because the Montanists insisted on being celibate, they weren't producing any new generations.

The Montanists are regarded by Christian historians as heretics. They are an example of a group of Christians who went astray by a misreading of the Bible. They are also a case of some very sincere believers who turned their backs on normal Christianity because they found it too dry and unemotional. Like many groups throughout the centuries, they turned to the Bible and found it full of references to the work of the Holy Spirit, which made them emphasize the vital role of the Spirit in the religious life. In other words, the Montanists had a few wrong beliefs mingled in with some very right beliefs. Their fascination with the book of Revelation and its prophecies of the millennium and the New Jerusalem (Revelation 20–22) had the negative effect of making many Christians neglect or ignore Revelation.

A Thousand Years of Saints Reigning?

The New Testament gives the impression that the early Christians expected Christ to return to earth very soon. So for several decades Christians hoped that the thousand-year reign of the saints of earth would begin soon. As time passed and Christ did not return, fewer people believed they would live to see the millennium in their lifetimes. Augustine, one of the most influential theologians in the Roman empire, put forward a new theory: The thousand years of the saints reigning with Christ had already begun, and it was visible in the life of the church across the world. In other words, the millennium is already here spiritually. Augustine totally spiritualized the thousand years described in Revelation 20. In his view, it referred to neither a literal thousand years nor to a literal reign of the saints.

This theory might have sounded plausible in Augustine's day (he died in 430), but as the centuries went by and church officials became more materialistic and corrupt, any sensitive Christian could see that the millennium and the church were *not* the same thing. If anything, the least saintly people seemed to be the ones who reached high positions in the church. Augustine had implied, "Don't expect the millennium, it's already here," but Christians in later times would have responded, "You call this immoral church bureaucracy a reign of *saints?*" So the expectation and hope that Christ would return to earth and usher in the millennium regained popularity.

David Koresh and Company

At a tender age, Vernon Howell had memorized long passages from the Bible. He took the Bible prophecies seriously and expected the millennium to come in his generation. Howell joined a community called the Branch Davidians, believing they were a righteous remnant destined to play a part in the final Armageddon. Howell changed his name to David Koresh, and the group hailed him as the Lamb destined to open the seven seals of Revelation and explain their meaning. Before they shared in Christ's victory at Armageddon, they believed they had to survive the coming tribulation and the reign of Antichrist, which is why the group stocked provisions and weapons.

Former members of the group revealed that Koresh created a harem (including girls as young as 14) and fathered at least a dozen children. Authorities also received evidence of widespread child abuse and statutory rape. In April 1993, after a 51-day siege, federal agents acting under orders of Attorney General Janet Reno killed Koresh and 74 other men, women, and children.

Look for the Union Label

Some Christians claim to believe that the European Union is the beast with ten horns from Revelation, as the addition of Greece in 1981 brought the total number of nations in the Union to ten. However, Portugal and Spain were added in 1986, making it 12, so the interpretation shifted to the image of the woman wearing a crown with 12 stars. That theory exploded as several other nations were added to the Union. However, considering the incredible power that the European Union has over millions of people—power held by people who were not democratically elected—the Union may yet enter a "beastly" phase.

A Very Short Antichrist

In the Napoleonic Era, many Europeans believed French

emperor Napoleon Bonaparte was the Antichrist. In fact, the classic novel *War and Peace* opens with some Russian nobles talking of the invader Napoleon as the Antichrist. Supposedly Napoleon's original name in Corsican was N'Appolione, so some people assumed he was the fiendish Apollyon, the "angel of the bottomless pit" of Revelation 9:11. Also, some had noted (or believed) that 666 members of the French Convention controlled France until Napoleon took power. On the other side of the political fence, King Louis XVI's name (in Latin) supposedly added up to 666. In other words, nearly everything connected with the French Revolution and the reign of Napoleon seemed to add up to 666. We now know that Napoleon wasn't the Antichrist or the Beast, but considering all the harm Napoleon's wars did, he was about as beastly a person as any who lived in that period.

The Rastafarians

This offbeat messianic movement began in Jamaica in 1930 when some Jamaicans decided that Ras Tafari, who was crowned as Haile Selassie of Ethiopia, was the fulfillment of prophecies. He assumed the biblical titles "King of Kings" and "Conquering Lion of the Tribe of Judah," both from Revelation 19:16. The Jamaican group believed he was the Black King and Redeemer—in fact, that he was God Himself. The group is probably more famous for their music and for such practices as wearing their hair in dreadlocks and smoking marijuana, which they call *ganja*.

The Albury Conferences

In the 1800s in England, many noted ministers, along with several members of Parliament, set up the Albury Conferences. These had one main theme: examining the Bible to determine if the Lord's coming was at hand. The conferences decided that at the French Revolution, which began in 1789, the vials of wrath from the book of Revelation had begun to be poured out on mankind. Considering the bloodshed of the Revolution, we can easily see how people might connect it with the end of time.

Joanna Southcott

She was quite the phenomenon of her day, this Methodist woman who believed she had received revelations of the destruction of Satan and the coming of Christ's kingdom. Miss Southcott (1750–1814), an English farm woman, became convinced she was the "woman clothed with the sun" (Revelation 12:1) and "the bride, the Lamb's wife" (Revelation 21:9). Though a virgin (so she said), she convinced many followers that she was pregnant through the Holy Spirit, but before she could bear the child who would rule all the nations (Revelation 12:5), she died. Some of her faithful followers kept the flame burning into the twentieth century.

The Buchanites

Many sad and deluded people have been misled by their reading of the book of Revelation. One of these was Elspeth Buchan, a woman of the village of Irvine, Scotland. In the 1780s she claimed to be the third person of the Godhead and the "woman clothed with the sun" of Revelation 12:1. She and Hugh White, a young minister who believed her, led a band of followers who awaited their rapture into heaven. The event was delayed time after time, until finally only one follower remained, keeping watch over the corpse of Elspeth Buchan and expecting her resurrection.

Resurrection Pills

In the 1840s in America, the followers of William Miller (who later evolved into the Adventist churches) were predicting the second coming of Christ, and some entrepreneurs began to advertise resurrection pills and even muslin for ascension robes. Since the second coming did not occur as Miller foretold, we can assume these products ceased to sell well.

Bengel's Apocalypse

German scholar Johann Albrecht Bengel (1687–1752) was a noted commentator on the New Testament, and many of his writings were incorporated into the *Notes on the New Testament* by Methodist founder John Wesley. Bengel, like many Bible readers, tried to determine the date of the end-time events foretold in the book of Revelation. He predicted that the millennium (Revelation 20) would begin in 1836. He was wrong (as have been all the predictors so far), but his New Testament notes are still widely read.

Stiefel the Calculator

Michael Stiefel was a German pastor, a follower of Martin Luther, and also a mathematician. In 1532 he published a small book called *Apocalypse on the Apocalypse: A Little Book of Arithmetic about the Antichrist.* From his reading of the book of Revelation, Stiefel had calculated that the day of judgment would occur on the morning of October 9, 1533. On that day many peasants laid their work aside and trudged to the village where Stiefel was pastor. When nothing happened, they bound him and dragged him to a nearby village, where some sued him for damages. A few years later, Stiefel published a pamphlet, *A Very Wonderful Recalculation,* in which he admitted he had made a mistake earlier.

Noyes, the Perfect Man

Christians have been arguing for almost two millennia about when the millennium described in Revelation 20 will occur.

American minister John Humphrey Noyes had the answer: It occurred a generation after the time of Christ and was still present on earth. (And obviously it had lasted longer than just a thousand years because Noyes lived in the 1800s.) Noyes was fascinated with the idea of Christian perfection, and he believed that some people, himself included, could live with no sin in their lives. He applied the angel Gabriel's words to the virgin Mary to himself: "The Holy Ghost shall come upon thee, and the power of the Highest shall overshadow thee" (Luke 1:35). He proclaimed himself a perfected Christian and started a magazine called *The Perfectionist.* Noyes established a community of other perfected Christians, where monogamy gave way to a sort of communal marriage. Every man and every woman was free to enjoy sex as easily as they enjoyed food with no sense of shame. As you might imagine, this scandalized many people, and Noyes was often in trouble with the law. Eventually his millennial community settled in Oneida, New York. (They became famous for making silverware, and the Oneida brand is still available.) Needless to say, this attempt at a Christian form of communism (including free love) did not endure because jealousy and other deep emotions have a way of surfacing even among "perfect" people.

The Fifth Monarchy Men

The description of the millennium (the thousand-year reign of the saints on earth) in Revelation 20 often has been merged with other Bible references to the end of time. One of those passages is Daniel 2, where Daniel interprets a dream of a statue made of four metals (gold, silver, bronze, and iron) but with feet of clay. Some Christians believed that the metals represent four empires, the fourth one (iron) being the Roman empire, and they tack on the belief that the next world empire will be the reign of the saints, the millennium. In the English Civil War of the 1640s, a group known as the Fifth Monarchy Men believed that the armies that fought against King Charles I were ushering in the millennial kingdom, the Fifth Monarchy. After the execution of the king, however, England did not turn into the heaven on earth they expected. Some of them not only turned against the new ruler, Oliver Cromwell, but even led rebellions against him.

New (Lack of) Harmony

In 1803, German minister Johann Georg Rapp led 1200 followers to Pennsylvania to establish a thoroughly Christian community and await the second coming of Christ, who would appear as the "woman clothed with the sun" in Revelation 12. They established a village called Harmony and tried to recreate the first Christian church described in Acts, where believers shared their property. The band moved to Indiana in 1814 and established New Harmony. In spite of all their good intention, Rapp and his followers did not prosper, perhaps partly because of their enforced celibacy, and of course the millennium did not arrive.

Monsters in Munster

Most of the Christian attempts to usher in the millennium have been peaceful—but not all have. In 1534, some radical Christians took over the town of Munster, Germany, and instituted a "reign of the saints." The city was fortified, and all property was made communal. The leader, an actor named Johann Beukels, ran naked through the town and proclaimed himself the king, assisted by 12 elders. He called the city the New Jerusalem, after Revelation 21. All books except the Bible were burned, and people could be executed instantly for swearing, adultery, and even malicious gossip. Men were free to marry as many wives as they liked, and an unmarried woman had to say yes when a man proposed.

Beukels himself had several wives, all under age 20. Forty-nine women were killed for refusing to marry. This violent and oppressive situation was more a reign of terror than a reign of the saints, and it lasted barely two years. Beukels was caught and tortured to death slowly with red-hot tongs.

Y1K

Most of us remember all the hoopla and weird speculation about what might happen on January 1, 2000. What happened? Nothing, really. This was also the case on January 1, 1000, except even more expectation (and fear) arose then because so many people believed that the second coming would occur at the end of this first thousand years, and the thousand-year reign of the saints described in Revelation 20 would begin.

Joachim and His Three Ages

One of the most influential early commentators on the book of Revelation was Joachim of Fiore, head of a monastery in Italy. Joachim wrote several books, including *Exposition of the Apocalypse.* He is remembered today because he taught the world would pass through three ages. First was the age of the Father, when people lived under the Old Testament law. Next was the age of the Son, which began with the birth of Christ and would continue (so Joachim predicted) until around 1260, when the third age, the age of the Spirit, would begin. This heavenly age would be the "reign of the saints" prophesied in Revelation 20. Joachim himself died in 1202, so he never knew if his prophecies were correct. But many people were aware of his writings and were seriously disappointed when 1260 passed without the age of the Spirit beginning.

The Taborite Army

The Taborite movement was born in Bohemia, an area that is in the modern-day Czech Republic. They held to an early form of Protestantism because they opposed the Catholic clergy, the belief in purgatory, praying to saints, and other extrabiblical practices. They believed that Jesus' second coming was about to occur, ushering in the millennium of Revelation 20. In 1419 about 40,000 of them gathered on a hill that they gave the biblical name Tabor. They had some able military leaders (one of whom was blind, oddly enough) and were able for a time to fight off the armies that regarded them as heretics. By 1434 the movement was crushed and all its leaders were killed, which has tended to happen to millennial movements that use violence.

Tabor, incidentally, was the name of the mountain where Jesus' transfiguration took place. The group chose this name for their mountain fortress because it was the name of a mountain where Jesus appeared in glory.

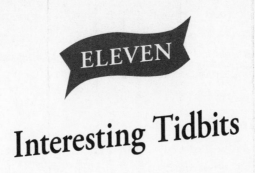

Interesting Tidbits

Sibling Devilry

In Charles Schulz' long-running comic strip *Peanuts*, Linus was often feuding with his domineering older sister, Lucy. On one occasion, Linus decided after Lucy hit him that he would retaliate by not giving her a Christmas present that year. Lucy responded by paging through the Bible and then running to Linus with this bit of news: "I found the word *sister* in the Bible! That *proves* you have to give me a Christmas present!"

Poor Cainy

English author Thomas Hardy's classic novel *Far from the Madding Crowd* has a character named Cain Ball, a farm boy. When the owner of the farm inquires about how a man came to be named for the Bible's first murderer, this is the reply: "Oh, you see, ma'am, his poor mother, not bein' a Scripture-read woman, made a mistake at his christening, thinkin' 'twas Abel killed Cain, and called 'im Cain, but 'twas too late, for the name could never be got rid of in the parish. 'Tis very unfortunate for the boy." On the brighter side, the locals had taken to calling him Cainy, thinking it softened the blow a little. Hardy claimed that he based this fictional character on an actual man who had been named Cain. If that was so, we have to question the Bible literacy of the minister who christened the child.

Shakespeare and the Bible

The late 1500s and early 1600s were the golden age of English literature, the age of Shakespeare and other great writers and also of some fine Bibles, including the King James Version. By the time the KJV was published in 1611, however, Shakespeare had already retired. Like most of his contemporaries, he had been raised on the popular Geneva Bible of 1560, and when he quotes the Bible in his plays, the wording is usually from the Geneva. In one amusing episode, he deliberately misquotes the Bible: In the fantasy play *A Midsummer Night's Dream,* the character Bottom (who is given a donkey's head in a magical spell) awakes from the spell and misquotes Paul: "The eye of man hath not heard." Bottom was evidently a little confused about anatomy. Probably most of the people in the audience at that time would have been familiar with 1 Corinthians 2:9: "Eye hath not seen, nor ear heard, neither have entered into the heart of man, the things which God hath prepared for them that love him."

Jesus of Japan

Followers of other religions often admire Jesus even if they don't accept Him as the New Testament presents Him. For example, some followers of the Shinto religion of Japan believe that Jesus was really a Japanese and that the Bible errs in stating that He died on the cross. Instead, the man who actually died on the cross was a younger brother of Jesus. The real Jesus left Jerusalem and journeyed across Asia to His real homeland, Japan.

The Bible's Author—Live and in Person?

One of the best one-man translations ever made was that by Scotsman James Moffatt, whose readable version of the Bible was published in 1924. Moffatt frequently lectured on the Bible, and after his translation was published, one lecture hall that booked him had him billed on the marquee as "Author of Bible to Lecture Tonight."

Still Latin After All These Years

The Protestant Reformation was a "back to the Bible" movement, and Martin Luther led the Protestants in making Bible translations from the original Hebrew and Greek writings. The Catholic church resisted this for centuries and maintained that the Latin Bible from around the year 400 was the one and only true Bible. When the Catholics finally allowed translations into the languages people actually spoke, those translations could only be made from Latin. As late as 1944 a Catholic translator named Ronald Knox published a new translation into English...from Latin. Thankfully, the Catholic church now allows—and even encourages—translations from the Hebrew and Greek.

The Truth, the Whole Truth...

Getting our hands on a copy of the complete Bible is so easy that we take it for granted. In the Middle Ages, this wasn't so easy. A complete Bible was a rarity. Much more common were volumes that contained just the Gospels, or the Psalms, or the Prophets. An entire Bible was referred to as a *pandect* (a word that was also applied to a country's complete body of laws), and Bible pandects were rare. (Most people couldn't read in those days anyway.) Not only was it difficult to get the whole Bible in one volume, but the books containing parts of the Bible frequently mingled legends about the Catholic saints, traditions about the Virgin Mary, and even stories from pagan mythology. In short, all these books circulating tended to blur the distinction between inspired Scripture and other writings. That would change dramatically in the 1500s with the Protestant Reformation, which insisted on getting all the books of the Bible between two covers in languages the people could understand.

Wicked Wycliffe?

You might recognize the name John Wycliffe as a saintly Englishman of the Middle Ages. Wycliffe was shocked, as most sensitive Christians were, by the corruption and wealth of the institutional church. He wanted to reform it and believed clergymen should behave as if (gasp!) they guided their lives by the Bible. Some of Wycliffe's followers dared to disobey the church authorities and to translate the Bible into English, the language the common people understood. This was done from the Latin translation, the only Bible the church officially approved. It all had to be done by hand, since Wycliffe lived before the invention of the printing press. Even so, the English translation was popular, despite being illegal and being so laborious to produce.

Wycliffe probably would have been executed as a heretic if he hadn't had some protective friends among the English royal house. He died a natural death, but after his death the church condemned him for heresy, dug up his bones, and burned them. Thomas Arundel, the archbishop of Canterbury (the head of the English church), wrote to the pope in 1411, referring to "this pestilent and wretched John Wycliffe, of cursed memory, that son of the old serpent" who "endeavored by every means to attack the very faith and sacred doctrine of the Holy Church, devising—to fill up the measure of his malice—the expedient of a new translation of the Scriptures into the mother tongue."

Troublemaking Tyndale

The great scholar William Tyndale had to live outside England while he completed his monumental translation of the New Testament—the first English New Testament made from the ancient Greek manuscripts. Living in England, he risked being arrested for violating the laws that prohibited translation into languages the people actually spoke—what the church authorities called the "vulgar tongues." At the very time Tyndale was laboring away at his translation, a young man in England was burned alive. His crime? Owning a piece of paper that had the Lord's Prayer in English.

Tyndale's New Testament was printed in Germany in 1526 and smuggled into England. The English church's bishops reacted with horror. The bishop of London, with the cumbersome name Cuthbert Tunstall, complained about "that pestiferous and most pernicious poyson dispersed through London." He claimed he found 2000 errors in Tyndale's translation. In fact, Tyndale made very few errors, and Tunstall's big mistake was thinking that the old Latin Bible was the most accurate version. Tunstall told the bookseller not to sell Tyndale's New Testament (many did so anyway), and whenever he could he bought up copies of it and burned them publicly, preaching that it was God's will that the Bible be only in Latin. (Actually, at this time, all the other European countries printed Bibles in the people's languages.) Tyndale joked that if the church authorities were trying to brand him as a heretic (which they eventually did), at least they had to read his English New Testament in order to convict him.

King James Cut Down to Size

If you are a "King James only" person, here's a bit of information you ought to know: The original King James Version of 1611 was *not* a new translation. It was a revision of the officially approved (and unpopular) Bishops' Bible of 1568. The KJV scholars were really revisers, not translators. They started from the Bishops' Bible but were also free to borrow phrasing from the other English versions available, including the very popular Geneva Bible of 1560. In the long preface to the King James Version, the scholars freely admitted that their version was not a new translation but merely a "new and improved" version.

Also, your King James Version probably doesn't contain the Apocrypha, but all KJVs *did* have the Apocrypha until the early 1800s.

Read Those Footnotes!

When the King James Version was published in 1611, one huge difference between it and earlier English Bibles was that it had very few footnotes. The more popular Geneva Bible of 1560 had lots of notes, most of them including very useful explanations of the text. For example, consider Ezekiel 9:6: "Destroy utterly the old, and the young, and the maids, and the children, and the women." Taking that verse out of context, and not having any note to explain the verse, some crackpot might say, "Ah, the Bible tells me to destroy people indiscriminately." But the Geneva Bible's footnote for Ezekiel 9:6 explains that the destroyers are angels.

Blake in All His Weirdness

The English poet-artist William Blake (1757–1827) was an odd and amazing character, a man who claimed to be able to communicate with his dead brothers, with angels, and even with fairies. He wrote some highly readable but puzzling poetry and produced his own illustrations. He obviously knew the Bible thoroughly, but he incorporated its people and events into his own personal mythology, which was a long way from Christianity. In his poem *The Everlasting Gospel,* Blake stated that the gospel was the forgiveness of sins, nothing more.

In Blake's poetic world, the Creator God was a cold, merciless being that Blake called Urizen, and he saw Urizen as the enemy of imagination and love. Among Blake's famous pictures was one called *The Ancient of Days,* a name for God borrowed from the book of Daniel. In Blake's pictures, this God is a cold, distant being with a long flowing beard, creating the world with a compass in his hand. In the picture *Elohim Creating Adam,* Elohim (God) again appears cold and merciless, and the newly created Adam seems to be in agony with a snake entwined around his leg.

Near the end of his life, Blake created some famous illustrations for the book of Job. Here he followed the Bible closely but, as usual, gave his own unique spin to the characters involved.

Hebrew New Testament?

In 1870, one of the bishops of the Church of England proposed that the church make "a revision of the Authorized Version of the New Testament" which would correct the "clear errors, whether in the Hebrew or Greek text." Perhaps the bishop overlooked the fact that the New Testament is all in Greek, not Hebrew.

Boot-Sized Bibles

According to an old story, in the English Civil War (the mid 1600s), soldiers in the armies of Parliament carried Bibles in their boots. Needless to say, they would have had to have been extremely large men—or worn extremely loose boots—to carry entire Bibles with them. What many of them did carry was the Soldiers' Pocket Bible, a mere 16 pages, roughly about the size of a modern passport. Its quotations were from the popular Geneva Bible (the King James

Version was available but wasn't as popular yet) and included such gems as "Love your enemies" and "Be strong in the Lord, and in the power of his might." The title page said that the quotations were "useful for any Christian to meditate upon, now in this miserable time of war." More than two centuries later, in America's own Civil War, about 50,000 copies of the Soldiers' Pocket Bible were distributed to Union troops.

The LXX Book

You might be aware that the New Testament was written in Greek. Well, so was the Old Testament—or, to be precise, it was translated from Hebrew into Greek around 250 BC. At that time, many Jews were living outside of Palestine and had ceased to speak or read Hebrew. As the legend goes, 70 (or 72) Jewish scholars, six from each of the 12 tribes of Israel, worked in their own separate cells and, amazingly, each one of them made exactly the same translation from Hebrew into Greek. This happened in Alexandria, Egypt, supposedly at the request of a ruler with the cumbersome name of Ptolemy Philadelphus. Because 70 (or 72) men worked on the translation, it is referred to as the Septuagint, although Bible scholars usually refer to it by LXX, the Roman numeral for 70.

This is an interesting story, and it illustrates the high regard the Jews had for making faithful copies of things. However, the Septuagint certainly was completed not in one time period but more likely over more than a century. Jews regarded the first five books—the Torah, or books of Moses—as the most important, so these were translated first. Then came the Prophets and then the Psalms and other books. The Septuagint was the only Bible for the many Jews who spoke Greek and not Hebrew. When Christianity began, most of the Christians were Jews, many of them Greek-speaking, and they thought the Septuagint was sacred. When the New Testament writers quoted the Old, they clearly referred to the Septuagint. In fact, as time passed, the Jews realized that Christians had taken the Septuagint to heart. The Jews reacted in two ways: They began using other Greek translations of the Old Testament, notably one by a scholar named Aquila. And, more importantly, they went back to the Hebrew originals and emphasized studying Hebrew in order to know the real truth of the Bible. In short, the Greek Septuagint became the Christians' book, and the Hebrew version was the Jews'.

What, a Jewish Old Testament?

Around the year 400, the Christian scholar Jerome began his amazing translation of the Bible into Latin, a project that became known as the Vulgate, and that became *the* Bible for almost a thousand years. Jerome logically translated from the original languages—Greek in the New Testament, Hebrew in the Old. But not everyone approved of this. Some said his translation of the Old Testament should have been based on the Septuagint, the Greek version of the Old Testament. Jerome thought the Hebrew text, being older, was the best to translate from, and practically every scholar now would agree. But some of Jerome's enemies—and as a rather sharp-tongued character, he had lots of enemies—said his translation was "tainted with Judaism" because he translated from Hebrew.

Swine Who Can Read

"Do not throw your pearls to pigs. If you do, they may trample them under their feet, and then turn and tear you to pieces." So said Jesus in Matthew 7:6 (NIV). Believe it or not, for many centuries, church leaders applied these words to the translation of the Bible into languages the people could actually understand. For more than a thousand years, the only authorized Bible was in

Latin—a dead language. The more the church increased in power (and corruption), the less the authorities wanted the people to understand the Bible.

In the 1300s, the English minister John Wycliffe worked to translate the New Testament into English. Many of his fellow ministers were scandalized. One of them said, "The jewel of clerics [pastors] is turned to the sport of the laity, and the pearl of the gospel is scattered abroad and trodden underfoot by swine." In other words, the common people had no business knowing the actual words of the Bible. They were "swine" who hadn't enough sense to understand it on their own. Translations were not only unnecessary but also dangerous.

Wycliffe had a clever response to such criticisms: He pointed out that the authors of the four Gospels were themselves translators because Jesus and the apostles had spoken in Aramaic, not Greek. If God blessed the Greek writings of the apostles, couldn't He also bless translations of those Greek writings into English, French, German, and other languages? The church authorities did not agree and banned English Bibles.

More than a century later, William Tyndale began translating the Bible into English. With the law against such translations in place, he had to live outside England and have his translation smuggled back in. In the preface to his New Testament, Tyndale made no mention of the institutions of the church—bishops, priests, the rituals. No wonder the bishops burned copies of Tyndale's translation whenever they could find them. He was presenting the Bible to people as if they needed no one or no thing to mediate between them and the Word of God.

King Henry VIII had his favorite scholar, Thomas More, write books condemning Tyndale and his translation. More claimed that the translation was "so corrupted and changed from the good and wholesome doctrine of Christ that it was a clean contrary thing." Oddly, in More's younger days he had spoken out against the corruption of the church in the same way Tyndale did, but as he aged he claimed the church never erred. More was offended that Tyndale believed the apostle Paul did not write the letter to the Hebrews—although practically every scholar of ancient languages now agrees that whoever wrote Hebrews, it wasn't Paul. But More's main concern was that Tyndale wanted the Bible to be read by everyone, not just the brain elite—that is, More's own class. Tyndale's replies to More were more charitable than the abuse More heaped on him. Tyndale wrote that "Christ's elect church is the whole multitude of all repenting sinners that believe in Christ, and put all their trust and confidence in the mercy of God"—that is, the church was the body of all Christians, not just the bishops, priests, and Latin scholars who wanted to keep the Bible locked away from the common folk. In all, More wrote more than a thousand pages of anti-Tyndale material.

More was very useful to Henry as a persecutor of "heretics." He gloated that "hell doth receive them, where they burn forever." Ironically, Henry eventually had More beheaded. Even more ironic, Henry eventually changed his tune about having the Bible in English and ordered that every church in the country possess an English Bible. And here's one more irony: The Bible that Henry approved was about 70 percent the work of William Tyndale. And despite all the harsh words More wrote against Tyndale, More admitted that Tyndale was a man of "right good living, studious and well learned in Scripture."

Later, Henry had another change of heart. Hearing that the laypeople were reading the Bible for themselves and (heaven forbid!) arguing about it, he ordered that only the ministers and the nobility could read the Bible. The common people should refer their questions to "men of higher judgment." But it was too late to make an order like that stick. Once English Bibles were in circulation, people were determined to read them—and think for themselves.

Some people had more faith in the common folk than King Henry did. One of these was Thomas Cranmer, the archbishop of Canterbury and head of the English church. In a preface to the 1540 Bible, Cranmer noted that with the Bible people could "learn all things, what they ought to believe, what they ought to do, and what they should not do, as well concerning Almighty God as themselves and all other."

We take Cranmer's sentiments for granted. Of course people should be able to read the Bible in their own language and interpret it for themselves. The men who wrote the Bible weren't members of an intellectual elite. Some of them were working-class people, and most of the people who hearkened to their words were not intellectuals either. And the New Testament is pretty clear about common folk making wise decisions based on the Bible. Consider Acts 17:11 (NIV), where we are told that the people of Berea "received the message with great eagerness and examined the Scriptures every day to see if what Paul said was true." Tyndale and other Protestant translators in the 1500s took these words to heart.

The church resisted this. Meeting in the 1500s, the Council of Trent decreed that the old Latin Bible was "not only better than all other Latin translations, but better than the Greek text itself in those places where they disagree." When the Catholics did allow translation into the common languages, they required that the translations be from Latin, not the original languages. They said that the Greek and Hebrew texts the Protestants used were impure, "foully corrupted by Jews and heretics." In England, the Catholic poet John Dryden mocked the Bible in his native language:

> The Book thus put in every vulgar hand,
> Which each presumed he best could understand,
> The common rule was made the common prey
> And at the mercy of the rabble lay.

Fortunately, the English as a whole did not agree with Dryden's low opinion of their intelligence.

The Much-Altered KJV

If you are a "King James only" person, you'll find this interesting. The King James Version printed today is *not* the same as the original one printed in 1611. As noted elsewhere in this book (see page 259), the 1611 KJV had the Apocrypha, and very few KJVs today do. But the original KJV also had lots and lots of words that, over the centuries, were modernized, either by updating the spelling or, in many cases, substituting a word that was more understandable. Consider this list of words, with the original KJV form on the left and the modern equivalent on the right:

botch = boil

by and by = at once

byss = fine linen

Candy = Crete

cavillations = legal quibbles

complexion = temperament

debite = deputy

despitions = outrages

duetie = what is due

earer = plowman

egalness = equality

groundly = profoundly

grece = flight of steps

leaings = lies

liefer = rather

meeked = tamed

noosell = nurture

parlous = perilous

peased = pacified

pickers = petty thieves

pyght = pitched

silverlings = shekels

trying-fire = fire for testing, purifying

wealth = well-being

weet = know

wot = know

A few of these, like *wealth,* remain in most modern printings of the KJV, but most have been altered over the years. Here are a few more original KJV morsels: creeple, ayre, middes, thorow, murther, fornace, ancres, damosel, fet, habergeon, wimples, cracknel, besom, neesing. Any guesses? And have you ever seen a KJV where these words appear? Probably not.

Like most older versions, the KJV was not consistent about spelling words. Also, some names familiar to us had unfamiliar spellings—such as Hierusalem (Jerusalem) and Moyses (Moses).

The "Bible Only" Language

Bible colleges and seminaries offer courses titled "New Testament Greek." Is that different from some other type of Greek? Definitely. It is generally a simpler (and easier-to-learn) Greek than the classical Greek of Homer's epic poems, Plato's philosophical writings, and the plays of Sophocles. The Greek of the New Testament is called *Koine,* which means "common."

Strangely enough, scholars once believed that the Greek of the New Testament was very *un*common. They observed that the

Greek of the Bible was not classical Greek—in fact, they had never read anything else written like the Greek of the New Testament. They concluded that this type of Greek was a special language of the Holy Spirit because no other documents have ever been found in that language. But archaeologists laid this notion to rest when they began digging up, mostly in Egypt, papyrus letters, bills, invitations, deeds, contracts, and other everyday documents written in exactly the type of Greek found in the New Testament. These dedicated diggers discovered that New Testament Greek was actually a common language, an international language used over most of the Roman empire at the time of Jesus. In fact, it was still being used as late as the year 250 in many locales.

The Name Game

In any English Bible you'll encounter personal names that are not spelled the same as the names in the Hebrew and Greek originals. For example, Jesus in the Greek is *Iesous,* with the *I* pronounced with a *y* sound. Caesar is actually *Kaisar,* Moses is *Mouses,* Paul is *Paulos.* Obviously the names morph when moved from one language to another. The oddest morph of all has to be James, the name of several men in the New Testament. In Greek the actual name is *Iakobos,* which is a variation of the Old Testament name Jacob. Since Jacob was the ancestor of the 12 tribes of Israel, many Jewish families named their sons after him. But how did we get from *Iakobos* to James? Apparently when the New Testament was translated from Greek into Latin, the name became *Iacomus*—the *b* sound in *Iakobos* shifting to an *m* for some odd reason. So our James is a slightly compressed form of *Iacomus.*

Dutch and French in the Bible

One of the best English Bibles ever published was the Geneva Bible of 1560, the most popular version before the King James came along in 1611. (In fact, the KJV took several decades to catch on while the Geneva was still popular.) The Geneva had excellent footnotes, explaining words and phrases that are hard to understand. Occasionally, though, the translators got carried away and wrote some bizarre footnotes. For example, verse 20 of the tiny book of Obadiah mentions the locales of Canaan, Zarephath, and Sepharad—places in the Middle East. But the footnote in the Geneva Bible has this: "By the Canaanites the Jews mean the Dutchmen, and by Zarephath, France, and by Sepharad, Spain."

Another place where the Geneva notes got a little goofy was in the note for Jeremiah 44:17, which refers to people worshipping the "queen of heaven." This probably was some goddess worshipped in the ancient Middle East, but the footnote in the Geneva Bible claims that the verse applies to Roman Catholics and their worship of Mary as "queen."

Manna for Breakfast

The cereal that later became well-known as Post Toasties first had the very biblical name Elijah's Manna—which is slightly wrong because Elijah the prophet was fed something else by ravens in the wilderness. Manna was the miracle food God provided for the Israelites in the days of Moses.

Other Great Harvest House Reading

KNOWING THE BIBLE 101
Bruce Bickel and Stan Jantz

With extensive biblical knowledge and a contemporary perspective, Bruce Bickel and Stan Jantz provide a manageable approach to understanding God's written message—its origin, themes, truth, and personal relevance. Formerly titled *Bruce & Stan's Guide to the Bible*.

KNOWING AND LOVING THE BIBLE
Catherine Martin

This powerful, interactive journey transforms reading and studying the Bible into acts of love and brings you closer to God as you discover nourishment for daily living and build a foundation on His promises.

SEARCHING FOR THE ORIGINAL BIBLE
Randall Price

Randall Price brings expert knowledge to examine faith-challenging topics: what the key ancient manuscripts reveal, whether mere humans composed the writings, the archaeological record, the gathering of inspired texts into one book, those texts' transmission to us. All available evidence, concludes the author, indicates the Bible is a trustworthy divine revelation.

101 MOST PUZZLING BIBLE VERSES
Tim Demy and Gary Steward

This solid, easy-to-access resource clarifies cultural, historical, and doctrinal issues regarding confusing Bible verses, ending your frustration and helping you enjoy and benefit from the Scriptures. Includes list of resources for further, in-depth study.

HOW TO STUDY THE BIBLE FOR YOURSELF
Tim LaHaye

From nationally recognized Bible teacher and author Tim LaHaye, this thirtieth anniversary edition of his bestselling *How to Study the Bible for Yourself* helps you uncover the wisdom and truth of Scripture for yourself.

HARVEST HOUSE
PUBLISHERS